GLOBAL ACTION

 Nuclear
Test Ban Diplomacy
at the End of the
Cold War

PHILIP G. SCHRAG

WESTVIEW PRESS

Global Action

Global Action

Nuclear Test Ban Diplomacy at the End of the Cold War

Philip G. Schrag

Westview Press

BOULDER • SAN FRANCISCO • OXFORD

This Westview softcover edition is printed on acid-free paper and bound in library-quality, coated covers that carry the highest rating of the National Association of State Textbook Administrators, in consultation with the Association of American Publishers and the Book Manufacturers' Institute.

Copyright © 1992 by Westview Press, Inc.

Published in 1992 in the United States of America by Westview Press, Inc., 5500 Central Avenue, Boulder, Colorado 80301-2847, and in the United Kingdom by Westview Press, 36 Lonsdale Road, Summertown, Oxford OX2 7EW

Library of Congress Cataloging-in-Publication Data
Schrag, Philip G., 1943–
  Global action : nuclear test ban diplomacy at the end of the Cold War / Philip G. Schrag.
    p. cm.
  Includes bibliographical references and index.
  ISBN 0-8133-1112-8
  1. Nuclear weapons—Testing. 2. Nuclear arms control. I. Title.
JX1974.7.S23 1992
327.1'74—dc20   92-60
                                                                            CIP

Printed and bound in the United States of America

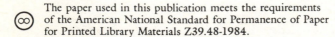 The paper used in this publication meets the requirements of the American National Standard for Permanence of Paper for Printed Library Materials Z39.48-1984.

10   9   8   7   6   5   4   3   2   1

*To the people who work for nuclear arms control and disarmament
in governments, parliaments, and citizen organizations
throughout the world*

Contents

Acknowledgments

I deeply appreciate the assistance of many people who cooperated with my research, including Olafur Ragnar Grimsson, Kennedy Graham, and Aaron Tovish of Parliamentarians for Global Action; Bernard Lown, Bill Monning, and Norm Stein of International Physicians for the Prevention of Nuclear War; the many diplomats who filled me in on behind-the-scenes negotiations; William Epstein, who helped me with the historical background; Tom Zamora, who allowed me to consult his archival material on the Fourth NPT Review Conference; Frank Polek, who provided able research assistance; and Victor Navasky, who helped me to obtain a United Nations press pass.

I am also very grateful to Georgetown University Law Center and the Ford Foundation, which provided generous grants to make the writing of this book possible.

And Lisa, I thank you for encouraging me at all the right times.

Philip G. Schrag
Georgetown University Law Center

Acronyms

AEC	Atomic Energy Commission
CD	Conference on Disarmament (the forty-nation group that meets twice a year in Geneva to discuss disarmament issues)
CTB	Comprehensive Test Ban
CTBT	Comprehensive Test Ban Treaty
IPPNW	International Physicians for the Prevention of Nuclear War
kt	kilotons (a measure of the explosive yield of a nuclear weapon—the bomb that destroyed Hiroshima had a yield of about 15 kt)
NPT	Non-Proliferation Treaty
PGA	Parliamentarians for Global Action
PTBT	Partial Test Ban Treaty (known as the Limited Test Ban Treaty in the United States)
PWO	Parliamentarians for World Order (original name of PGA)
TTBT	Threshold Test Ban Treaty
U.K.	United Kingdom
U.N.	United Nations
UNGA	United Nations General Assembly
U.S.	United States
USSR	Union of Soviet Socialist Republics

For the convenience of readers, I have employed the acronym "PGA" to refer to the organization that organized the drive for the Partial Test Ban Treaty Amendment Conference. Parliamentarians for Global Action never refers to itself by this or any other acronym.

Note on Sources
and National Actors

We are all used to reading newspaper stories that quote unidentified "sources." Journalists sometimes decry government officials' insistence on not being quoted by name, but faced with the choice between quoting an "authoritative source" or foregoing a story, virtually all of them will accede to the conditions imposed on them.

For an academic writer, an official's insistence on anonymity is even more problematic, and for a law professor, such a demand is at odds with a strong tradition. Law professors are accustomed to meticulous—some would say excessive[1]—footnoting to support every assertion and are generally loathe to make any claim that cannot be independently checked by reference to documentation or at least by re-interviewing a person who made an oral statement.

While I would have preferred not to relax these traditional standards, it would not have been possible to recount the history of the Partial Test Ban Treaty Amendment Conference without relying on sources who could not allow themselves to be identified. Many of the meetings leading up to and during the conference were held behind closed doors and without any documentary records, and while many of the relevant officials were quite willing to cooperate on a historical project they would not have been able to obtain authorization from their governments or organizations to be quoted by name. Like a member of the working press, I was required to honor their insistence on anonymity or to forego the full story. I chose a more complete narrative rather than a fully documented silhouette of the event.

I would have preferred as well not to have had to use the convention of referring to nations as though they were individual persons, as in the sentence, "Nigeria favored negotiation of a comprehensive test ban." In his great work *Essence of Decision,* Professor Graham Allison showed that such claims are only a shorthand and conceal the rich texture of bureaucratic and interpersonal conflict that inheres in much national security policy-making.[2] The claim that "Nigeria favored negotiation of a test ban" does not mean that everyone in Nigeria had that view, or even that every person or government agency in Nigeria was in accordance with that policy, but only that the final result of the Nigerian government's decision-making process was that some official spokesperson was authorized to make that statement on behalf of the nation. I have argued in an earlier Westview Press book that Allison's insights about the value of probing beneath the surface of governmental decisions is applicable even to relatively minor aspects of arms control policy.[3] This book might have explained more if it had been possible to expose and to study internal conflicts within the many governments that have expressed views on ending nuclear testing. A deeper exposition of such disputes was never a possibility, however, given the large number of governments involved, the relative lack of media attention to the nuclear-testing issue, and the understandable reluctance of governments to air their internal disagreements.

Notes

1. Arthur D. Austin, "Footnote Skulduggery and Other Bad Habits," *U. of Miami L. Rev.*, vol 40, p. 1009 (1990).

2. Graham T. Allison, *Essence of Decision* (Boston: Little, Brown, and Co., 1971).

3. Philip G. Schrag, *Listening for the Bomb: A Study in Nuclear Arms Control Verification Policy* (Boulder: Westview Press, 1989).

Introduction

Between July 16, 1945, and July 16, 1991, six countries detonated at least 1919 nuclear explosions.[1] Two of these explosions were the atomic bombs used against Japan, and about a hundred and fifty were Soviet and American experiments with the "peaceful" use of nuclear explosive devices.[2] All of the others were nuclear weapon tests.[3]

During most of the atomic age, dozens of national governments, along with several non-governmental peace movements, have sought to persuade the countries with nuclear explosive technology to stop testing these weapons. Indeed, the cessation of nuclear testing was the first concrete goal articulated by the postwar peace movement in the United States,[4] and it soon became an international priority.[5] The international demand to stop testing reached a crescendo in the early 1960's, when fallout from atmospheric tests threatened public health throughout the world.

After the Partial Test Ban Treaty of 1963 led the United States and the Soviet Union to move their tests underground, the public clamor to stop nuclear testing subsided, but it did not end. Calls for a complete halt in nuclear testing—a negotiated "comprehensive test ban"—continued to be made by governments, international organizations and citizen groups; in 1990 a senior United Nations official could note that "no other item on the disarmament agenda has attracted so much attention and persistent efforts as the achievement of a comprehensive test ban,"[6] a goal that still had not been achieved.

By the end of the 1980s, several countries' governments had little sympathy with the ongoing nuclear weapon testing programs of the superpowers and little patience with the apparently low priority that those who continued to test gave to negotiating a ban on the practice. At the same time, a number of contemporary events suggested that renewed international pressure on the superpowers might have some effect.

First, the cold war appeared to be ending. The United States and the Soviet Union had agreed to eliminate their intermediate-range nuclear missiles, and to accept intrusive measures to verify compliance with that agreement.[7] Both superpowers were experiencing severe budget crises, impelling them to search for further ways to reduce military expenditures. Early in 1989, the Soviet Union had begun to democratize its national government, electing first a Congress of People's Deputies and then, through the Congress, a revamped Supreme Soviet to which real legislative power devolved. Later that year, the Soviet Union refrained from intervening as Communist governments were ousted from power in Poland, Hungary, Czechoslovakia and East Germany. The destruction of the Berlin wall and the opening of negotiations for reunification of Germany provided dramatic evidence that new constellations of forces in international politics would inevitably emerge.

Second, ending nuclear tests was already a high priority of the Soviet leadership, and it was likely to become a still more urgent matter. President Gorbachev's first arms control initiative had been an unsuccessful attempt to press the United States on this issue by declaring a unilateral moratorium on Soviet testing. A mutual halt in testing became all the more important to Moscow as Soviet environmentalists began a powerful campaign to end testing in that country whether or not the United States responded.

Third, the issue of verifying a ban on nuclear testing, which had always seemed to be the insuperable obstacle to agreement, appeared to be receding as an issue. Although the Soviet government had once resolutely resisted intrusive verification on its soil, it had agreed in the Intermediate Nuclear Forces Treaty to the stationing of American observers outside of a Soviet missile factory for a period of years. Even more to the point, beginning in 1986, it had allowed American scientists to establish seismic monitoring stations on its soil to demonstrate that a test ban could be verified adequately.

Fourth, the United States Congress had begun to become an active player in the test ban effort. In 1986, 1987 and 1988, the House of Representatives had passed legislation cutting off funding for testing nuclear weapons at yields greater than one kiloton if the Soviet Union verifiably observed that limit. The Senate had not concurred in the fund cutoff, but the American government seemed less monolithic on nuclear testing than it had been for years.

Finally, the non-aligned countries had a vehicle for forcing the testing issue, if not to a successful conclusion, then at least to a public confrontation. Early in 1989, these countries invoked a provision in the 1963 Treaty to require the United States and the Soviet Union to participate in a multinational negotiation, the Partial Test Ban Treaty Amendment Conference, that would have the power to amend the 1963 Treaty so as to forbid all nuclear tests by any of its parties.

Notwithstanding all of these developments favorable to their cessation, underground nuclear tests continue to take place. The Partial Test Ban Treaty Amendment Conference could not, at least in the short run, force an end to such testing. In the United States, the Bush administration had inherited from its predecessor a policy of refusing all overtures for further restrictions of nuclear tests, much less a complete prohibition. Along with its British ally (whose only testing, at minimal levels, was conducted in Nevada), the American government was willing to refuse the entreaties of the vast majority of the nations of the world, and to brandish its legal right to veto an amendment to the 1963 accord.

This book explores the strategies of the global movement to change American test ban policy, and the sources and nature of the Bush administration's resistance to change. Chapter 1 traces the history of the domestic and international test-ban effort over its thirty-five year life and the alternating attitudes of the American and Soviet governments. Chapter 1 also includes a brief summary of the major arguments regarding American test ban policy as of the late 1980s.[8] Chapter 2 explores the emergence of a new international strategy for changing the policy of the United States government. It tracks the Amendment Conference from its conception by an American peace activist in 1984, until March, 1989, when it became certain that a global meeting would actually take place. Chapter 3 recounts the diplomatic skirmishes surrounding the birth of this new negotiating forum, between March, 1989 and the end of May, 1990, when the two-week organizational "Meeting" of the Conference began. Chapters 2 and 3 also set the organization of the Conference into its political context, including the changes made in Soviet policy by Mikhail Gorbachev and the efforts by Soviet and American activists to make the test ban a priority issue for their governments.

Chapters 4 through 6 examine the period from the opening of the organizational meeting through the Conference itself, including the behind-the-scenes negotiations over the outcomes of these events and the failure to achieve consensus at the intervening Fourth Non-Proliferation Treaty Review Conference. These chapters also provide an opportunity to explore with care the fabric of routine multilateral diplomacy; Chapters 4 and 6, in particular, report the day-by-day events of negotiation (including strategic planning by the major players and reports, based on interview data, of the closed-door meetings) at a level of detail rarely elaborated even in journalistic accounts, much less academic works.[9] The concluding chapter provides my commentary on the outcome of the Amendment Conference, my prediction about the future of nuclear testing, and my recommendation for strategies to advance the date on which a comprehensive test ban agreement enters into force.

Notes

1. For 1910 tests through October, 1990 see "Known Nuclear Tests Worldwide, 1945 to December 31, 1990," *Bulletin of the Atomic Scientists* April, 1991, p. 49. During the first six and a half months of 1991, France conducted six tests and the

United States conducted three. Agence France Presse, "France carries out nuclear test at Mururoa," July 16, 1991; "U.S. discloses general range of underground nuclear test," *Chicago Tribune,* April 17, 1991, p. 4; "Nuclear test goes off after 51 protesters arrested," *Chicago Tribune,* April 5, 1991, p. 4; "U.S. tests nuclear weapon under nevada desert," Xinhua General Overseas News Service, Item 0308072, March 8, 1991. The total number of tests may be somewhat understated because some low-yield explosions may not have been announced or detected.

2. *Ibid.*

3. India exploded one nuclear explosive device in 1974, which it claimed was for "peaceful" purposes.

4. Milton S. Katz, *Ban the Bomb* (New York: Praeger, 1987) pp. 14, 20.

5. "Regulation, Limitation and Balanced Reduction of All Armed Forces and All Armaments; Conclusion of an International Convention (Treaty) on the Reduction of Armaments and the Prohibition of Atomic, Hydrogen and Other Weapons of Mass Destruction," United Nations Resolutions Adopted by the General Assembly (New York: General Assembly Official Records, 1957), Resolution Number 1148, Session XII, adopted November 14, 1957.

6. Yasushi Akashi, United Nations Under-secretary General for Disarmament Affairs, addressing the Meeting of the States Parties to the Treaty Banning Nuclear Weapon Tests in the Atmosphere, in Outer Space and under Water for the Organization of the Amendment Conference, prepared text p. 3 (May 29, 1990). In affording primacy to work directed toward an end to nuclear testing, Mr. Akashi was referring to multilateral efforts; certainly the United States and the Soviet Union had devoted considerably more time and effort to negotiating mutual curbs on the numbers of their intermediate-range and strategic nuclear delivery systems.

7. Treaty Between the United States of America and the Union of Soviet Socialist Republics on the Elimination of their Intermediate-Range and Shorter-Range Missiles, in U.S. Arms Control and Disarmament Agency, *Arms Control and Disarmament Agreements: Texts and Histories of the Negotiations,* p. 350 (Washington: U.S. Arms Control and Disarmament Agency, 6th ed., 1990).

8. The description of the policy arguments is not intended to be comprehensive. More thorough analyses of the policy issues, including a considerable amount of technical detail, can be found in several recent writings including Steve Fetter, *Toward a Comprehensive Test Ban* (Cambridge, Massachusetts: Ballinger Publishing Company, 1988); R.E. Kidder, *Maintaining the U.S. Stockpile of Nuclear Weapons During a Low-Threshold or Comprehensive Test Ban,* UCRL-53820 (Livermore, California: Lawrence Livermore National Laboratory, 1987); Congress of the United States, Office of Technology Assessment, *Seismic Verification of Nuclear Testing Treaties,* OTA-ISC-361 (Washington, D.C.: U.S. Government Printing Office 1988); The Belmont Conference on Nuclear Test Ban Policy (David A. Koplow and Philip G. Schrag, Rapporteurs), "Phasing Out Nuclear Weapons Tests," *Stanford Journal of International Law,* v. 26, 1989, p. 205; and The International Foundation, *Toward a Comprehensive Nuclear Warhead Test Ban* (Moscow and Washington, D.C.: The International Foundation, 1991).

9. The author's other descriptions of official processes at this level of detail include "Bleak House 1968—A Report on Consumer Test Litigation," *N.Y.U.*

Law Review, vol. 44, p. 115 (1969) (litigation); *Counsel for the Deceived* (New York: Pantheon Books, 1972) (civil law enforcement by local government); *Behind the Scenes: The Politics of a Constitutional Convention* (Washington, D.C.: Georgetown University Press, 1985) (a constitutional convention), and Chapter 4 of *Listening for the Bomb: A Study in Nuclear Arms Control Verification Policy* (Boulder: Westview Press, 1989) (national security decision-making).

1

Thirty Years of Frustration

In 1985, a small group of peace activists, politicians and diplomats began a new campaign to achieve an objective long sought by many nations. They wanted to force the United States, Britain, and the Soviet Union—and eventually France and China—to end the testing of nuclear weapons, and to prevent all other nations from embarking on their own series of tests.

Their vehicle was novel; they proposed to amend the 1963 Treaty that had banned testing in the atmosphere. But their cause had a very long and disappointing history. For thirty years, many citizens and governments had tried to bring an end to testing. At various times, the heads of state of all three major nuclear powers had joined the effort, but big power advocacy of this objective was often hesitant, ambivalent, or subordinate to other goals. Furthermore, the superpowers appeared to take turns championing a test ban, or advocating particular provisions of a proposed treaty, so that whenever one of them really seemed ready to end testing on a reciprocal basis, the other was not. At least three times, in 1960, 1963, and 1978, the United States, Britain and the Soviet Union appeared to be within reach of agreement, but each time, a failure of will by one or more of them blocked the negotiation of a treaty.

In any event, for more than a generation, all efforts to end the tests had failed, and in 1984, a nuclear explosion had been detonated, somewhere in the world, on the average of every six days.[1] Indeed, the new campaign to end testing attracted the attention and support of many nations in large measure because the non-aligned countries had become bitterly frustrated by the fact that for decades, the major powers had been admonishing other countries to refrain from acquiring nuclear weapons, while they themselves constantly improved their own nuclear stockpiles through repeated cycles of development and testing.

Eisenhower, Macmillan,
and Khrushchev: 1954–60

Nuclear testing by the United States and then by the Soviet Union had proceeded, with little public opposition in either country, from 1945 to 1954. The first protest came from India, and the dramatic incident that sparked it involved Japan, the nation that had suffered history's only atomic bombing.

In February, 1954, in the Bikini Atoll, the United States tested its first practical design for a hydrogen bomb. The device produced two surprises: a yield twice as great as had been expected, and radioactive fallout so intense and so widespread that the crew of the Japanese trawler *Lucky Dragon,* 85 miles away, became ill. Many crew members were sick when the ship returned to Japan, and panic broke out when fish at Japanese markets, taken from the vessel, were found to be radioactive. All 23 crew members had to be hospitalized for months, and one died.[2]

Two weeks after the ship reached Japan, Prime Minister Jawaharlal Nehru spoke out in the Indian Parliament against nuclear weapons testing, particularly in or near Asia, and he called on the United States and the Soviet Union to stop testing and to work in the United Nations for a broader disarmament agreement.[3] The British Labor Party unsuccessfully called upon the Conservative government to try to bring about a world-wide halt to testing, and Pope Pius XII devoted most of his Easter message to the dangers of radiation caused by nuclear weapons.[4]

Despite growing domestic and international concern about the health dangers resulting from atmospheric testing, for four years the Eisenhower administration rejected making an end to testing a goal for American policy. Within the administration, the Department of Defense and the Atomic Energy Commission (AEC) argued that the need to develop a variety of deliverable fusion weapons outweighed the health dangers.[5] As early as February, 1955, the U.S. government had completed its first policy review, and President Eisenhower had announced that he was not interested in what he characterized as a "piecemeal approach" to disarmament.[6] As testing continued, scientists periodically reminded the public of the potential health menace. World-wide protest continued to build. In his 1955 Easter message, the Pope repeated his warning about the genetic risks caused by the fallout from testing, and at Christmas he called for an international agreement to put "a check on experiments in nuclear weapons."[7] At a conference of leaders of non-aligned countries in Bandung, Indonesia, President Sukarno of Indonesia joined Prime Minister Nehru in calling for a ban on testing, and delegates to the conference adopted a call for a negotiated prohibition and a temporary suspension.[8] The Soviet Union took up the call; it proposed a United Nations General Assembly resolution calling for an indefinite suspension of testing. The United States strenuously opposed this call and succeeded in defeating it in the UN's First Committee by a vote of 36–17.[9] It also refused a direct call by the Soviet Union for a reciprocal halt in tests.[10]

In 1956, the test ban issue began to become a significant topic of public debate within the United States, in large measure because the Democratic Presidential candidate, Adlai Stevenson, made it a major topic of his campaign, devoting an entire nationwide television address to the issue.[11] The Eisenhower administration continued to oppose a test ban in its public statements, and it even rejected a British proposal for private bilateral discussions on the issue, but with 69% of the public favoring a negotiated ban, the President quietly authorized a new study of the issue by his National Security Council.[12] Early in the following year, the U.S. government made the first small shift in its test ban policy, stating its willingness to negotiate a test ban treaty, but only after all nuclear weapons production had ended under strict international supervision.[13] At about the same time, Britain announced plans to test its first hydrogen bomb, in the Pacific. Japan protested both formally and in private approaches to London, and the West German Bundestag called on Britain, the U.S. and the Soviet Union to negotiate an end to testing.[14] That spring, the American editor Norman Cousins went to Gabon to ask Dr. Albert Schweitzer, a Nobel Peace Prize winner and one of the most esteemed people in the world, to speak out on the testing issue.[15] After receiving encouragement from Prime Minister Nehru, Schweitzer delivered a lengthy radio address, rebroadcast in fifty countries, in which he urged the people of the world to demand that testing be halted.[16] In the United States, the Nobel laureate Linus Pauling responded by speaking out against testing and by circulating among scientists a petition calling for an internationally negotiated agreement. Within two weeks, more than 2000 American scientists had signed the call, despite the fact that no organization had been involved in circulating it.[17]

As domestic and international demand for a halt in testing continued to build, and as the Soviet Union continued to press the point, President Eisenhower began to reconsider his view of the issue.[18] His disarmament advisor, Harold Stassen, suggested that a test ban might be a good first step toward nuclear disarmament, but Admirals Lewis Strauss, the AEC Chairman, and Arthur Radford, the Chairman of the Joint Chiefs of Staff opposed this concept vehemently, and Radford went public against it. After a "stormy session" with them, Eisenhower allowed Stassen to suggest to the Soviet Union a brief test suspension in exchange for future limitations on weapons production. The Soviet government responded quickly, expressing its interest in a two to three year moratorium as well as in a permanent halt, and expressing its willingness to accept international controls with monitoring posts on its soil.[19]

Alarmed that a test ban might become a reality, the American scientists and officials who were opposed to limitations on testing began campaigns both to persuade the President not to agree to a ban and to undercut him in Congress (where a test ban treaty would fail if not approved by a two-thirds vote of the Senate) if he rejected their advice. The opposition to restraints on testing was centered in the two national weapons development laboratories, Livermore and Los Alamos, whose scientists were responsible for designing new types of nuclear weapons. Opposition was particularly fierce at Livermore, which had been founded a few years earlier to develop new types of thermonuclear (hydrogen) explosives. On June 24, 1957, three Livermore officials, led by Edward Teller (known popularly as the father of the H-bomb), met with Eisenhower for 40 minutes. They argued that testing should continue to develop a "clean" hydrogen bomb, one that was free of fallout, for use as battlefield weapons and for peaceful purposes such as harbor excavation. Indeed, many argued, it would be a "crime against humanity" not to test such weapons. The scientists made the same case to a closed hearing of the Congressional Joint Committee on Atomic Energy. Two days after meeting with Teller, Eisenhower appeared to retreat from a suspension of testing, stating at a press conference that with four to five years of additional testing, an "absolutely clean bomb" could be developed. The United States did offer to suspend tests for two years, but only if the Soviet Union agreed to a mutual halt in weapons production, a condition that the Soviets promptly rejected.[20]

Public pressure for an end to testing continued to mount, however. During the summer of 1957, many liberal and religious organizations began to speak out on the issue; they included the Federation of American Scientists, the World Council of Churches, the American Friends Service Committee and Americans for Democratic Action.[21] At the same time, Americans opposed to testing founded a new organization, the Committee for a SANE Nuclear Policy, which would work primarily on the test ban issue. In November, SANE placed a full-page advertisement against nuclear testing in the New York Times; contributions in response to the statement recovered its cost within days, and by the following summer, SANE had 25,000 members in 130 chapters across the country.[22] Scientists around the world continued to sign Dr. Pauling's statement; in January, 1958, he presented the petition, with 9235 signatures of researchers (including 37 Nobelists), to the Secretary-General of the United Nations.[23] When the Soviet Union called again for a moratorium on testing (this time, for the years 1958 and 1959), Nehru urged Eisenhower to agree to it. Turning down the Soviet proposal, the President again linked its acceptance to a cutoff on the production of nuclear weapons.[24]

But within the United States government, an important change had taken place. In reaction to the shock of observing the Soviet Union become the first country to orbit a satellite, Eisenhower had created a post for a Presidential science advisor, had asked MIT President James J. Killian to fill the position, and, at Killian's urging, had created a President's Science Advisory Committee of prominent non-governmental scientists. This action had the incidental effect of providing him with scientific advice on the nuclear testing issue that was independent of the information provided by Los Alamos, Livermore, and the Joint Chiefs of Staff, "allowing the ideas of academic scientists to compete with the more parochial and defense-oriented views of Pentagon and AEC officials."[25] A few months later, the AEC was further undermined when it appeared to conceal the United States' ability to detect distant underground nuclear explosions. In March, 1958, it announced that the United States' first underground nuclear test, RANIER (with a yield of just 1.7 kilotons (kt)), had been detected by seismographs only to a distance of 250 miles from the Nevada test site.[26] Senator Hubert Humphrey noted that in fact, the U.S. Coast and Geodetic Survey station in College, Alaska, 2300 miles away, had detected the explosion and accused the AEC of distorting the evidence. The AEC apologized and said that the error had been caused by a bureaucratic mix-up.[27]

A few days later, Nikita Khrushchev, who up to then had been only General Secretary of the Communist Party, became head of state of the Soviet Union as well. Four days after assuming the office, he stunned the world; the Supreme Soviet suspended testing in the U.S.S.R., appealed to the American and British parliaments to adopt similar measures, and stated that the Soviet Union would be free to resume testing if other countries continued to test.[28] Secretary of State Dulles called the move "propaganda," and Eisenhower labelled it a "gimmick," but in fact, Eisenhower was furious because the Soviet Union had scored an impressive victory in the Cold War battle for world opinion.[29]

Within the United States and throughout the world, people called for American and British reciprocity.[30] Eisenhower replied that the United States shouldn't suspend testing until it had learned all that it needed to learn about the nuclear weapons then being developed, but he privately asked his officials—now including the independent scientists of the President's Science Advisory Committee—to conduct a review of American test ban policy.[31] Meanwhile, without consulting the AEC or the Defense Department, he proposed to Khrushchev that technical experts from the United States and the Soviet Union meet to discuss the verifiability of a test ban agreement, noting that "with the practicalities already worked out, the political agreement [to stop testing] could begin to operate very shortly after it was signed and ratified."[32] After a three-day meeting, the President's

Science Advisory Committee recommended that the President should try to negotiate a "sustained test cessation" to take effect as soon as possible after completion of the HARDTACK test series scheduled for the summer of 1958. This timing, suggested the Committee, would "leave the U.S. in a position of technical superiority for at least several years."[33]

Immediate reconciliation of the disparate views with the United States government was not necessary, because Khrushchev accepted Eisenhower's proposal for a Conference of Experts.[34] Meeting in Geneva, the experts designated by the United States, the Soviet Union and their allies agreed on a report in less than two months. They concluded that "it is technically feasible to establish . . . a workable and effective control system to detect violations of an agreement on the worldwide suspension of nuclear weapons tests."[35] A network of seismic stations that included 37 posts in Asia would identify as earthquakes (rather than explosions) 90% of all seismic events equivalent to more than 5 kt. On two issues, however, the experts were silent or ambiguous, and these issues would later become central in negotiations. They did not specify the nationality of the personnel who would operate the control posts, and they did not specify the criteria for triggering an on-site inspection to resolve the events that remained of uncertain origin after analysis of seismographic records.[36]

Within the Eisenhower administration, John McCone succeeded Admiral Strauss as Chairman of the AEC, and, supported by the Department of Defense, he continued to fight against a test ban, preventing the consensus that Eisenhower sought.[37] Nevertheless, as the Conference of Experts came to a close in mid-August, a political decision had to be made; over the objections of the AEC and the Joint Chiefs of Staff, Eisenhower decided that when the Geneva meeting ended, he would call for full-scale test ban talks and would suspend American testing temporarily. Eisenhower wanted British participation, and to obtain it, he had to make a fateful decision. The British had planned a series of tests for the early fall, which they did not want to cancel. Eisenhower therefore resolved that the Western test suspension would not begin until October 31, and he allowed the AEC to accelerate its HARDTACK II test series, which had been planned for 1959, into September and October, 1958. Included in this accelerated American series were four underground tests, although to this point the United States had undertaken only one such explosion.[38]

The day after the Conference of Experts ended, Eisenhower proposed full-scale test ban negotiations to begin October 31, and he stated that the U.S. would suspend testing for one year beginning on that date if the Soviet Union also refrained from testing. He added that the United States would renew the suspension annually if an inspection system were established and "satisfactory progress" were made toward nuclear disarmament.[39] The British issued a parallel statement. The Soviet Union agreed to begin the negotiations, but Khrushchev noted that with U.S. and British tests continuing until November, the Soviet government would resume its own testing.[40] The United Nations General Assembly urged a moratorium on tests while the Geneva negotiations were in progress, and the Soviets stopped testing on November 3 without formally announcing a new moratorium policy.[41]

On the day the negotiations opened, nineteen world leaders, including Albert Schweitzer, Dimitri Shostakovich, Bertrand Russell, Eleanor Roosevelt and Martin Luther King, Jr., signed a full-page advertisement in the New York Times appealing to the negotiators to achieve successful results.[42] But progress was slow. During the first two months, the delegates worked primarily on the question of decision-making by the control commission, with the Soviets essentially arguing for a veto that would, in the U.S. view, make the inspection system self-policing.[43] When the Conference resumed after a Christmas break, the U.S. and the U.K. relaxed their announced policy, making their willingness to enter into a ban on testing contingent only on adequate verification of compliance, and not on satisfactory progress toward disarmament.[44] But in the same week, the U.S. delegation made a move that made agreement much more difficult.

The four underground tests conducted as part of HARDTACK II appeared to show that identification of ambiguous seismic events was considerably more difficult than the American experts, extrapolating from the single RANIER test, had believed. To achieve the capability that the system described by the Conference of Experts would have had (90% identification above 5 kt based on seismic records alone) would now require either 500 seismic stations or between 200 and 1000 inspections a year.[45] Fearful that inspectors could be spies seeking to investigate their military capabilities, the Soviets refused to discuss the new data, but they quietly hinted to Britain's Prime Minister, Harold Macmillan, that they might agree to on-site inspection if the number of such inspections could be capped by a quota.[46] Eisenhower was furious at having to backtrack, and although he did not like the idea of a quota, he arranged for a new scientific panel to investigate ways to make the inspection system work without requiring more of the Soviets than the system jointly proposed by the experts in 1958.[47]

Livermore's Dr. Teller, meanwhile, had been busily seeking further ways to reverse the President's policy. At Teller's suggestion, Albert Latter, a RAND corporation scientist, had calculated that an explosion clandestinely detonated in a large underground cavity could be "decoupled" from its environment to create a seismic signal only one three hundredth as large as a corresponding explosion in hard rock. These calculations were later shown to have been vastly overstated; the decoupling factor turned out to be only about seven, rather than 300.[48] But they were published in classified form in the spring of 1959, and later that year, they were presented to the Soviets, increasing their suspicion that the Americans were intent on sabotaging the talks.[49] James J. Wadsworth, the American ambassador, later observed that during this period, "several times . . . my instructions contained positions which—from the Russians' point of view—were scarcely negotiable. They seemed to be designed to break off the talks. But [because of the test ban opponents' representation in senior policy-making ranks in Washington] it was not always easy to persuade Washington to modify the instructions."[50]

The idea of a quota on on-site inspections appeared to be the only available device for assuring the Western nations that Soviet evasion of a test ban might be established by conclusive evidence of radioactivity while allaying Soviet concerns of unlimited opportunities for espionage. Although Eisenhower authorized his ambassador to explore the idea, his AEC Chairman publicly advocated breaking off the talks.[51] Though the Geneva talks appeared stalemated over the issue of the verification system, Eisenhower announced an extension of the U.S. moratorium through the end of December, while Khrushchev, going a step further, said that the Soviet Union would not resume testing unless "the Western Powers" did so.[52] Meanwhile, the French government was preparing to begin nuclear weapons testing, and when the United Nations General Assembly voted 51–16 to request France to abstain, the United States and Britain opposed the resolution.[53] At the year's end, Eisenhower noted that no satisfactory agreement was in sight, and he announced that the U.S. would no longer be bound by the moratorium.

Early in 1960, the U.S. suggested a new approach: a ban on tests in the atmosphere and on underground tests with seismic magnitudes above 4.75 on the Richter scale; that is, on those tests that, as of that time, could be detected and identified with only about 20 annual on-site inspections in the Soviet Union.[54] The Soviets accepted this proposal, provided the U.S. and the U.K. agreed to continue to observe a "moratorium" on underground explosions below this threshold for an unlimited period (during which both sides would investigate ways to lower the threshold through scientific research), and with the proviso that the quota of on-site inspections be negotiated in advance.[55]

Senior American officials soon met to decide on their response. McCone continued to oppose agreement, but the Deputy Secretary of Defense, representing the Pentagon, joined with the Secretary of State, the CIA director, and others to support an agreement that would at last involve some international inspection in the Soviet Union. McCone took his dissent to Eisenhower, who rejected it "in a sharp voice."[56]

In a meeting at Camp David a few days later, Eisenhower and Macmillan agreed to accept the Soviet proposal, while trying, in the final negotiations, to hold down the duration of the moratorium on low-yield tests. Eisenhower wanted a moratorium of about a year; the Soviets had hinted that they wanted a four to five year period. Macmillan suggested compromising on a three year moratorium, and they announced publicly their readiness to avoid low-yield testing for a period "of agreed duration". The two leaders did not agree on what the maximum annual on-site inspection quota should be, but they decided to negotiate this figure with Khrushchev six weeks later at the summit conference scheduled to take place in Paris.[57]

The Eisenhower-Macmillan response to the Soviet counter-offer set the stage for the signing of an agreement halting all nuclear tests by the three nuclear powers; France had refused to participate in the talks, but the treaty would have put enormous pressure on France to cancel its test program. After a year of difficult and disappointing negotiations, the relief in Western capitals was palpable. The Secretary of State said he was "reasonably optimistic" that testing would be ended. Macmillan, aware that Eisenhower "would accept further concessions [at Paris] to get [a treaty]" believed that "all the omens were good." Ambassador Wadsworth later said that "[o]nly the final details of the agreement remained to be worked out at the 'summit'. . . . [I]t appeared all efforts to delay the agreement would fail. . . . [T]here was widespread expectation that a test ban would be concluded."[58]

McCone prepared to take the battle one step further, persuading the Joint Committee on Atomic Energy to hold a public hearing to explore the risks of the impending ban. He called the pending agreement a "national peril" and threatened to resign as Chairman of the AEC. His purpose, according to the President's science advisor, was to set the stage for defeat of the treaty in the U.S. Senate.[59]

The treaty never got that far. The summit was to open on May 16. On May 1, an American U-2 spy plane was shot down over the Soviet Union; its pilot, Francis Gary Powers, was captured. Arriving in Paris, Khrushchev was furious that Eisenhower would not apologize to him publicly (although the President did announce that the overflights would stop), and he stormed out of the meeting.[60] "The chances for agreement on . . . the ending of nuclear tests had been blown to bits."[61] No further progress on the issue was made during the Eisenhower administration, and the President later said that he regarded the failure to conclude a test ban agreement as the greatest regret of his presidency.[62]

Kennedy and Khrushchev: 1961–63

As a candidate for President, John F. Kennedy stated that he had always thought that concluding an international ban on "all tests" was of "extreme importance . . . because new advances in technology have brought atomic weapons within reach of several additional nations." But he also warned that if progress were not achieved within "a reasonable but definite time limit," he would resume underground testing.[63] When he entered office a few months later, the unofficial moratoria were still being observed, although France had begun to test atomic weapons in the Sahara. In the continuing Geneva negotiations, the Soviet Union had addressed one of the two issues left outstanding by the Paris collapse, stating its willingness to accept three on-site inspections a year. This number was much smaller than the 20 inspections the U.S. had thought necessary, but it had been regarded as a positive move by American negotiators that the Soviets had at last committed themselves, with more than hints, to a particular number of inspections.[64]

When the talks resumed after the inauguration of the new President, the United States government at last had internal agreement on the desirability of a comprehensive test ban; even the new AEC Chairman, Glenn Seaborg, supported the President, although his bureaucracy did not and he therefore felt constrained to play "a double game" and be "an honest broker" between "the AEC community" and the President.[65] The United States quickly agreed that the moratorium on tests below the 4.75 threshold could last for three years, with discussions during the last several months on what would be done about the threshold after that. But the Soviet Union, which also changed its position, appeared to be moving further from what would be acceptable to the West. Reflecting its anger over actions that the United Nations' Secretary-General had taken in the Congo, it demanded that the treaty be administered not by a single official acceptable to all sides but by a three-person group, one of whom would be a Soviet appointee with a veto over any decisions. It also warned that continued French testing might provoke it to resume its own series of tests.[66] Despite severe disagreement with the Soviet move on treaty administration, the United States made a further compromise with regard to on-site inspections, declaring its willingness to have as few as 12 inspections per year if, applying agreed criteria, there were as few as 60 ambiguous seismic events in the U.S.S.R.[67]

But Soviet interest in achieving a test ban seemed to have waned after the summit debacle and particularly after East-West tensions increased with the building of the Berlin Wall and President Kennedy's mobilization of the National Guard in the summer of 1961. The Soviet ambassador to the test ban negotiations said in late August that while a test ban in 1958 or 1959 might have been "a step toward disarmament . . . the present situation shows beyond all doubt that the question of discontinuing nuclear weapon tests can be solved only in conjunction with that of disarmament."[68] Two days later, Radio Moscow announced that the Soviet Union would resume testing, and the following day it began an intensive test series that must have required months of preparation.[69]

Throughout the world, anger and disappointment followed the Soviet test series and the subsequent resumption of American testing. Nehru denounced the Soviet Union; Ghana's President Kwame Nkrumah called Soviet testing "a shock which forcibly brings home to us the supreme danger facing mankind," Canada announced that radiation counts in Toronto went up 1000-fold as a result of the Soviet tests, and a new organization, Women's Strike for Peace, generated demonstrations against testing in cities throughout the United States.[70] The United Nations General Assembly noted the resumption of testing with regret.[71]

Despite the setback, Kennedy continued to want to pursue a comprehensive test ban. In 1962, negotiations moved to a new forum, the Eighteen Nation Disarmament Committee (subsequently enlarged to 40 countries and now known as the Conference on Disarmament, or CD). The Committee included eight non-aligned nations as well as the superpowers and their allies. Verification of compliance was still the critical question, and the non-aligned group had its own ideas. Sweden took a particularly active role. Its scientists knew, from the scholarly literature, that on-site inspections could deter violations of an agreement but that they were not as important as the West had claimed because it would be very difficult to locate accurately the site of a suspicious seismic signal. Therefore only very rarely would an on-site inspection turn up incriminating evidence even if a clandestine test had taken place. Accordingly, the non-aligned group proposed a system under which scientists from neutral countries would report on any suspicious events, suspected parties could invite inspectors to clear their reputations, and if an invitation were not forthcoming, other parties could decide whether to withdraw from the treaty.[72] The non-aligned proposal included many ambiguities, which each side interpreted in its own favor, precluding a narrowing of their positions.[73]

Two events moved the United States in the direction of further compromise. First, it reviewed its verification requirements in the light of research results showing that seismic detection and identification could be improved significantly by putting instruments in deep holes, filtering the data, using ocean-bottom seismometers, and discarding inaccurate assumptions about the number of ambiguous seismic events that would take place each year in the Soviet Union.[74] Second, the Cuban Missile Crisis in the fall of 1962 caused the President and other world leaders to believe that nuclear war could actually occur, and that intensified efforts to begin a disarmament process were essential.[75] In the fall, the United Nations General Assembly called for an end to testing by the beginning of the new year.[76] The United States offered to reduce the number of seismic stations that would be required on Soviet soil, and to permit Soviet staffing under international supervision, and it stated its willingness to consider still further reductions in the quota of on-site inspections.[77] But Khrushchev only reiterated the Soviet offer of two to three inspections.[78] In the spring of 1963, still trying to allay Soviet concerns about spying, the United States made a further offer to reduce the inspection quota to eight, and then to seven. The President had authorized an additional fallback to six, and Harold Brown, then a senior Pentagon official, mentioned the number five in public.[79]

But Khrushchev, apparently believing that he had been told by senior Western officials that three inspections would suffice, had with some difficulty persuaded other Soviet officials to accept that number and was unwilling or unable to go higher, despite Kennedy's obvious efforts to provoke movement that would result in a final compromise on what had become the most difficult issue of the negotiations. The source of his belief is uncertain, but there appear to be two possibilities, and both may have had some bearing. First, Macmillan may have told Khrushchev in 1959 that the West would accept a quota of three to four inspections. William Epstein, a career United Nations official who worked on the test ban issue during the 1960s, learned from a senior member of the British delegation to the Geneva negotiations that while Macmillan was in Moscow that winter, he confidentially proposed these numbers; when the British delegates heard what he had done, "they were aghast, and the Americans were livid."[80] This report is consistent with the claim made by the Soviet ambassador to the Geneva negotiations, on April 19, 1961, that "the Soviet quota of three inspections a year was 'very close' to one of the numbers mentioned by Prime Minister Macmillan in his visit to Moscow in February, 1959."[81] Second, Khrushchev wrote to Kennedy that Kennedy's Ambassador, Arthur Dean, had told a Soviet Deputy Minister of Foreign Affairs in October, 1962, that two to four inspections in the Soviet Union would suffice. Dean may in fact have inadvertently exceeded his instructions, for he was known to be "often vague" and on a previous occasion he had incorrectly said that the United States would be willing to forego seismic stations within the Soviet Union.[82]

Khrushchev went even further to signal the Soviet Union's failing interest in a comprehensive test ban; he accused the United States of repudiating its offer of two to four inspections and appeared to withdraw—and then withdrew—the offer to submit to any quota of on-site inspections.[83] But he agreed to a proposal from Kennedy that he talk further with Averell Harriman, whom the President would send as a personal emissary in Moscow, and, in a surprising reversal of policy, he responded favorably to a long-standing American offer, recently reiterated by Kennedy in Kennedy's now-famous 1963 speech at American University, to ban tests in the atmosphere, under water and in outer space without any seismic stations, on-site inspections or other intrusions in Soviet territory.[84]

Kennedy told Harriman to try, in Moscow, to achieve a comprehensive test ban, but if that were unobtainable, he could settle for a ban that allowed underground testing to continue. Harriman carried a personal letter from Kennedy to Khrushchev, telling the Premier that "we continue to believe that it will be best if we can get a comprehensive agreement on the end of all nuclear testing."[85] In Moscow, the American and British delegations tried one last time to interest Khrushchev in working out arrangements to end underground as well as atmospheric testing by suggesting that the three nations' scientific advisors meet at once as a "preliminary step toward what all sides hope for, namely, ultimate extension [of a limited treaty to a] comprehensive ban." But the Soviets said that such a meeting would serve no purpose, and the scientific advisors flew home.[86] The United States, the Soviet Union, and Britain quickly signed and ratified the Partial Test Ban Treaty (PTBT),[87] and within two months, more than 100 countries (not including France or China) had signed it.[88] But the comprehensive test ban had foundered on Soviet fears of espionage, and more than a decade would pass before any further constraints would be imposed on nuclear testing.

The Viet Nam and Watergate Years: 1964–76

The PTBT is a dramatic illustration of the principle that as a practical matter, a good solution to a problem may prevent achievement of its best solution. The end of atmospheric testing alleviated concern about radioactive fallout. The United States and the Soviet Union increased the rate of nuclear testing.[89] Nevertheless, within the United States, opposition to continued testing virtually disappeared. Membership in SANE dwindled; less than a year after ratification of the Treaty, the organization's unpaid bills exceeded $25,000.[90]

In the Preamble to the Treaty, the parties had noted that the agreement was only the beginning of the process of ending nuclear tests. They declared themselves to be "seeking to achieve the discontinuance of all test explosions of nuclear weapons for all time [and] determined to continue negotiations to this end." Most countries were determined to complete this task, and they expected the United States and the Soviet Union to lead the way, as they had done with the PTBT. Three months after the PTBT was signed, the General Assembly voted 104 to 1 (Albania) to request continued negotiations for a comprehensive ban.[91] The United States and the Soviet Union both supported the resolution. The urgency of the issue was reinforced the following year, when China detonated its first atomic explosion.[92] In response to this development, President Lyndon B. Johnson declared that the United States would work for a "solid" and "verified" comprehensive test ban.[93]

But for a long time, the Soviet Union continued to block progress because of its fears of the intrusive verification that would have to accompany a comprehensive ban. Within the Eighteen Nation Disarmament Committee, it opposed technical discussions.[94] Although the United States and Britain continued to demand the assurances of compliance that a verification system would provide, their view of what would be required softened as seismological research continued to lower the thresholds at which tests could be detected and identified by seismic means. In 1965, the United States announced that "if [scientific] exploration indicated that verification requirements can be satisfied by a different number and type of inspections from those previously discussed, we will take those facts into account gladly," and Britain stated, more directly that "a significantly smaller number of inspections would now be acceptable." Despite this showing of flexibility, and American attempts to have the Eighteen Nation Disarmament Committee work on a CTB as "a matter of priority," the Soviet government continued to rule out all inspection on Soviet soil. By the end of 1965, it was abstaining on the annual General Assembly vote calling for a comprehensive test ban.[95]

The following year, Sweden proposed a variant of the idea that the non-aligned states had put forward in 1962. Under its plan for "challenge" inspections, no numerical quota would be established. However, a nation on whose territory a suspected test had occurred would not be the only party entitled to take the first step in initiating an inspection. If it did not act to clear its reputation, it could be challenged by another treaty party to allow an on-site inspection. No one could force the inspection to take place, but a refusal to permit it would seem very suspicious and could lead to disintegration of the test ban agreement. Both the United States and the Soviet Union rejected the Swedish proposal when it was made,[96] but years later, it would become the basis for resolving the long-standing on-site inspection issue.[97]

For about a decade, progress ground to a halt. The General Assembly continued to vote by large majorities (which again included the Soviet Union) to urge negotiation of a treaty banning underground tests, but the United States and the Soviet Union focussed their attention on other disarmament agreements—the Non-Proliferation Treaty and then the SALT I accords.[98]

The central concept of the Non-Proliferation Treaty (NPT) was to increase world security by creating a global norm that armament should be only of conventional types. Countries that did not already have nuclear weapons would refrain from acquiring them, and countries that did have them would not share their weapons or their bomb technology with others.[99] The Treaty was negotiated in 1967 and 1968, and it entered into force in 1970. Within fifteen years, 124 countries had become parties to it, although France, China, and several other countries thought to have nuclear weapon capability, or to be capable of acquiring it, had not signed. The other important non-signatories included Israel, India, Pakistan, South Africa, Argentina, and Brazil.[100]

Many countries signed the NPT with some reluctance, for although it increased their security by discouraging, slowing, or preventing local nuclear arms races, it froze the status quo, allowing the major military powers to keep their monopoly on the world's most awesome weaponry, and prevented others from acquiring a "great equalizer." This feature of the Treaty led one of the American negotiators privately to characterize the agreement as "one of the greatest con games of modern times."[101] In order to reduce this inherent discrimination, they demanded and received a modest "quid pro quo;" in the Treaty each of the parties agreed to "pursue negotiations in good faith on effective measures relating to cessation of the nuclear arms race at an early date."[102] During the negotiations in the Eighteen Nation Disarmament Committee, several countries spoke of the primacy of a CTB.[103] Some of them, led by Sweden, wanted the Treaty to include an explicit textual commitment to the importance of negotiating that particular agreement.[104] In the end, these nations agreed that to keep the textual language to "modest dimensions" it would suffice to recall, in the Treaty's Preamble, the commitment that the PTBT parties had made to continue negotiations toward a CTB, and Sweden's amendment to the draft Preamble was adopted.[105]

The nuclear powers did, in subsequent years, achieve some significant measures of arms control, including the Anti-Ballistic Missile Treaty and the Intermediate Nuclear Forces Treaty. But progress toward a CTB was always regarded by most non-aligned states as the main measure by which to judge whether the nuclear powers were keeping their part of the NPT bargain; their continuing to develop and deploy new types of nuclear weapons would widen the technological gap between the nuclear "haves" and the "have nots."[106]

A further issue during negotiation of the Non-Proliferation Treaty was the duration of that agreement. The United States and the Soviet Union wanted a treaty in perpetuity, like the PTBT. Most NATO countries, particularly West Germany, opposed an unlimited commitment not to have their own nuclear weapons and took exception to the US-Soviet proposal. Some non-aligned countries, including Brazil, Switzerland and India, wanted at least the initial duration of the treaty to be short, in order to put pressure on the superpowers to fulfill their Article VI obligations to negotiate an end to the arms race.[107] Eventually, the Parties agreed to a treaty with an initial duration of 25 years, at the end of which a Conference of all parties would decide, by majority vote, whether to make the duration permanent, or to extend the Treaty for one or more specified periods of years.[108] Although that Conference does not appear to have authority to cause the Treaty to terminate abruptly at the end of the 25-year period in 1995, it could decide to extend the Treaty for only a brief period, such as a year or two, making a collapse of the Treaty regime at the end of that time a likely possibility.

Between 1968, when negotiation of the NPT was completed, and 1974, the War in Viet Nam preoccupied the leaders of the superpowers and diverted the attention of the American peace movement.[109] The main flurry of test ban activity occurred in 1970, when the United States Defense Department's Advanced Research Project Agency sponsored a conference at Woods Hole, Massachusetts, at which experts discussed improved seismic detection and identification capabilities. At the conference, scientists presented new techniques that enabled remote detection and identification of nuclear tests at levels down to one or two kilotons. When Senator Clifford Case, the ranking Republican member of the Senate's Arms Control Subcommittee, tried to obtain public release of this document, a copy was sent with the summary "ripped out and the summary was the only portion of the report comprehensible to the layman." It turned out that the Defense Department had disagreed with the summary, had designated it for "Official Use Only" to prevent public release, had planned to write its own summary, and had claimed, in a press interview, that the original summary reflected only the views of one of the conferees. But Senator Case received letters from six scientists who had been at the conference, attesting to the accuracy of the original summary; three of the authors said that "the discrimination problem [distinguishing between explosions and earthquakes] has essentially been solved down to magnitude 4.0." Senator Case instigated a Congressional hearing at which he charged the government with "overt manipulation or suppression of the frank opinion of scientists . . . an abuse of authority which cannot be tolerated."[110]

In 1974, the United States and the Soviet Union took the test ban process a small step further. As early as 1971, President Richard M. Nixon had stated his support for efforts to negotiate a comprehensive test ban, although some believed it to be "half-hearted."[111] In February, 1974, the Soviet Union tested Nixon's commitment, proposing bilateral negotiation of a CTB at a summit scheduled for June of that year. Under General Secretary Leonid I. Brezhnev's proposal, the agreement would not become effective without adherence by France and China. With the advice of Secretary of State Henry Kissinger, Nixon rejected the idea, not wanting to pressure those countries (and perhaps particularly not China, which was entering into a new relationship with the United States). But Brezhnev raised the alternative of banning tests below a stated threshold. The two leaders knew that no other significant arms control arrangement would be ready in time for signing at the summit. Nixon's arms control achievements had already been impressive; reeling from the threat of impeachment for his cover-up of the Watergate scandal, he wanted another arms control treaty to boost his Presidency. At the summit, Nixon refused still another CTB overture from the Soviet leadership, but he did agree to a bilateral Threshold Test Ban Treaty (TTBT) setting a 150 kiloton limit on underground testing.[112]

The treaty was not well received in other countries. While it was being negotiated, India detonated its first nuclear explosion, which it claimed was for "peaceful" purposes, although the laws of physics do not distinguish between devices intended for war and those to be used in other ways.[113] The Indian explosion shocked the world, making serious efforts to stop the arms race seem imperative. American experts predicted that the political effect of the TTBT would be "minimal at best, and very possibly negative, particularly now that a comprehensive treaty would be so welcome and seems within reach."[114] These forecasts proved accurate; the Treaty "was received with a great feeling of indifference on the part of United Nations member States."[115] Perhaps one reason for the disappointment was the level of the threshold, which was set to accommodate military requirements in the United States and was far higher than the capabilities of existing seismic technology.[116]

During the brief administration of President Gerald T. Ford, the United States and the Soviet Union negotiated, as contemplated by the TTBT, a companion agreement limiting underground explosions for peaceful purposes to the same 150 kiloton threshold. But during the Ford administration, both countries conducted numerous explosions with yields higher than 150 kilotons, taking advantage of the fact that the effective date of the TTBT had been put off for two years, perhaps for the very purpose of enabling the parties to test their latest weapons fully.[117] Perhaps the most significant aspect of the two treaties is that the TTBT committed the United States and the Soviet Union to "continue their negotiations with a view towards achieving a solution to the problem of the cessation of all underground nuclear weapon tests."[118] For the first time, this commitment was expressed as a legally binding treaty commitment rather than in a precatory preamble.

Carter and Brezhnev: 1977–80

Like John F. Kennedy, Jimmy Carter entered the oval office with a personal commitment to ending nuclear weapons tests. As a candidate, he'd criticized the TTBT, saying that "we can and should do more," and he had called for "an agreement to bar all nuclear tests for five years . . .

subject to renewal."[119] Interviewed by four wire service correspondents on his third day in office, he said that "I would like to proceed quickly and aggressively with a comprehensive test ban treaty. I am in favor of eliminating the testing of all nuclear devices, instantly and completely. . . . And whether or not the Soviets will agree to do that, I don't know yet. . . ."[120] But at this early moment in his Presidency, his administration had not worked out a plan of action. Asked whether the United States would take "unilateral action" challenging the Soviets to an immediate moratorium, Secretary of State Cyrus R. Vance, Jr. was at first unable to respond because he had not "had a chance to discuss that point" with Carter; later, his spokesman said that the President was not "advocating" a unilateral halt.[121]

Less than ten days later, Carter showed just how serious he was about seeking a negotiated ban when he told Soviet Ambassador Anatoly Dobrynin, in their first meeting, that he wanted a CTB.[122] But Carter had already planted the seeds for the failure of this venture by appointing Dr. Zbigniew Brzezinski as his national security advisor. Brzezinski saw the CTB issue as a "nonstarter" and had "little confidence that we would make any progress," but "out of deference to the President's zeal" for a test ban, he "went through the motions of holding meetings, discussing options, and developing negotiating positions."[123] Although Carter wanted to ban all tests and Vance advised him privately that "there is substantial support in the country . . . and that [with a five year rather than unlimited duration] it will be possible to muster support from the Joint Chiefs," Brzezinski "did what [he] could to move the bureaucratic machinery" toward proposals "which would not jeopardize our ability to continue the minimum number of tests necessary for our weapons program."[124] Carter also appointed James Schlesinger as Secretary of the new Department of Energy (which had succeeded to the AEC's function of developing and testing nuclear weapons). Like Brzezinski, Schlesinger opposed a CTB.[125] The Secretary of Defense supported the President, but the Joint Chiefs of Staff, relying on advice relayed from the directors of Livermore and Los Alamos, opposed his policy "openly and strongly."[126]

Brezhnev responded to Carter's overtures by altering the Soviet Union's stance on on-site inspection. In a March, 1977, speech, he accepted the Swedish plan for an unlimited number of "challenge" inspections, a compromise that the United States also accepted because it concluded that no country would actually allow an on-site inspection if it had violated a test ban agreement and that refusal to allow a "challenge" inspection would have virtually the same political consequences for a potential violator as refusal to allow an inspection pursuant to a quota.[127] A few months later, as the first serious CTB negotiations since 1963 were getting under way, Brezhnev also conceded to the American position that a comprehensive test ban would have to include a contemporaneous ban on nuclear explo-

sions for peaceful purposes.[128] This policy change removed the last fundamental obstruction to negotiation of an agreement.

Two parallel developments followed. In Geneva, delegates from the
United States, Britain and the Soviet Union began to make rapid progress
in drafting a comprehensive test ban treaty. In Washington and at Livermore and Los Alamos, Brzezinski and bureaucrats who were opposed to a
CTB worked to undercut the negotiations.

At the bargaining table, the Soviets accepted an American proposal to
install ten unmanned but tamper-detecting seismic stations on their territory, although they argued that the United States and Britain should each
be required to have ten stations as well.[129] The three parties agreed on
many of the less controversial aspects of a multilateral treaty (including
procedures for entry into force, amendment, a review conference, an
international seismic data exchange, and challenge inspections) and of a
supplemental trilateral agreement that would provide for more stringent
verification procedures among themselves.[130]

But other issues, including the duration of the treaty and the Western
response to the Soviet demand for ten British stations, remained unresolved. The American delegation constantly required negotiating instructions from Washington to introduce initiatives on any issue and to respond
to Soviet proposals. But more than half of the people on the "working
group" writing the instructions (and most of the people on the delegation
itself) "were generally opposed to holding the negotiation at all," an
administrative arrangement that Carter's ambassador to the talks characterized as "wrong" and "stupid."[131] Test ban opponents in Washington
forced every attempt to formulate instructions into a bureaucratic deadlock,
slowing progress considerably:

> It was possible for these opponents to take every small issue and raise it to a
> cabinet-level issue so that it took several months [because the senior, cabinet-
> level National Security Council groups met only every month or so] to decide
> anything. [They also employed] other mechanisms by which it was possible
> for them to slow things down to the point where the negotiations couldn't
> move at all. . . .[132]

Bureaucratic opposition to a CTB within the U.S. government was
mirrored within the British government. The Labor Party, which was in
office during the critical period of the talks, strongly favored a CTB, but
test ban opponents in the Ministry of Defense succeeded in helping to put
a brake on the talks by persuading the government to refuse the Soviet
demand for ten stations on British territory.[133]

When policy issues were finally confronted by U.S. officials at the cabinet
level, Carter's senior officials often reflected the disagreements that had

been expressed at lower ranks. In that event, only Carter could decide policy, but the high-level meetings were chaired by Brzezinski or his deputy, and Carter had not been present to hear the discussion. He made his decisions on the basis of summaries written by Brzezinski and not shown to Vance or other test ban supporters before being given to the President. Although it is not yet known whether the test ban summaries were accurate, Vance has reported that generally speaking, "the summaries quite often did not reflect adequately the complexity of the discussion or the full range of participants' views. Sometimes [when I did get to see them later] I found discrepancies, often serious ones from my own recollection of what had been said, agreed, or recommended."[134]

Not satisfied by slowing down the process of providing guidance to the delegation, or by withholding instructions that could move the negotiations forward, the bureaucrats who opposed the President resorted to three additional tactics. First, they proposed reversals in important aspects of the President's stated policy, although steps backward by the U.S. delegation at the bargaining table would have the effect of causing the Soviets to doubt the seriousness of the American government's desire for progress. Carter had declared himself in favor of a ban on all testing, but some test ban opponents wanted the delegation to propose that small nuclear experiments be exempted.[135] That toe having been wedged into the doorway of the inter-agency discussions, others wanted to redefine a comprehensive test ban to permit explosions up to five kilotons.[136] Carter had signed a Presidential Directive directing his negotiators to seek a five-year treaty, but opponents insisted, successfully, that the negotiators' instructions be changed to limit the duration of the agreement to three years.[137]

Second, they began to take their case against the President to the public and to Congress. Donald Kerr, a ten-year veteran of Los Alamos National Laboratory who was serving as the Acting Assistant Secretary of Energy for Defense Programs, told a House Armed Services subcommittee hearing in March, 1978, that "in the long run without testing we could not maintain the same confidence in our nuclear weapon stockpile that we have today."[138] In August, he repeated his argument in a second hearing.[139] The effect of this testimony was to "lock in" the view of the Energy Department on the public record, so that if a Treaty were actually negotiated, Departmental support for it would be perceived by the Senate as a political afterthought and would be difficult for the President to justify.[140] Although Kerr was reprimanded for failing, as directed, to share his written testimony with other agencies so that they could coordinate administration policy statements,[141] he was not fired; in fact, on Schlesinger's recommendation, he was soon promoted to become the Director of Los Alamos.[142] Actually, Kerr's testimony had been developed with the help of another Los Alamos and Department of Energy veteran, Seymour Shwiller, who at the time was on loan to the House Armed Services Committee as a member of its professional staff. Shwiller had "worked some of the questions [to Kerr] out with the Department of Energy;" when challenged by a Congressman, he claimed that he did not usually coordinate questions and answers with witnesses, and that his having done so this time (with the witnesses of the Departments of Energy and Defense) was "a random occurrence" for which he had "no reason."[143]

Finally, Los Alamos and Livermore took their opposition directly to the President. Schlesinger secured a 90-minute appointment at which he and the laboratory directors spoke directly with Carter about their objections to his policy.[144] The meeting was almost a rerun of Teller's session with Eisenhower twenty-one years earlier. One of the laboratory directors believed that the discussion changed Carter's views on the desirability of a test ban; more probably, as Carter's CTB ambassador put it years later, after having discussed the CTB negotiations with the former President, Carter came to understand "that the opposition to a test ban [within his administration] was deeper and stronger than he had realized."[145]

A further force pushing Carter to slow down the CTB negotiations was the increasing controversy about the emerging strategic arms treaty, SALT II. The administration had hoped to have the strategic treaty signed and ratified by early 1978, but a series of controversies dragged out completion of the agreement until the middle of 1979, and it never was ratified.[146] Carter "did not want to 'muck up' SALT with the [extremely contentious] test ban," and in late September or early October, 1978, he and Soviet Foreign Minister Gromyko agreed to conclude SALT ahead of CTB.[147] In 1979, the CTB negotiations went into slow motion, and with the Soviet invasion of Afghanistan at the end of the year, they froze. The window of opportunity that had opened in 1977 had slammed shut.

Reagan and Brezhnev

The Reagan administration, elected on a platform advocating a military buildup, surprised no one by its decision, in 1982, not to keep the CTB talks going. At first it cited verification concerns, but administration officials eventually conceded that they would oppose a CTB even if all verification problems were solved.[148]

The administration offered several different justifications for its opposition to a test ban. First, it was unpersuaded by CTB advocates' claim that a test ban was desirable because it would slow the superpower arms race. Proponents of a comprehensive test ban acknowledged that it would have limited impact on slowing the development of new types of weapons, since nuclear explosive technology had not changed drastically since the early 1960s.[149] On the other hand, they argued that a CTB in the late 1980s could still forestall an emerging arms race of space-based nuclear explosive weapons based on "third generation"[150] principles; that is, weapons that would work by steering or aiming their energy.[151] Weapons designers in both superpowers were working on designs for X-ray and optical anti-missile lasers powered by nuclear explosions in space; nuclear weapons whose energy would be transformed into microwaves that would be directed against communications and other electronic systems; and nuclear kinetic energy weapons, in which tiny pellets would be focused and hurled by nuclear explosions in space at enormous speeds toward other targets in space.[152] The Reagan administration rejected a CTB in part because it wanted to keep open the option to run, and win, a race to develop and deploy weapons incorporating these new technologies, which were at the heart of one of its concepts of "Star Wars" defenses against ballistic missile attack.[153]

Opponents of a test ban, in and out of government, also rejected the claim that a test ban could slow the proliferation of nuclear weapons. CTB advocates believed that an end to testing by the superpowers would make it harder for national leaders in the third world to justify their own acquisition of nuclear weapons, and that India and Pakistan, which had justified their refusal to sign the Non-Proliferation Treaty by pointing to its failure to impose the same obligations on both nuclear and non-nuclear powers,[154] would be unable to withstand international political pressure to adhere to a CTB equally binding on all countries. Those favoring continued testing argued, however, that potential proliferators, such as South Korea, Taiwan and South Africa "will be governed by detailed assessment of the external danger as they view it, and their internal politics," and will not be influenced by the superpowers' adherence to a CTB.[155]

Furthermore, Reagan administration officials asserted that a CTB could harm American national security. In addition to claiming that "third generation" weapons would help to defend the United States against a missile attack, they asserted, as the laboratory directors had done in 1978, that testing was necessary to maintain confidence in the reliability of the nuclear stockpile. They made two types of claims for this view. First, they said that small changes in the design of particular types of nuclear warheads would inevitably be made because as components or materials wore out, they would surely be replaced not with identical components or materials, but with the latest improvements; after an accumulation of small changes, a test would be needed to determine that the weapon still had its advertised yield.[156] Test ban advocates agreed with the premise that design changes could necessitate tests and advocated a freeze on such changes,[157] claiming that CTB opponents were obscuring the issue of whether the United States was *willing* to freeze warhead designs by asserting the inevitability of design alteration.[158]

The second type of stockpile reliability claim made by the administration was that even if physical inspection of dismantled warheads and non-nuclear testing, rather than nuclear explosive testing, could be relied on to maintain stockpile confidence,[159] it would be essential to maintain a core of weapon designers at the national laboratories so that any doubts could be resolved by experts. But "in the absence of an experimental program," the experts "would gradually move into more dynamic areas [of science]."[160] Needless to say, test ban advocates were unimpressed by the argument; they believed that the experts could be enticed by other interesting work to remain at the laboratories or assembled on an *ad hoc* basis if necessary, and that to the extent that the loss of a center of expertise was a real concern, it would be equally problematic for the Soviet Union.

While cancelling the CTB negotiations initiated by its predecessor, the Reagan administration also increased the frequency of U.S. testing, and it initiated a policy of not announcing some of its tests.[161] In addition, it adopted a much more confrontive stance internationally. At the end of 1981, the administration abstained (as it had traditionally done) on the annual United Nations test ban resolution, which called on the three negotiating nuclear weapon States to resume their talks.[162] A year later, essentially the same resolution passed by a vote of 111 to 1, with the United States in opposition.[163]

The Reagan administration even reversed the small progress that Presidents Nixon and Ford had achieved, announcing that the verification provisions that the United States had sought and agreed to a decade earlier for the still-unratified Threshold Test Ban Treaty were now regarded as inadequate, and that the United States would not ratify that pact until the Soviet Union accepted additional verification equipment and procedures. This move was widely viewed as a tactic to obstruct any further progress toward a CTB.[164]

For the new President's first term, the Soviet Union's interest in the issue was unclear, a result, in all likelihood, of the leadership crisis occasioned by the successive deaths of Brezhnev and his two immediate successors.[165] In 1985, Mikhail Gorbachev came to power as committed to a CTB Treaty as Carter had been in 1977.[166] But his Western partners were unwilling to dance.

The Missed Opportunities

By the time of Gorbachev's accession, the thirty year cycle was complete. The United States and the Soviet Union were back to the positions they had taken in 1955, with the Soviet Union the vigorous champion of an end to tests, and the United States opposed to the very idea.

Three opportunities to end nuclear testing had been squandered through bureaucratic infighting and unlucky timing. In the late 1950's, Eisenhower might have been able to take advantage of Soviet commitment to a test ban (as reflected in its policy statements and its moratorium), but he was unwilling or unable to resolve disagreements within his administration until it was almost too late. If the mutual moratorium of 1958 had begun a few months earlier, or if the four underground explosions within the HARDTACK II series had been canceled, there would have been no "new data" to undercut the findings of the Conference of Experts the following January. Despite the "new data," if Khrushchev had been more flexible on verification, a comprehensive test ban could probably have been negotiated at any time in 1959, for by that time Eisenhower was strongly in favor of negotiating an agreement, and from the American administration's perspective, the only problem was ensuring Soviet compliance. Despite the limited flexibility of the Soviet government with respect to verification, a test ban would probably have been signed in 1960 if the U-2 flight had not disrupted the Paris summit, or if Khrushchev had regarded negotiation of a CTB as of sufficient importance to warrant agreement despite the U-2 affair (particularly in light of Eisenhower's cancellation of future U-2 surveillance of the Soviet Union). In light of the fact that satellite reconnaissance of the Soviet Union replaced airplane overflights within a few years, the fact that the CTB foundered over the U-2 issue seems absurd a generation later.

A second opportunity appeared during the Kennedy administration, because the President personally believed in a CTB and had appointed officials who were loyal to him. Kennedy's keen interest in resolving the outstanding questions was reflected in his constant reduction in the number of inspections that the United States demanded, from twenty to eight, seven, and what would have been six or five if the Soviets had shown any willingness to compromise. But as the American government's desire for a treaty grew steadily from 1957 to 1963, the Soviet government's interest appeared to fall inversely, so that Harriman was virtually imploring Khrushchev, during the Moscow negotiations, to negotiate a CTB, only to be rebuffed by a Premier who was more willing to settle for a partial agreement.

Both American and Soviet interest in ending nuclear testing waned during the war in Viet Nam, but a third opportunity emerged as both countries warmed to the idea in 1977. This time, the endeavor crashed for several reasons. First, the Soviets probably did not realize that if they were to reach agreement with the United States and Britain, they would have to move quickly and not dicker at length over minor details such as the design of the robot seismic stations.[167] Second, if the Soviets had not invaded Afghanistan, SALT II might have been ratified and a CTB negotiated in

1980. But most important, President Carter simply did not enjoy sufficient loyalty within his government, even from senior officials, and he acted as though he were "a broker instead of a leader" on the CTB issue.[168] He declined to "put down some of the more extreme demands of internal opponents."[169] Of course, even if Carter had exercised stronger leadership within his administration, he would have had to mount a powerful campaign—perhaps drawing on the strong domestic support for a CTB that has always existed—in order to obtain Senate approval.[170]

In any event, by 1985, the three opportunities had come and gone, and leaders in most of the countries that had watched the action from the sidelines were disgusted. In 1980, at the Second Non-Proliferation Treaty Review Conference, some of them had attacked the apparent hypocrisy of the big powers, citing their failure to agree on a CTB, and some of them warned that they might renounce the NPT.[171] The Conference ended, ominously, without a declaration of support for the NPT.[172] In the Conference on Disarmament (formerly the Eighteen Nation Disarmament Committee, now expanded to 40 members) in Geneva, the non-aligned countries, supported by the Soviet Union and its allies, sought a resolution permitting that body to begin to draft a CTB itself, but the United States and Britain opposed them; the resolution had to fail because the Conference makes its decisions only by unanimous consent.[173] The Secretary-General of the United Nations noted that the General Assembly had adopted far more resolutions calling for an end to nuclear testing than on any other issue of disarmament, and that most countries had come "to regard the achievement of a comprehensive test ban as a litmus test of the determination of the nuclear-weapon States to halt the arms race."[174] The General Assembly responded with still more resolutions, fruitless annual appeals calling for negotiation of a comprehensive test ban.[175] By the late 1980s, the United States and France were often the only nations opposing these resolutions.[176] Yet the Reagan administration seemed not even slightly distressed that it had reversed the stated policy of six American presidents and was out of step with the thinking of nearly all other governments. The stage was set for the non-aligned countries to undertake a dramatic new initiative in order to get the CTB back onto the bargaining table.

Notes

1. Known nuclear tests worldwide, 1945 to December 31, 1990, *Bulletin of the Atomic Scientists* April, 1991, p. 49.

2. Richard L. Miller, *Under the Cloud: The Decades of Nuclear Testing* (New York: Free Press 1986) 188–94. Miller describes in graphic detail the events at the test site and on the trawler.

3. Robert A. Divine, *Blowing on the Wind: The Nuclear Test Ban Debate 1954–1960* (New York: Oxford University Press, 1978), p. 20. Divine's book provides an excellent, detailed history of the first six years of test ban debate and negotiations.

4. *Ibid.* p. 21.

5. National Academy of Sciences, *Nuclear Arms Control Background and Issues* (Washington, D.C.: National Academy Press, 1985), p. 188; Allen G. Greb, "Survey of Past Nuclear Test Ban Negotiations" in Jozef Goldblat and David Cox, *Nuclear Weapon Tests: Prohibition or Limitation?* (London: Oxford University Press, 1988), p. 96.

6. Divine, p. 62.

7. Divine, p. 59; "The Nuclear Weapons Test Ban," *Bulletin of the Atomic Scientists* November, 1956, p. 268.

8. Milton S. Katz, *Ban the Bomb: A History of SANE, the Committee for a Sane Nuclear Policy* (New York, N.Y.: Praeger, 1987), p. 15.

9. Divine, p. 64.

10. *Ibid.,* p. 66.

11. Statement of May 12, 1956, in "The Nuclear Weapons Test Ban," *Bulletin of the Atomic Scientists* November, 1956, p. 268; Divine, pp. 72, 93; Katz, pp. 15–16.

12. Divine, pp. 67, 139, 85; Greb, p. 96 (British proposal).

13. Divine, p. 113.

14. Divine, pp. 120, 124–25.

15. Katz, p. 16. Schweitzer had achieved by this time "virtually cultic status" within the United States because of his saintly character and his humanitarian activities. *Ibid.*

16. Albert Schweitzer, "A Declaration of Conscience," *Saturday Review* May 18, 1957, p. 17 (text of address); Divine, p. 122 (fifty nations); Letter to Norman Cousins from Jawaharlal Nehru, March 16, 1957, in Norman Cousins, *Albert Schweitzer's Mission* (New York: W.W. Norton & Co., 1985) (Nehru's encouragement).

17. Linus Pauling, "An Appeal by American Scientists to the Governments and People of the World," *Bulletin of the Atomic Scientists* September, 1957, p. 264. Pauling eventually won a second Nobel Prize, the Peace Prize, for his efforts to encourage a halt to testing. Katz, p. 17.

18. Between the Schweitzer appeal and the first British H-bomb test, the Supreme Soviet offered the West a reciprocal termination of testing. Divine, p. 125.

19. *Ibid.,* p. 144–46.

20. *Ibid.,* pp. 148–55; Statement by President Eisenhower, Aug. 21, 1957, *Department of State Bulletin,* September 9, 1957, p. 418.

21. Katz, p. 20.

22. *Ibid.,* pp. 26–28.

23. Divine, p. 182.

24. *Ibid.,* pp. 175–76.

25. *Ibid.,* p. 171.

26. Every test is given a name, a process "done on a casual, often comical basis" by scientists at the Los Alamos and Livermore laboratories where nuclear

explosives are designed. "How scientists play games with names," *Business Week* December 30, 1967, p. 66.

27. Divine, p. 188.

28. U.S. Department of State, *Geneva Conference on the Discontinuance of Nuclear Weapons Tests* (Washington: U.S. Government Printing Office, 1961), p. 13.

29. Divine, p. 201. Divine notes that Eisenhower had only himself to blame, because he had personally come to favor a change in U.S. policy, but he had allowed the AEC and the Defense Department to kill test ban proposals offered by the State Department. *Ibid.,* pp. 201–02.

30. SANE was able to maintain a nineteen-day rally in New York City. Katz, p. 32.

31. "U.S. Will Consider Atomic Test Halt," *New York Times* April 10, 1958, p. 1 (Eisenhower's public statement); Divine, p. 201 (new policy review).

32. Letters to Premier Nikita S. Khrushchev from President Dwight D. Eisenhower, April 8 and 28, 1958, *Geneva Conference* p. 14; Divine, p. 211 (lack of consultation of AEC and DOD).

33. Divine, p. 209.

34. *Geneva Conference,* pp. 14–15.

35. "East-West Technical Experts Conclude Talks at Geneva," *Department of State Bulletin* September 22, 1958, p. 452, 460.

36. The Experts reported that "when the control posts detect an event which cannot be identified by the international control organ and which could be suspected of being a nuclear explosion, the international control organ *can send* an inspection group to the site." (emphasis added) Ibid. 461. For a careful critique of the inadequate guidance given to the Western delegates, see Robert Gilpin, *American Scientists and Nuclear Weapons Policy* (Princeton, N.J.: Princeton University Press, 1962). The responsibility for the lack of adequate guidance must rest with the President, who at this time, as later, was unwilling to resolve conflicts among his advisors and consequently left the experts to their own devices. For example, the chairman of the American delegation "tried desperately to obtain a judgment from Washington as to whether or not the [British proposal for a compromise on the number of control stations, which the Americans eventually accepted] would present an acceptable risk to the United States, but he could not obtain this assurance." Harold Karan Jacobson and Eric Stein, *Diplomats, Scientists and Politicians* (Ann Arbor, Michigan: University of Michigan Press, 1966), p. 77.

37. Divine, p. 219; "Fateful Decision," *Time* September 1, 1958, p. 7.

38. Divine, pp. 228, 232.

39. *Geneva Conference,* p. 19.

40. *Ibid.,* pp. 19–20.

41. *Ibid.,* p. 21.

42. Katz, p. 35.

43. *Geneva Conference,* pp. 22–29.

44. *Ibid.,* pp. 29–30.

45. Divine, p. 246.

46. *Geneva Conference,* p. 31 (refusal to discuss data); Divine, p. 252 (quota concept).

47. Divine, pp. 246–47, 252.

48. United States Congress, Office of Technology Assessment, *Seismic Verification of Nuclear Testing Treaties* (Washington: U.S. Government Printing Office; 1988), p. 102.

49. Divine, p. 293. Even at the time, scientists doubted the validity of Latter's "big hole" scenario. Hans Bethe, who had presented the theory to the Soviets at the Geneva talks late in 1959 gave a public speech a few months later in which he noted that it would take two and a half years and ten million dollars to wash out a salt dome to decouple a 20-kiloton explosion; that salt domes were uncommon; and that the washed-out salt could be detected. "I really think that we are all behaving like a bunch of lunatics to take any such thing as the big hole seriously. . . . The opponents of a test-cessation agreement have forced us into considering more and more and smaller and smaller technical details which become more and more absurd. . . . I think the problem is not a technical problem; [it is] a political problem." "The Test Ban and 'the Hole,'" *Scientific American,* June, 1960, p. 81.

50. Letter to Sen. Edmund Muskie from James. J. Wadsworth, July 14, 1971, *Hearings on Prospects for Comprehensive Nuclear Test Ban Treaty before the Senate Subcommittee on Arms Control, International Law and Organization,* 92d Cong., 1st Sess. (July 22, 1971), pp. 5, 7.

51. Divine, pp. 282–84.

52. *Geneva Conference,* p. 66.

53. *Ibid.,* p. 67.

54. *Geneva Conference,* pp. 84–86. For a fully coupled explosion in hard rock (such as the rock at the Soviet Union's nuclear test site at Semipalatinsk), a seismic magnitude of 4.75 corresponds to a nuclear yield of about 15 kilotons, or about the magnitude of the Hiroshima bomb. See Henry J. Myers, "Extending the Nuclear-Test Ban," in *Arms Control: Readings from Scientific American* (San Francisco: W. H. Freeman and Company, 1974), p. 283.

55. *Ibid.,* p. 90.

56. Divine, pp. 300–01, quoting George Kistiakowski, *A Scientist at the White House* (Cambridge, Mass.: Harvard University Press, 1976).

57. Divine, pp. 301–02; *Geneva Conference* p. 91 ("agreed duration").

58. Divine, pp. 304 (Sec. of State Herter), 302 (Macmillan); Letter to Sen. Edmund Muskie from James. J. Wadsworth, July 14, 1971, in *Hearings on Prospects* pp. 7–8 (Wadsworth).

59. Divine, p. 310.

60. Divine, pp. 311–313.

61. A.M. Rosenthal, "Collapse Feared for Geneva Talk," *New York Times* May 18, 1960, p. 1

62. Greb, p. 100.

63. Open letter to Thomas E. Murray from Senator John. F. Kennedy, Oct. 9, 1960, reprinted in *Bulletin of the Atomic Scientists* November, 1960, inside back cover.

64. *Geneva Conference,* p. 105; Gilpin, p. 251.

65. Glenn T. Seaborg, *Kennedy Khrushchev, and the Test Ban* (Berkeley, California: University of California Press, 1981), p. 35.

66. *Geneva Conference,* pp. 125–128, 177.

67. *Ibid.,* pp. 150–54.

68. *Ibid.,* pp. 584–85.

69. National Academy of Sciences, p. 191. The Soviets did not technically break a moratorium, because they had declared only that they would refrain from testing if the "Western nations" refrained and had explicitly included France, a NATO member, as a Western nation. United States officials were surprised that the Soviets were willing to accept international condemnation for being the first superpower to test after President Kennedy had hinted in public that the United States was itself on the verge of deciding to end its moratorium on testing. "End of the Test Ban," *Science* September 8, 1961, p. 656. In June, President Kennedy had ordered that preparations at the Nevada Test Site begin for tests that might occur at the end of the year. Seaborg, p. 69.

70. Divine, p. 316 (Nehru); "More Bombs," *Scientific American* October, 1961, p. 80 (Nkrumah); "A Hundred Million More," *Scientific American* December, 1961, p. 72 (Canada); "Test: A Tentative—and Probable—Yes," *Newsweek* November 13, 1961, p. 21 (women).

71. Resolution number 1648, "Continuation of Suspension of Nuclear and Thermo-nuclear Tests and Obligations of States to Refrain from Their Renewal," adopted November 6, 1961, *Yearbook of the United Nations* (United Nations, NY: Office of Public Information, 1961), vol. XVI, 1961, pp. 24–5.

72. United States Arms Control and Disarmament Agency, *International Negotiations on Ending Nuclear Weapon Tests, September 1961–September 1962* (Washington: U.S. Government Printing Office, 1962), pp. 216–18.

73. Seaborg, p. 149.

74. *Ibid.,* p. 162.

75. Greb, pp. 101–02.

76. Resolution 1762a and b, "The Urgent Need for Suspension of Nuclear and Thermo-nuclear Tests," adopted November 6, 1962, *Yearbook of the United Nations* (United Nations, NY: Office of Public Information, 1962), vol. XVI, 1962, pp. 97–98.

77. *International Negotiations* p. 95.

78. Seaborg, p. 179.

79. Arthur H. Dean, *Test Ban and Disarmament: The Path of Negotiation* (New York: Harper and Row, 1974), p. 95 (eight and seven); Seaborg, p. 188 (six); Steve Fetter, *Toward a Comprehensive Test Ban* (Cambridge, Massachusetts: Ballinger Books, 1988), p. 9 (five).

80. Telephone interview with William Epstein, June 6, 1990.

81. *Geneva Conference,* p. 143.

82. Seaborg, pp. 162, 179–80.

83. *Ibid.,* pp. 209, 227, 240.

84. *Ibid.,* p. 227.

85. *Ibid.,* p. 240.

86. *Ibid.,* p. 242.

87. Treaty Banning Nuclear Weapon Tests in the Atmosphere, in Outer Space and Under Water (1963). The Treaty is reproduced as Appendix A. It is commonly

known as the Limited Test Ban Treaty in the United States and the Partial Test Ban Treaty elsewhere in the world. Because of its focus on the international debate, this book uses the informal name by which the agreement is more frequently cited.

88. "Beyond the Test Ban," *Scientific American* November, 1963, p. 64.

89. See "Forty Five Years of Nuclear Testing," *Arms Control Today,* November, 1990, pp. 6–7; *Threshold Test Ban and Peaceful Nuclear Explosion Treaties: Hearings on Executive N Before the Senate Comm. on Foreign Relations,* 95th Cong., 1st Sess. 111 (1977) (testimony of Dr. Herbert Scoville, former Assistant Director of the Central Intelligence Agency, on behalf of the Arms Control Association).

90. Katz, p. 87.

91. "Urgent Need for Suspension of Nuclear and Thermo-nuclear Tests," Resolution number 1910, adopted November 27, 1963, *Yearbook of the United Nations* (United Nations, New York: Office of Public Information, 1963), vol. IX, 1963, pp. 139–40.

92. "And Now There are Five," *Newsweek,* Oct. 26, 1964, p. 54.

93. *Hearings on Prospects,* p. 29. For a counter argument, see Steve Fetter, *Toward a Comprehensive Test Ban* (Cambridge, Massachusetts: Ballinger Publishing Co., 1988), p. 11, expressing the view that a "CTB remained part of Johnson's official arms control agenda largely for propaganda purposes."

94. *Hearings on Prospects,* p. 28.

95. *Ibid.,* p. 29.

96. *Ibid.,* p. 30.

97. National Academy of Sciences, p. 201.

98. National Academy of Sciences, p. 196. The bilateral SALT I agreements included the Anti-Ballistic Missile Treaty and the first agreement limiting deployments of strategic offensive missiles. See Treaty Between the United States of America and the Union of Soviet Socialist Republics on the Limitation of Anti-Ballistic Missile Systems and the Interim Agreement Between the United States of America and the Union of Soviet Socialist Republics on Certain Measures With Respect to the Limitation of Strategic Offensive Arms, in U.S. Arms Control and Disarmament Agency, Arms Control and Disarmament Agreements (Washington: U.S. Arms Control and Disarmament Agency, 6th ed. 1990), pp. 150–76.

99. Treaty on the Non-Proliferation of Nuclear Weapons, Article I (nuclear weapon states) and Article II (non-nuclear weapon states), in U.S. Arms Control and Disarmament Agency, Arms Control and Disarmament Agreements (Washington: U.S. Arms Control and Disarmament Agency, 6th ed. 1990), pp. 98–102.

100. Leonard Spector, *The Undeclared Bomb* (Cambridge, Massachusetts: Ballinger Publishing Co.) pp. 164–93 (Israel), 80–153 (India and Pakistan), 286–305 (South Africa), 233–79 (Argentina and Brazil).

101. Quoted in William Epstein, *The Last Chance: Nuclear Proliferation and Arms Control* (New York: Free Press, 1976), p. 118.

102. Article VI.

103. The West German Government noted that under the treaty, "the non-nuclear weapon powers alone would be accepting substantial self-restrictions and obligations. . . . It is incumbent on the nuclear weapon powers to . . . aim at a comprehensive test ban [among other arms control measures]." Memorandum from

the Federal Republic of Germany to Other Governments: Nonproliferation of Nuclear Weapons, April 7, 1967, in United States Arms Control and Disarmament Agency, *Documents on Disarmament* (Washington, D.C.: U.S. Government Printing Office, 1968) (hereafter cited as Documents on Disarmament 1967), pp. 179–80. The Swedish ambassador said that a CTB was logically part of a "package" with the NPT and an agreement cutting off production of fissile materials and added that since 1963, "instead of signs of any advanced preparation for a comprehensive test ban we find underground tests proceeding in a relentless crescendo in regard both to tempo and to yield. What was meant to be a temporary exemption from prohibitory rules seems instead to have been interpreted as a legitimization of underground testing." Statement by the Swedish Representative to the Eighteen Nation Disarmament Committee, May 30, 1967, in *Documents on Disarmament 1967,* pp. 239–47. The Canadian representative, summing up the negotiations, noted that with respect to other measures needed to reduce the danger of nuclear war, "priority seems to be given to an agreement on the complete prohibition of nuclear tests." Statement by the Canadian Representative to the Eighteen Nation Disarmament Committee, Aug. 3, 1967, in *Documents on Disarmament 1967,* pp. 315–18.

104. Statement by the Swedish Representative to the Eighteen Nation Disarmament Committee, May 30, 1967, in *Documents on Disarmament 1967,* p. 247.

105. Statement by the Swedish Representative to the Eighteen Nation Disarmament Committee, together with Swedish Working Paper, Feb. 8, 1968, in United States Arms Control and Disarmament Agency, *Documents on Disarmament 1968* (Washington, D.C.: U.S. Government Printing Office, 1969), pp. 41–45. The Preamble notes that the parties are "recalling the determination [of the PTBT parties] to seek to achieve the discontinuance of all test explosions of nuclear weapons for all time and to continue negotiations to this end."

106. On the essential "bargain," and the importance of the CTB, see Epstein, pp. 181, 183, 198. Fetter notes that "[m]ost nonweapon states implicitly understood this language [in Article VI] to refer to a [comprehensive test ban], which is clearly demonstrated by the fact that, despite a steady stream of SALT negotiations, the nonnuclear states have complained consistently that the nuclear states are not living up to their obligations under Article VI. Fetter, p. 13. See also National Academy of Sciences, p. 196.

107. Mohamed I. Shaker (Ambassador of Egypt to the United Nations), *The Nuclear Non-Proliferation Treaty: Origin and Implementation 1959–1979,* v. 2 (London: Oceana Publications, 1980), pp. 859–66; Swiss Aide-Memoire to the Co-Chairmen of the Eighteen Nation Disarmament Committee, Nov. 17, 1967, in *Documents on Disarmament 1967,* pp. 572–73 (Switzerland).

108. Article X, Sec. 2.

109. See Katz, pp. 93–125.

110. *Hearings on Prospects,* pp. 58–61. For a more detailed summary of the state of seismic verification capabilities *circa* 1970, see Henry R. Myers, "Extending the Nuclear-Test Ban," *Scientific American,* January 1972, p. 13–23.

111. *Hearings on Prospects,* p. 32 (official support); Fetter, p. 13 ("half hearted").

112. Raymond L. Garthoff, *Detente and Confrontation, American-Soviet Relations from Nixon to Reagan* (Washington, D.C.: The Brookings Institution, 1985),

pp. 421–27. The agreement is the Treaty Between the United States of America and the Union of Soviet Socialist Republics on the Limitation of Underground Nuclear Weapon Tests.

113. Robert Gillette, "India: Into the Nuclear Club on Canada's Shoulders," *Science* June 7, 1974, p. 1053.

114. George W. Rathjens, and John P. Ruina, "Should We Ban Nuclear Testing Now?" *Science* July 5, 1974, p. 11.

115. Shaker, "The NPT: The First 15 Years and the Current Crisis," in Sadruddin Aga Khan, *Nuclear War, Nuclear Proliferation and their Consequences* (Oxford: Clarendon Press, 1986), p. 43.

116. *Hearings on Executive N, the Threshold Test Ban and Peaceful Nuclear Explosion Treaties, Before the Senate Committee on Foreign Relations,* 95th Cong., 1st Sess. 49, 1977 (testimony of Adm. Patrick J. Hannifin on behalf of the Joint Chiefs of Staff) (military requirements); Fetter, p. 15 (relationship to seismic technology).

117. See Robert S. Norris and Ragnhild Ferm, "Nuclear explosions, 16 July 1945–1 July 1987," in Jozef Goldblat and David Cox, *Nuclear Weapon Tests: Prohibition or Limitation?* (London: Oxford University Press, 1988), p. 399.

118. Article I, Section 3.

119. "Carter urges nuclear plant curbs," *Facts on File World News Digest,* May 29, 1976, p. 374.

120. "President Carter Interviewed by AP and UPI Correspondents," *U.S. Department of State Bulletin* February 14, 1977, p. 123.

121. Murray Marder, "Goals on Arms: A Formidable Challenge for Administration," *Washington Post* January 25, 1977, p. A4.

122. Jimmy Carter, *Keeping Faith: Memoirs of a President* (New York: Bantam Books, 1982), p. 217 (diary entry, February 1, 1977).

123. Zbignew Brzezinski, *Power and Principle: Memoirs of the National Security Advisor 1977–81* (New York: Farrar, Straus and Giroux, 1983), p. 172.

124. Cyrus R. Vance, *Hard Choices: Critical Years in America's Foreign Policy* (New York: Simon and Schuster 1983), p. 453; Brzezinski, p. 172.

125. Herbert F. York, *Making Weapons, Talking Peace* (New York: Basic Books, 1987), p. 286.

126. *Ibid.,* p. 288.

127. National Academy of Sciences, p. 201.

128. David K. Shipler, "Brezhnev, in a Shift, Says He Would Halt Civil Nuclear Tests," *New York Times* November 3, 1977, p. 1.

129. York, pp. 302–06. Like the Swedish "challenge" concept, the idea of using robot stations to avoid the issue of whose personnel would operate monitoring stations had a long history. It was first developed by Soviet and American scientists, meeting informally at the Tenth Pugwash Conference on World Affairs in September, 1962. "Test Bans and the Black Box," *Bulletin of the Atomic Scientists* January, 1963, p. 34. See also L. Don Leet, and Philip G. Schrag, Letter to the Editor, *New York Times* October 19, 1962, reprinted in "Test Bans and the Black Box," (proposal for a CTB incorporating the robot station and other concepts).

130. Tripartite Report to the Committee on Disarmament: Comprehensive Test Ban, July 30, 1980 (United States Arms Control and Disarmament Agency,

Documents on Disarmament 1980 (Washington, D.C.: U.S. Government Printing Office, 1981), p. 317.

131. Amb. Herbert F. York, in Warren Heckrotte and Smith, *Arms Control in Transition, Proceedings of the Lawrence Livermore National Laboratory Arms Control Conference* (Livermore, California: Lawrence Livermore National Laboratory 1983), p. 75.

132. *Ibid.*

133. The internal politics of the British rejection of the Soviet Union's demand for ten monitoring stations on British territories (in various parts of the world) has been documented by the American ambassador to the CTB negotiations, Herbert York. In essence, the deputy chief scientist in Britain's Ministry of Defense was part of a group of senior officials in both the United States and Britain who collaborated in"thwarting [President] Carter's desire to negotiate a test ban," and he effectively used the anticipated cost of the ten stations to persuade the Labor government's prime minister to reject the Soviet request. Carter later recalled that he had agreed with the British government that the British would propose a compromise of three stations on British territory, but this idea was never communicated to the ambassador from either country, much less to the Soviets. Herbert York, *Making Weapons, Talking Peace* (New York: Basic Books, 1987), pp. 305–10).

134. Vance, p. 37. Vance was so distressed by Brzezinski's distortions that he advised his successor, Edmund Muskie, to insist on the right to review the summaries in draft form before they were given to Carter. *Ibid.*, pp. 37–38.

135. Garthoff, p. 757.

136. Walter Pincus, "U.S. Sees No Early Nuclear Test Ban Accord," *Washington Post* August 9, 1978, p. A6, and correction, Aug. 10, 1978.

137. George C. Wilson, "Carter to Seek Five Year Ban on Atomic Tests," *Washington Post* May 27, 1978, p. A1; York, p. 305 (three years).

138. *Current Negotiations on the Comprehensive Test Ban Treaty, Hearings before the Intelligence and Military Application of Nuclear Energy Subcommittee of the House Committee on Armed Services,* 95th Cong., 2d Sess., March 15, 1978, p. 22.

139. *Effects of a Comprehensive Test Ban Treaty on United States National Security Interests, Hearings before the Panel on the Strategic Arms Limitation Talks and the Comprehensive Test Ban Treaty of the Intelligence and Military Application of Nuclear Energy Subcommittee of the House Committee on Armed Services,* 95th Cong., 2d Sess., Aug. 14, 1978, pp. 9–10.

140. A candid illustration of a government official's use of legislative testimony to limit the President's range of action is provided by Elmo Zumwalt, Chief of Naval Operations (and therefore a member of the Joint Chiefs of Staff) under President Nixon. Nixon, his Secretary of State, and his National Security Advisor were about to go to Moscow for a summit meeting at which Zumwalt feared that Nixon would enter into arms control agreements that Zumwalt did not support. Shortly before the summit, Senator Henry Jackson held a closed hearing. "I was delighted with Senator Jackson for doing it. I judged that if anything would restrain the pilgrims to Moscow, it would be a written record in the files of the Senate Armed Services Committee . . . that suggested . . . that the administration had

failed . . . to heed . . . the advice of those professional advisors whom the law bade it consult and listen to carefully." Elmo R. Zumwalt, Jr., *On Watch* (New York: Quadrangle Books, 1976), p. 505.

141. California Senate Subcommittee on Health and Human Services, *Forum on the Involvement of the University of California in Nuclear Testing at Lawrence Livermore and Los Alamos National Laboratories,* Feb. 11, 1987, p. 32 (testimony of Dr. Richard Garwin).

142. Nicholas Wade, "Defense Scientists Differ on Nuclear Stockpile Testing," *Science* September 22, 1978, p. 1105 (duty to share statements, prior Los Alamos experience); Norman Solomon, "The Atom-Weapons Lobby is Gaining," *The Nation* October 11, 1978, p. 334 (promotion).

143. *Effects of a Comprehensive Test Ban Treaty on United States National Security Interests,* pp. 96–98.

144. Pincus, p. A6.

145. York, pp. 287, 309.

146. Brzezinski, p. 54 (1978 expectation).

147. Greb, p. 109, quoting a videotaped statement of Frank Press, Carter's science advisor ("muck up"); Carter, p. 231 (meeting with Gromyko).

148. "Even if we could verify compliance with a comprehensive test ban at this point, it would not be in our interest or the interest of the world to undertake such a ban." *Hearings on Nuclear Testing Issues before the Senate Committee on Foreign Relations,* 99th Cong., 2d Sess., May 8, 1986, p. 21 (testimony of Richard Perle, Assistant Secretary of Defense for International Security Affairs).

149. Steve Fetter, *Toward a Comprehensive Test Ban* (Cambridge, Massachusetts: Ballinger Publishing Company, 1988), p. 61. The neutron bomb was conceived in the 1950s, but its development might have been precluded by a CTB in the 1960s or early 1970s. The significance of failure to preclude the neutron bomb is diminished by the facts that it is only a tactical weapon and that political objections in Europe have precluded neutron weapons from being stored outside of the United States.

150. Atomic weapons such as the ones used against Japan were the in the "first generation," while hydrogen bombs, using a combination of fission and fusion for their explosive energy, are considered "second generation."

151. See Fred Hiatt and Rick Atkinson, "Lab Creating a New Generation of Nuclear Arms," *Washington Post* June 9, 1986, p. A1. Space-based third-generation nuclear weapons would have to be tested in space before military commanders would rely on their use. Their development would generate pressure to abrogate or amend the Limited Test Ban Treaty, the Anti-ballistic Missile Treaty, and the Outer Space Treaty to accommodate such tests. CTB advocates argued that a CTB that precluded development would help the emergence of such pressures.

152. See Theodore Taylor, "Third Generation Nuclear Weapons," *Scientific American* April, 1987, p. 30; Dan L. Fenstermacher, "The Effects of Nuclear Test Ban Regimes on Third-Generation Weapons Innovation," *Science and Global Security* March, 1990, p. 187.

153. Fetter, p. 51; see Peter Clausen, "Limited Defense: The Unspoken Goal," in *Empty Promise: The Growing Case Against Star Wars* ed. John Tirman (Boston: Beacon Press, 1986), pp. 147–160; Matthew Bunn, *Foundation for the Future: The*

ABM Treaty and National Security (Washington, D.C.: The Arms Control Association, 1990), p. 34.

154. Gerard A. Smith, "End Testing, Stem the Bomb's Spread," *Arms Control Today*, November, 1990, p. 9.

155. *Effects of a Comprehensive Test Ban Treaty on United States National Security Interests, Hearings before the Panel on the Strategic Arms Limitation Talks and the Comprehensive Test Ban Treaty of the Intelligence and Military Application of Nuclear Energy Subcommittee of the House Committee on Armed Services*, 95th Cong., 2d Sess., 1978, pp. 52–54 (testimony of Dr. Michael May, Associate Director, Lawrence Livermore National Laboratory).

156. See Jack Rosengren, Some Little-Publicized Difficulties With a Nuclear Freeze (report to the Department of Energy), reprinted in *Nuclear Testing Issues: Hearing Before the Senate Committee on Foreign Relations*, 99th Cong., 2d Sess., 1986, p. 161.

157. Letter to President Jimmy Carter from former nuclear weapon designers Norris E. Bradbury, Richard L. Garwin and J. Carson Mark, August 15, 1978, in *Effects of a Comprehensive Test Ban on United States National Security Interests, Hearings Before the Panel on the Strategic Arms Limitation Talks and the Comprehensive Test Ban Treaty of the Intelligence and Military Application of Nuclear Energy Subcommittee of the House Committee on Armed Services*, 95th Cong., 2d Sess., 1978, p. 181; J. Carson Mark, "Do We Need Nuclear Testing?" *Arms Control Today*, November, 1990, p. 12.

158. Dr. Richard Garwin, a former nuclear weapons designer who supported a CTB, in a conference transcript quoted in Hugh E. DeWitt, and Gerald E. Marsh, "Stockpile reliability and nuclear testing," *Bulletin of the Atomic Scientists* April, 1984, pp. 40, 41.

159. Stockpile reliability has historically depended primarily on these methods rather than on nuclear testing. Only about a dozen nuclear tests were undertaken for the purpose of stockpile reliability in all the years before President Reagan took office, and only about one such test was conducted annually even in the Reagan years. (Even at the much accelerated Reagan rate of reliability testing—which some CTB proponents believe was instituted to forestall a CTB—each type of stockpiled weapon is tested only about once every twenty years). See sources cited in The Belmont Conference on Nuclear Test Ban Policy (David A. Koplow and Philip G. Schrag, Rapporteurs), "Phasing Out Nuclear Weapons Tests," *Stanford Journal of International Law*, v. 26, 1989, p. 230, n. 77.

160. This paraphrase of the argument is from Herbert F. York, *Making Weapons, Talking Peace* (New York: Basic Books, 1987), pp. 285–86. See also Donald M. Kerr, "The purpose of nuclear test explosions, Paper 2," ed. Jozef Goldblat and David Cox, *Nuclear Weapon Tests: Prohibition or Limitation?* (Oxford: Oxford Univ. Press, 1988), pp. 45–46 (related argument that loss of "the best weapon scientists [who would] leave for more promising careers" would make it hard for the U.S. to respond to an eventual need to resume testing).

161. Fred Hiatt, "12 Unannounced Tests Held for Nuclear Arms," *Washington Post* Jan. 15, 1986, p. A5.

162. A/36/85 (Dec. 9, 1981). See *Plenary Meetings of the General Assembly*, 36th Sess., p. 1608.

163. A/37/73 (Dec. 9, 1982). See *Plenary Meetings of the General Assembly*, 37th Session, p. 1633 (roll call vote).

164. The deputy assistant secretary of defense for nuclear forces and arms control policy wrote that "the more time wasted on discussions and experimentation of monitoring techniques irrelevant to the verification of an environment in which there are no legal tests, the easier it will be to stave off demands for the more constraining comprehensive test ban." Frank Gaffney, Jr., "Test Ban Would be Real Tremor to U.S. Security," *Defense News* Sept. 5, 1988, pp. 36–37. At about the same time, Scientific American reported that "privately officials in the White House have acknowledged to Scientific American that they have another aim. By creating the appearance of progress towards a test ban, officials said, they hope to divert attention from the achievements of genuine test ban proponents and so reduce their momentum." John Horgan, "Test-Ban Countdown," Scientific *American October,* 1988, p. 16. In addition, the Reagan administration may have proposed the additional verification proposal in the "mistaken belief that its intrusiveness would result in its unacceptability by the Soviets" and therefore a perpetual stalemate on test ban issues. Letter to Sen. David Boren from Ray E. Kidder, Department of Theoretical Group Physics, Livermore National Laboratory, Jan. 24, 1990, reprinted in *Congressional Record,* p. S 13731, Sept. 25, 1990.

165. Greb, p. 109.

166. See Chapter 2.

167. The details of the seismometers were not settled for two years, and the Soviets were never willing to discuss the details of the radio equipment through which the seismic stations would communicate with the monitoring country. York, p. 311. Soviet negotiators "continued to argue over essential details [regarding on-site inspections] until the very end." *Ibid.,* p. 317.

168. William H. Kincade, "Banning nuclear tests: cold feet in the Carter administration," *Bulletin of the Atomic Scientists November,* 1978, pp. 8, 9.

169. York, p. 320.

170. Solomon, 334 (Harris Poll shows 3 out of 4 Americans favored a CTB in 1980); see York, p. 321, for his pessimistic view (in 1987) on Senate ratification of a CTB until a time when the great powers are moving away from dependence on nuclear weapons.

171. Paul Lewis, "Short Fuses at the Nuclear Treaty Review," *New York Times* August 17, 1980, Sec. 4, p. 4.

172. William Epstein, "A Critical Time for Nonproliferation," *Scientific American* August, 1985, p. 33, 37.

173. CD/PV.276 (July 26, 1984).

174. Report of the Secretary General to the General Assembly of the United Nations, A/35/257 (May 23, 1980).

175. A/38/63 (Dec. 15, 1983); A/39/53 (Dec. 12, 1984).

176. A/RES/42/27 ("Urgent need for a comprehensive nuclear test ban treaty"), adopted by a vote of 143 to 2 (France, United States), with 8 abstentions (including Great Britain), A/PV.84, Nov. 30, 1987; A/RES/43/64 ("Urgent need for a comprehensive nuclear-test-ban treaty"), adopted by a vote of 146 to 2 (France, the United States), with 6 abstentions (including Great Britain), A/PV.73, December 22, 1988.

2

From Concept
to Conference Call

Tovish, Grimsson, and PGA

Aaron Tovish was an unlikely candidate to mobilize the staid players of the world of diplomacy. The son of the noted sculptors Harold Tovish and Marianna Pineda, he grew up in the suburbs of Boston. Like many other high school students in the middle 1960s, he was troubled by what he read about the United States' role in the war in Viet Nam. While in high school, he organized his friends to send anti-war postcards to Massachusetts Senator Ed Brooke; then, at the height of the war, he went to the Massachusetts Institute of Technology where he was, in the jargon of the time, radicalized.

As part of his assigned course work, he read William Hinton's *Fanshen*,[1] a description of the land reform campaign in 1948 China. He became convinced that the war in Viet Nam had to be stopped, and that change could occur only through the applied efforts of organizations. He became what he calls "something of a Maoist" and nearly joined the Progressive Labor Party. He was involved in the anti-war movement through the M.I.T. chapter of Students for a Democratic Society, participated in sit-ins, and was arrested for helping to take over a building at Harvard. His father brought bread to the jail for him and for the friends with whom he was locked up, and he bailed him out.

Undeterred by his encounter with a penal institution, he helped to take over the office of the President of M.I.T. For this he was suspended from college for a year, but on his return, he helped to take over the R.O.T.C. building. By this time, the tide of American opinion had turned against the war. Haiphong harbor had just been mined. To the frustration of the M.I.T. administration, the students charged in the R.O.T.C. incident turned their hearing into a trial of American war policy. The faculty-student committee acquitted all of them. Nevertheless, Tovish began to turn away from radical activism. He had become resigned to the notion that major social change would not come to the United States. Thinking about what interested him enough to warrant a life's work, he found geology. The field of plate tectonics was just being developed at M.I.T., and this new area of inquiry appealed to him.

He pursued geology for five years, getting his masters at U.C.L.A., publishing several papers on mantle fluid dynamics, and doing field work in seismology. But he gradually became disillusioned with geology, which was too slow-paced for him. New seismic data on plate tectonics were being acquired only over a period of decades; many new papers seemed to rehash old discoveries. He decided to switch sciences, and he settled on animal behavior studies, a field in which quantitative methodology was just beginning to take hold, enabling him to put his mathematical background to use.

A girl friend from California had gone to London to study, and he followed her there and began his animal behavior studies in 1979, a move that would bring him into contact with the international peace movement. In Britain, protests against American cruise missile deployments were beginning. He thought that his experience in popular protest in the United States would be helpful to British peace movement leaders, and he thought that he could be helpful in advising them how to avoid being taken over by groups at the far left of the spectrum. Keenly aware that the American peace movement was relatively ineffectual because any of its positions that coincided with those of the Soviet Union were immediately discredited, he also wanted to learn from Europeans how Americans dissidents could be more effective in their own country.

One idea that appealed to Tovish was international arbitration; perhaps neutral parties positioned between the United States and the Soviet Union could help to resolve some cold war conflicts. He started an organization called Third Party Intervention, raised funds to support it, began attending European conferences, and met groups with similar interests in Sweden, among other countries. Swedish acquaintances asked him to work with them, and in the early 1980s, he began to work at the offices of the Peace and Arbitration Society in Stockholm. In 1983, he was contacted by Nicholas Dunlop, a New Zealander whom he'd met through mutual friends in the peace movement. Dunlop was the Secretary-General (essentially the executive director) of an organization whose officers wanted to meet with Olaf Palme, the Prime Minister of Sweden. Drawing on connections he'd made in Stockholm, Tovish was able to help bring media attention to the idea of Sweden standing up to the big powers. The news columns Tovish generated helped Dunlop and his colleagues to have credibility with Palme. Impressed with his work, they asked Tovish to work with their organization, Parliamentarians for Global Action (PGA).[2]

PGA had been organized in London in 1977 by a small group of members of the parliaments of Britain, France, Canada and Japan who were interested in cooperating on disarmament issues.[3] By 1980, the organization had recruited 500 legislators in 18 countries and was working with national caucuses of parliamentarians interested in arms control and disarmament in Britain, France, India, Canada, Japan, Norway and New Zealand. Its statement of mission proclaimed that "one half of one percent of one year's world military expenditures would pay for all the farm equipment needed to increase food production and approach self-sufficiency in food-deficit, low-income countries by 1990."[4]

While PGA was in its formative stages, Olafur Ragnar Grimsson became a member of the Icelandic parliament. After studying political science in Great Britain and becoming the first Icelander to receive a Ph.D. in that field, Grimsson had founded the political science department at the University of Iceland. The concepts of that field of study were so new to his country that he had to create the Icelandic words for them.

During Grimsson's youth, his country had no army and no military tradition, although since 1951 it had hosted an American naval base. In his youth, Grimsson had participated in a movement to force his government to close the base on the ground that it existed not to defend Iceland, but to enable the United States to maintain its fleet of nuclear submarines in the North Atlantic. Grimsson believed that "for a nation with no armed forces to be in a military alliance is absurd." These views were strengthened during his studies in Britain during the late 1960s, when students throughout Western Europe began to challenge the policies of their governments.

Entering the parliament with an international background, he became a member of the Committee on Foreign Affairs and a member of the Council of Europe's Parliamentary Assembly, where he was the principal rapporteur on North-South issues. In 1982 he persuaded the Icelandic Parliament to send a delegation to observe the United Nations' second Special Session on Disarmament. While a member of the delegation, he met Nicholas Dunlop in New York, and he decided to join PGA.[5]

The following year, Grimsson was appointed to PGA's executive committee;[6] more significantly, he became part of an informal group of three PGA parliamentarians and two PGA staff members who began to develop new initiatives for the organization. This group included Relus ter Beek of the Netherlands (who at the end of the decade became Defense Minister and had to resign his PGA membership because Dutch cabinet members cannot remain in parliament), Congressman Tom Downey of the United States, Dunlop, and, within his first year on the staff, Aaron Tovish.[7] PGA's first new thrust was to try to create a significant third force in the cold war world, a group of non-aligned leaders who would make highly visible proposals to end the arms race, and who would offer to mediate between the superpowers.[8]

This idea became the Six-nation Peace Initiative, through which several heads of state, each of whom was individually an international celebrity, combined forces to issue public statements to which they hoped the American and Soviet leaders would react. PGA had access to these world leaders through its members, legislators who served in their parliaments. For example, Mexican Senator Sylvia Hernandez, a member of PGA's Board, helped the organization's officers to have access not only to her own President, Miguel de la Madrid, but also to the President of Argentina.[9] In May, 1984, Andreas Papandreo (Greece), Olaf Palme (Sweden), Indira Gandhi (India), Raul Alfonsin (Argentina), Julius K. Nyerere (Tanzania) and Miguel de la Madrid (Mexico) issued a joint statement, calling on the American and Soviet leaders to halt the testing, production and deployment of nuclear weapons.[10] They followed their statement with more dramatic activity, holding three summits among themselves in Delhi, Ixtapa (Mexico), and Stockholm, each time making statements that were reported throughout the world.[11]

A second PGA project involved a 1985 proposal by non-aligned nations to help monitor superpower compliance with a CTB. Although this effort could not succeed because the U.S. government would not agree to a CTB, it helped to launch a related project that was initiated by the Natural Resources Defense Council (NRDC). In April, 1986, when Grimsson and ter Beek met with Soviet Foreign Minister Edward A. Shevardnadze, they were accompanied by Professor Frank von Hippel of Princeton University, who suggested that the Soviet government convene a workshop on test ban monitoring. The Soviets agreed, and from the workshop the next month emerged the test ban demonstration project under which NRDC set up seismic monitoring stations in the Soviet Union and Soviet scientists set up similar stations near the United States' test site in Nevada.[12]

Grimsson developed the theory of what he believed was PGA's new approach to international relations. In his view, virtually all of the usual global actors were paralyzed. The superpowers were constrained by their enormous bureaucracies from taking new or risky initiatives for peace. The other governments were afraid to confront the superpowers because they would be embarrassed by a failure. The international organizations were staffed by bureaucrats more concerned with protecting their careers than with making policy; this focus ensured that they made no waves because in these organizations, causing any offense can jeopardize a career. So in the entire diplomatic world, Grimsson reasoned, it was nearly impossible for anyone to try anything new. PGA could become "the guys who can afford to lose face, the ones who are in the business of being turned down." Under his influence, PGA adopted a goal of testing new ground. "If we meet with a country's leader and are turned down," he said, "we go home and nothing has happened except that we have flown in and then out again. We accepted the role that the monks played in the Middle Ages. We could speak to the princes who couldn't speak to each other."[13]

PGA avoided all the formalities of protocol. Its officers chaired the early meetings of the six world leaders, so that they didn't have to decide which of them would be the leader of leaders. But Grimsson injected other elements of strategy as well as his new ideas and PGA's independence of national or international bureaucracies. He drew on experts, particularly those of the U.S. and Britain, to make it more difficult for the Western nations to dismiss PGA's work.[14] He also assiduously sought written support from the United States Congress, so that foreign leaders could see that although President Ronald Reagan might oppose a PGA idea, other American political leaders supported it. He hoped to convey the idea that disagreeing with President Reagan was not an "anti-American" political act.[15]

A New Idea

In 1984, the cold war was in one of its iciest periods. The Soviet army was still in Afghanistan, President Reagan had called the U.S.S.R. an "evil empire,"[16] the United States was engaged in a rapid military buildup, including "Star Wars" strategic defense research, and for the first time since the 1960s, a President was about to complete a term of office without reaching any arms control agreement with the Soviets. The issue of a comprehensive test ban had virtually disappeared from sight. In June of that year, in a speech to a convention of International Physicians for the Prevention of Nuclear War in Helsinki, Bernard Lown, its American co-president, had called on each superpower to declare a new, unilateral moratorium on nuclear testing, but to no one's surprise, neither country responded.[17] Lown persevered, travelling to Moscow in the fall to present the idea of a new moratorium to Soviet officials. He was scoffed at in the Foreign Ministry, where officials pointed out that a unilateral moratorium could only hurt the Soviet Union, because a short one would be treated as meaningless, while a long one would be unreciprocated and would produce an outcry against the U.S.S.R. when it finally resumed testing.[18]

In PGA's New York office, Aaron Tovish spent the summer and fall planning how the organization should relate to the Third Review Conference under the Non-Proliferation Treaty, scheduled for the summer of 1985. In the course of his work, he read the Treaty carefully, including its amendment clause. He was at once struck by the fact that one-third of the parties to the Treaty could require the United States, Britain and the Soviet Union (called the "depositary governments" because the original copies of the Treaty had been deposited with them) to convene a conference to consider a proposed change.[19] Quickly checking the text of the PTBT, he found that a conference to consider amendments to that treaty could be triggered the same way.[20] Both treaties required the concurrence of the U.S., the Soviet Union, and Britain in order for an amendment to be approved.[21] Nevertheless, Tovish realized at once that the provision for calling an amendment conference might be a lever through which the non-nuclear countries could put pressure on the major nuclear powers to agree to a comprehensive test ban. "A light went off in my head," he later recalled. "I realized that an organization like the one I happened to be working for could launch an amendment effort. But I had wild ideas about how to do it, and if I had known that it would take more than five years, I would have said to hell with it."[22]

Tovish quickly tried out his idea on William Epstein, a semi-retired United Nations official who was a PGA consultant. Epstein, a Canadian, was a career international civil servant; in the 1960's, he had been UN Secretary-General U Thant's personal representative to the Eighteen-National Disarmament Committee's deliberations in Geneva, and he had brokered some of the deals that had made the Non-Proliferation Treaty possible.[23] Epstein's reaction was instant and positive: "Aaron, you are a genius!"[24] Epstein offered more than compliments, however.

He commended Tovish's idea to Alfonso Garcia Robles, Mexico's Ambassador to the Conference on Disarmament, who came to New York every fall to participate in the disarmament debates of the United Nations.

Garcia Robles was a living legend. For decades, Mexico had played a major role in international disarmament negotiations, and Garcia Robles had always been Mexico's spokesman on these issues. He had helped to draft the United Nations Charter in 1945 and had represented his nation at the Eighteen-Nation Disarmament Committee during the 1960s; he had also drafted the Treaty of Tlatelolco, under which Latin America had become a zone free of nuclear weapons.[25] He had then achieved significant success by persuading nearly all of the Latin American governments to sign that Treaty, and for this work he had been awarded the Nobel Peace Prize in 1982. He was the last of the older generation of disarmament experts, the "dean of disarmament" in the United Nations.[26] He too was intrigued by Tovish's plan, and he offered to try to help.[27]

Tovish wanted to see quick implementation of his proposal. He wrote up a plan for how to bring it to fruition quickly, and two timetables for action: a slow version contemplating that the thirty-nine requests needed to convene the Conference would be submitted in April, 1985, with the Conference to be held the following spring, and a "short" scenario under which the Conference would be held in June, 1985, prior to the Non-Proliferation Treaty Review Conference.[28] Tovish wanted Grimsson, who had become PGA's President, to present the amendment conference concept to the representatives of the heads of state involved in the Six-nation Peace Initiative while they were preparing for the Delhi summit that they would hold early in 1985. But Grimsson refused, reasoning that the idea would be controversial, that careful groundwork would have to be undertaken, and that it would be better to approach the six leaders and their key advisors individually, so that they couldn't hear each other's objections.[29]

Grimsson began by obtaining the approval of the PGA executive committee to pursue the idea,[30] and by consulting informally with several of the leaders who attended the Six-nation Delhi summit.[31] It became clear to him that the project's appeal to world leaders would be significantly enhanced if it received the endorsement of creditable American politicians. Since the Treaty that would be amended was the legacy of President John F. Kennedy, Grimsson and his colleagues sought help from those who had been involved in Kennedy's government. Accordingly, PGA asked Abram Chayes, a Harvard law professor who had been the chief State Department lawyer during the Kennedy administration, to write a legal memorandum supporting the idea and to help the organization obtain endorsements for it from other former Kennedy officials. In April, eleven of them, including Averell Harriman, signed a letter supporting the PGA plan.[32] During the spring and summer of 1985, Grimsson sent letters to selected heads of state formally urging them to lead the effort, and he enclosed a copy of the Kennedy officials' letter.[33]

Meanwhile, Konstantin Chernenko, the Soviet leader, was dying. Some Soviet officials were emboldened, during the interregnum before a new leader could be selected, to advocate new policies. Bernard Lown successfully encouraged Evgeny Chazov, the Soviet co-chair of International Physicians for the Prevention of Nuclear War, to speak out in public for a Soviet unilateral test moratorium. Chazov was then a member of the Central Committee of the Communist Party and the personal physician to most of the Kremlin leadership; two months later, when Mikhail Gorbachev became General Secretary of the Communist Party, Chazov was named Minister of Health.

The Campaign Begins

Grimsson and Dunlop began to take Tovish's plan on the road, traveling first to Mexico City. The results of the trip were not encouraging. President Miguel de la Madrid "did not rule out initiating the process" at the end of 1985 but he "wished to study it more carefully."[34] Garcia Robles doubted that the project should be undertaken by the leaders of the Six-nation Peace Initiative at all, because that group included countries that were not party to the Non-Proliferation Treaty (India) or the Partial Test

Ban Treaty (Argentina).[35] In view of this reception, Grimsson aimed for a lower objective: not to obtain commitments from leaders immediately, but to ask each government to participate in a meeting to talk about the idea. Ambassadors concerned with disarmament from most of the countries of the world would gather in Geneva in August for the Non-Proliferation Treaty Review Conference. Grimsson sought to entice them to a meeting, sponsored by PGA, at which the idea would be presented. "No government could have called such a meeting," he reasoned. "That would have been a public act. But presidents of countries could let their ambassadors attend this meeting because it was not an official event. It was just a street caucus."[36]

In July, the test ban issue suddenly became a major international topic, when the new Soviet leader, Mikhail Gorbachev, followed Khrushchev's precedent and announced that on August 6, the fortieth anniversary of the Hiroshima explosion, the Soviet Union would initiate a unilateral test moratorium, which it would make permanent if it were reciprocated. The Reagan administration not only failed to reciprocate Gorbachev's first foreign policy initiative but it also refused to reopen CTB negotiations, rebuffing not only the Soviet Union but also the Republican-controlled Senate, which had voted 77–22 to urge him to resume the talks.[37] This most recent superpower rejection of a test ban initiative would not necessarily gain Grimsson any governmental endorsements of the PGA project, but it helped him to obtain a receptive ear in many countries' capitals. He and Dunlop hurried to Delhi, taking with them Sylvia Hernandez and Relus ter Beek, a member of the Dutch parliament and, like Hernandez, a PGA officer.

There they met with Rajiv Gandhi (who had succeeded his assassinated mother as Prime Minister) and his chief foreign policy advisor, Chinmaya Gharekhan. They told the PGA officials that India could not propose the Amendment Conference, indicating that to endorse the idea would put India in an awkward position, given that Pakistan had not signed the PTBT.[38] Nevertheless, Gandhi said that India would take "an active and constructive part" in the conference when it was held.[39] Gandhi made this statement believing that the conference would never be held, but Grimsson was now able to tell other countries about this near-endorsement of the Conference idea from a country that was central because of other nations' concern about its growing nuclear weapons capability.[40]

Back at home, William Epstein was helping to legitimate PGA's project by describing it in print. Writing in *Scientific American,* he described the frustration that the non-aligned countries were likely to experience at the coming Non-Proliferation Treaty Review Conference. "Some members of the [non-aligned] group talk of taking matters into their own hands by calling a conference to amend the test ban treaty," he wrote. Conceding that the United States and Britain could veto any amendment, he concluded that nevertheless, "majority approval of such an amendment would put considerable pressure on the three nuclear parties. A failure on their part to respond could have profound political repercussions."[41] As this article appeared, Hernandez and ter Beek began a tour of five Latin American countries, to persuade them to send their Ambassadors to PGA's meeting in Geneva, and Grimsson went to Yugoslavia. There, Vice President (later President) Lazar Mojsov not only agreed to send his ambassador to PGA's Geneva meeting, but also contributed a strategic idea that would prove central to PGA's later planning. He suggested that many countries would find it much easier to support the Conference, over American objections, if the United Nations General Assembly endorsed the idea.[42] Meanwhile, Tovish was calling on the ambassadors themselves as they assembled in Geneva, telling them that members of his organization had been talking to their foreign ministers and presidents, an unusual and startling message that in many cases, got their attention. Thirteen ambassadors assembled at the meeting, including representatives from three potential nuclear weapon states that had not ratified the Non-Proliferation Treaty.[43]

Meanwhile, Grimsson recruited Garcia Robles to chair the Geneva meeting. "This was a bit of a trick," Grimsson later revealed, because he and his colleagues had told all of the attending countries that PGA was holding an "informal meeting," implying that PGA would chair it. But he opened the meeting by saying that since everyone was assembled in the Palais de Nations, UN headquarters in Geneva, he thought it appropriate that Garcia Robles chair the discussion. "No one could object, because Garcia Robles was the grand old man of disarmament." This tactic not only gave the meeting greater significance, but left Grimsson freer to be an advocate.[44]

The meeting produced statements of support for the amendment conference effort from Yugoslavia and Sri Lanka, several indications of interest in continuing to explore the concept, and some indications of a negative attitude, particularly from Sweden. Sweden's lack of enthusiasm was important, for Sweden had traditionally been one of the strongest proponents of a comprehensive test ban. But the only forum in the world in which Sweden played a leading diplomatic role was the Conference on Disarmament, which it had helped to found, and the Swedish foreign ministry saw the amendment conference as a slight to the Conference on Disarmament, even though the United States was blocking all attempts to negotiate a test ban there.[45] Grimsson repeatedly warned Swedish officials that "when we get a comprehensive test ban through this route, we will let the world know that Sweden opposed it," but this threat did not worry the Swedes, who, like Gandhi, did not expect the conference to take place.[46]

A few days later, the Review Conference itself nearly collapsed over the test ban issue.[47] Led by the Mexican delegation, the non-aligned countries demanded a vote on a resolution calling for a resumption of CTB negotiations and a moratorium in the meanwhile. The United States opposed this language and was ultimately able to negotiate a compromise in which the Conference declared that "except for certain states" it called for negotiation of a CTB.[48] Meanwhile, in the United States and the Soviet Union, Lown and Chazov learned that their organization had won the Nobel Peace Prize.

Shortly after the Geneva meeting, as the UN General Assembly convened for its annual session, PGA held a luncheon for disarmament representatives at a restaurant on Second Avenue in New York. Garcia Robles led a discussion of a UN resolution that he had drafted, and the resolution began to gather support. PGA officials worried that their effort could collapse if the Soviets ended their moratorium before 39 countries called for a conference, but they were optimistic that their efforts would soon bear fruit; Dunlop reported to the PGA Executive Committee that by the end of the year, some countries might send a letter to the depositary governments, officially proposing the amendment.[49] His optimism was unfounded; no such letter was sent in 1985. But the General Assembly did approve Garcia Robles' resolution, recommending that the parties to the Partial Test Ban Treaty "carry out urgent consultations among themselves as to the advisability and most appropriate method of taking advantage of the provisions of its article II [to convert it to a CTB]."[50] The vote was 121 (including India, Pakistan, Brazil, and the Soviet Union) to 3 (the U.S., Britain, and France), with Sweden and most U.S. allies abstaining.[51]

With the effort to launch a conference call slowly gathering momentum, PGA began to refine its political strategy. Its officers had to confront the cold fact that the Reagan administration, which so strongly opposed a CTB, would be in office through 1988 and would therefore probably veto a Treaty amendment approved by a Conference held at any time in the next three years. Grimsson suggested holding the Conference in two sessions. One would be held in 1986 or 1987 to give some publicity to the test ban issue, but it would adjourn (without voting) for perhaps a year and a half. Holding a second session much later "would push the vote closer to 1989 with a possibly different, more receptive political climate."[52]

Grimsson's Odyssey

Early in 1986, Grimsson made what would be the most difficult of his many trips soliciting support for the Amendment Conference.[53] He flew from Iceland to Madrid and then to a PGA meeting in Rome. From Rome he flew to Buenos Aires for a planning meeting of the Six-nation Peace

Initiative. On the sidelines of that meeting, he separately sought out Garcia Robles and officials of the Swedish and Greek foreign ministries. Garcia Robles reported that he was unable to persuade the Mexican government to request the convening of the Conference. His colleagues in the foreign ministry were arguing, successfully, that Mexico was already at odds with the United States on several issues and couldn't take on the Americans on still another subject. He suggested that Grimsson talk directly with more senior officials in Mexico. The Swedish official was even more discouraging: Sweden would never back the proposal. Only the Greek official was encouraging; he thought that President Andreas Papandreo might be intrigued by the idea.

Grimsson flew on to New York, en route home, but there he was intercepted by Tovish, who had just learned that the foreign minister of Indonesia and the president and foreign minister of Sri Lanka would be willing to see Grimsson, in three days, in their capitals. The next day, he was off to Jakarta, where he joined up with John Langmore, an Australian member of parliament who was also a member of PGA's International Council.

Grimsson believes that he was able to gain a sympathetic audience in part because Mochtar Kusumaatmadja, the Foreign Minister of Indonesia, was fascinated that a member of the Icelandic Parliament would travel half way around the world to tell him what to do. "Foreign ministers never meet anyone but other foreign ministers and other diplomats," says Grimsson. "Besides, in that world nobody ever talks to each other except in the most circumspect ways. He was amazed that I had come all the way from Iceland to talk with him, and that I spoke so directly. In addition, Iceland is a small country with no ulterior motives, so I travel to other countries with no baggage resulting from my nationality."

Grimsson brought to Jakarta something more than a peculiar nationality. In New York, he had picked up from Tovish a letter that PGA had just received. It expressed support for the amendment conference idea, and it had been signed by more than eighty members of the United States House of Representatives. Grimsson laid a copy of this letter on the table of the of Foreign Minister of Indonesia. "That woke them up," he reports.

The next morning, Grimsson and Langmore flew on to their appointment in Sri Lanka. "The President didn't have a clue as to what I was talking about," Grimsson recalls. "But the fact that I had met with the President of Sri Lanka meant that everyone else in the government paid attention to what I was saying." Grimsson also met with the foreign minister, whom he discovered wanted to meet with the Icelandic stranger for purposes of internal political prestige. It was rare for foreign politicians to go to Sri Lanka to ask it for something, so the meeting was deemed newsworthy, and television stations covered the event.

Nevertheless, Grimsson was unable to obtain an explicit commitment from either country to initiate the amendment procedure. He flew home to Iceland, discouraged by the results of his 17-day excursion, during which he had slept on airplanes for nine nights. Just as he was at last falling asleep in his own bed, his telephone rang; Olaf Palme, the Prime Minister of Sweden who had been central to the Six-nation Peace Initiative, had been murdered, the second assassination (after the slaying of Indira Gandhi) of a Six-nation leader. On the day he was killed, Palme had signed the Six-nation group's appeal to President Reagan and General Secretary Gorbachev to refrain from nuclear testing until their next summit meeting.[54]

The Soviets were continuing to show enthusiasm about an end to testing in general and the amendment conference in particular. In January, Gorbachev had pronounced the amendment idea acceptable to the Soviet Union, and two days after the Six-nation appeal was made public, he responded to its authors by extending the Soviet moratorium.[55] Shortly thereafter, the Soviet Union agreed to allow American scientists of the Natural Resources Defense Council to set up seismic monitoring stations near the Semipalatinsk Test Site, the Soviet Union's main test area.[56] The United States continued to refuse to discuss the subject of a CTB; the Director of the U.S. Arms Control and Disarmament Agency dismissed a Soviet call for talks, saying that "we're not interested at this time."[57] Privately, PGA tried to stimulate even small movement within the Reagan administration. But a letter from members of Congress appeared to have no impact, and visits by Dunlop to senior officials of the Defense Department, State Department, and National Security Council were equally unavailing; "everyone said the U.S. must continue testing to maintain its defense."[58]

Appeasing the Sorcerers

American inflexibility and Palme's death stalled PGA for a few months. For many countries, the prospect that the Conference would probably end with an American veto put a "pall" over the whole idea.[59] But by the spring of 1986, the project had begun to recover its momentum.

The leaders of the Six-nation effort organized another summit, to be held in Ixtapa, Mexico, in August. President Miguel de la Madrid of Mexico had been reluctant to invite the other heads of state to his country, fearing negative publicity if they turned down the invitation. But Grimsson and other PGA officials had been able to act as go-betweens, ascertaining that the other presidents would accept, and thereby making it safe for the Mexican leader to invite them.

While in Mexico for the summit, Grimsson and Dunlop visited senior officials of the foreign ministry. Grimsson managed to get them more interested in the amendment idea. He then told the Sri Lankan and Indonesian governments of the greater Mexican interest, in the hope of creating the appearance of a bandwagon. From New York, Tovish furthered this impression by lining up endorsements of the amendment idea from celebrities such as Carl Sagan, and from Senators such as Edward Kennedy and Paul Simon. The celebrity endorsements were occasionally reported to foreign ministries by their missions to the United Nations, suggesting that PGA's project was a major global event.

Nevertheless, no country stepped forward to request a Conference. PGA's Executive Committee discussed ways to get around the "general feeling [among otherwise supportive governments] that the expected veto by Mr. Reagan would run the Conference into a stone wall."[60] Grimsson suggested several elements of a plan.

First, he reiterated the "two-session" strategy. PGA could propose that the Conference should begin before the next American election but should not vote until after President Reagan was out of office, so that a new American administration could develop a new policy. Second, PGA and its allies should try to make United Nations headquarters in New York the venue of the event, so that it would be reported more widely in the United States, requiring the 1988 Presidential candidates to take a stand on the CTB issue. Third, PGA should press for a stronger resolution of support at the 1986 General Assembly.[61] In addition, PGA would continue to collect endorsements from legislators (particularly in the United States) and from international bodies.[62]

Of these elements, the campaign to engender more support in the American Congress was the most immediately productive. Many members of Congress were distressed that the President had not responded more positively to the unilateral Soviet moratorium, which by this time had lasted for more than a year, and they put pressure on the Administration in several ways. The House of Representatives passed a test ban amendment to the defense authorization bill; had the Senate concurred, it would have prohibited the United States from conducting tests with more than one kiloton yield unless the Soviets tested at higher yields or refused to permit the installation of seismic monitoring equipment.[63] To head off possible testing restrictions in the Conference bill on the eve of the Reykjavik summit with General Secretary Gorbachev, President Reagan had agreed to tell Gorbachev that once the TTB and PNE Treaties were ratified, he would propose that the US and USSR "immediately engage in negotiations on ways to implement a step-by-step parallel program—in association with a program to reduce and ultimately eliminate all nuclear weapons—of limiting and ultimately ending nuclear testing."[64] At about the same time, eleven Senators sent Grimsson a letter calling the amendment concept "especially timely."[65]

The effort to obtain additional international endorsement also moved forward. PGA legislators who were members of the European Parliament introduced a resolution of support there, which the Parliament adopted in December.[66] The UN General Assembly passed a stronger resolution than it had in 1985, this time recommending not mere consultations, but rather that PTBT parties "undertake practical steps leading to the convening" of an amendment conference.[67] No concrete action toward convening a Conference had occurred, but symbolic statements of support continued to accumulate. PGA's officers hoped that in the new year, countries would slide from symbolic encouragement to political action.

In fact, 1987 would be another year of disappointment. In its opening weeks, the United States tested a nuclear weapon in Nevada, and the Soviet Union hinted that in view of continued U.S. testing, it would soon discontinue its unilateral moratorium.[68] Most test ban advocates were resigned to the resumption of Soviet testing, but Bernard Lown, the American co-chair of International Physicians for the Prevention of Nuclear War (IPPNW), made a last-ditch attempt to head off Soviet testing. After having won the Nobel Peace Prize, his organization had become more visible in the Soviet Union, and its press releases, ignored in most American papers, were often printed in *Pravda*. In February, Lown attended the Forum for a Nuclear Free World and the Survival of Mankind, an international "peace forum" that Gorbachev had convened in Moscow. There, he pleaded with Anatoly Dobrynin, former Ambassador to the United States, not to resume testing. Dobrynin scoffed, and he teased Lown. "I have a suggestion. I'll arrange for you to argue your case before the Politburo. One member will appreciate it, but he is the only one on the Politburo who supports you."

"Who's that?" Lown asked.

"Gorbachev," Dobrynin said. "As for the rest of them, you have to understand that the Central Committee has received 30,000 letters from Soviet citizens opposing our unilateral halt in testing."

Lown did not speak to the Politburo, but he did address the thousands of peace activists at the Forum. When he returned to the rostrum, Gorbachev reached into Lown's breast pocket, took out the speech that he had just given, and wrote on it, in Russian, "I agree with every word of your speech."[69] Nevertheless, the Soviets soon resumed testing.[70]

Through the spring, PGA continued to try to find governmental sponsors to call for an amendment conference. PGA members of parliaments met with foreign ministers in Peru in February, Brazil in April, and Yugoslavia in May, but the foreign ministers were noncommittal.[71] In June, Grimsson sent a series of letters to foreign ministers around the world. With these letters, he sent each of them the lengthy "Guide to an Amendment Conference" that Tovish had written. The Guide explained the theory and legal significance of PGA's plan and asked the foreign ministers to consider arranging for their countries to call for the conference.[72] The responses were, however, less than encouraging. The Belgian foreign minister called the amendment proposal "original" but noted that his country "wants to see the complex realities of international relations and the related security issues taken into account."[73] His Japanese counterpart expressed "profound respect" for Grimsson's test ban efforts but noted that "it is doubtful that a mere change of the forum [from the deadlocked Conference on Disarmament to the Amendment Conference] will produce a desirable result.[74] The West German government noted its support for a CTB but did not directly respond to Grimsson's amendment conference idea.[75]

Meanwhile, Garcia Robles was eager to lead the call for the conference, but the Mexican government continued to withhold authorization for such action.[76] It told him that Mexico could not request the conference until all of the countries that had been co-sponsoring the United Nations resolutions were prepared to act collectively.[77] By this time, Indonesia and Sri Lanka were ready to make the requests, but Yugoslavia was still dragging its feet, prompting Grimsson, ter Beek and Tovish to go to Belgrade to see President Lazar Mojsov. The meeting was, in Tovish's words, a "terrible disappointment." Mojsov claimed that Yugoslavia could not act because "you didn't get a statement of support from the last non-aligned meeting, in New Delhi." Descending the stairway after meeting Mojsov, Tovish reminded Grimsson that while Mojsov had long ago suggested getting a General Assembly resolution, he had never before said anything about having to get a statement from the New Delhi meeting. "This is like the problem of the prince in the fairy tale," he added. "He has to do a task to get the princess. But every time he completes the task and bring the token to the sorcerer, he leaves with another task."[78] In this case, the next opportunity to do the sorcerer's bidding would come in May, 1988, at the meeting of non-aligned countries in Havana.

Immediately after leaving Mojsov, the PGA officials spent two hours with Foreign Minister Raif Dizdarevic, who began to say that his government needed more time to study the amendment conference concept. Grimsson reports becoming very tough. "Your government has advocated a CTB for more than 30 years," Grimsson noted. "Reagan has no interest in it. We have a new idea for raising this issue internationally, and it's supported by Willy Brandt, Gorbachev, and more than a hundred members of the U.S. Congress. If you don't support it, you are saying that you don't really care about a test ban. Of course you are entitled to your foreign policy, but we will have to let the world know that Yugoslavia doesn't really mean what it says."

According to Grimsson, "no one representing a country could have been so blunt. But Yugoslavia would not want to have been unmasked before all the peace groups of the world, and they knew we could have done it. They knew that the Six-nation Peace Initiative had made headlines all around the world, and that we had access to leaders in parliaments and governments all over the world. I also knew that the Yugoslavian foreign minister was sophisticated enough to tolerate such blunt talk and not to be insulted personally by it."[79]

Soon thereafter, Grimsson headed for New York, where he met the Mexican foreign minister, Bernardo Sepulveda Amor. The meeting went badly; Despite the resolutions that Mexico had sponsored in the General Assembly, Sepulveda argued against the whole amendment conference idea, and for months thereafter, his ministry was slow to act on anything to do with the amendment conference project. Nevertheless, some officials in the Mexican foreign ministry liked the idea very much, and they continued to keep it alive.[80]

While he was in New York, Grimsson participated in a PGA press conference to celebrate the twenty-fourth anniversary of the signing of the Partial Test Ban Treaty and to declare a campaign for an amendment conference that would begin on the Treaty's 25th anniversary. The famous astronomer Carl Sagan spoke for the amendment conference, as did several former Kennedy and Carter administration officials, but the press conference received only minor media coverage.[81]

The fall brought with it the opportunity for still another General Assembly resolution. As in 1986, Garcia Robles drafted one that was much stronger than the resolution that had been approved in the previous United Nations session. PGA's strategy was to make countries that voted for the resolution "morally bound" to support any nations that, in response, called for an amendment conference to be convened. This time, the resolution called on the non-nuclear parties to the PTBT to "formally submit an amendment proposal . . . with a view to convening [an amendment] conference at the earliest possible date." The resolution was approved by the General Assembly by a vote of 128–3. Twenty-two countries abstained; as usual, these included Sweden, Japan, and most NATO members.[82]

Meanwhile, the United States and the Soviet Union began to fulfill the commitment they had made at Reykjavik to begin "step-by-step" test ban negotiations. They announced that by December, they would begin to negotiate, "as a first step," further measures for the verification of the 1974 Threshold Test Ban Treaty, and that they would eventually proceed "to negotiating further intermediate limitations on nuclear testing, leading to the ultimate objective of the complete cessation of nuclear testing as part of an effective disarmament process."[83] The statement set out no timetable for progress, even on the first step (which involved no further restrictions on testing), and in fact nearly three more years would pass before the two governments signed their additional protocol for Threshold Test Ban Treaty verification.[84]

Despite lack of real momentum toward a CTB by the superpowers, as 1988 began, the prospects for initiating the convening of an amendment conference seemed dim. At the January meeting of the PGA Executive Committee, Tovish reported that Peru and Sri Lanka remained ready to join a group to put the proposal forward, but they would not lead it. Dunlop thought that the stalled project was beginning to detract from other PGA activities, and he suggested that "if there had been no movement by the middle of the year, this project should be given a rest."[85] By the next meeting two months later, even Grimsson was discouraged. In June, PGA's International Council was scheduled to meet. If no country had introduced the amendment by then, Grimsson said, "a realistic assessment of the project would need to be made" at that session.[86] The Amendment Conference project had persisted for three and a half years and attracted many statements of support, but no government had been willing to take the lead and thereby to risk offending the United States and Britain. The effort now seemed a mere three months away from being shelved.

PGA's leadership had little choice but to make what could have been a final effort to launch the Conference. Fortuitously, the United Nations Disarmament Commission[87] was scheduled to hold its annual meeting in New York in May, and this event would bring to UN headquarters the leading disarmament spokespersons from a large number of countries. Grimsson successfully asked Garcia Robles to chair a private luncheon meeting, during the Commission's session, in the United Nations Delegates Dining Room, for the purpose of reaching "agreement . . . on a text [of a Conference call] to be forwarded by the participants to their capitals for further consideration."[88] The invitees were ambassadors or other senior diplomats from Mexico, Indonesia, Peru, Sri Lanka, Venezuela, and Yugoslavia; from PGA, Tovish attended, along with William Epstein acting as a PGA consultant.[89]

The meeting was an extraordinary success. While none of the representatives was yet able to commit any government to calling for the Conference, each of them agreed to request governmental authority to submit an amendment proposal to the Depositaries "if all six co-sponsors are willing to proceed together" and, once the Depositaries circulated the proposal to hold a Conference, to recruit two other countries to support it. They also set, as a target date for a public announcement of the Conference call, August 5, 1988—the 25th anniversary of the Partial Test Ban Treaty.[90] In addition, in order to provide the sorcerer with one more token, the four participants whose countries would be at the non-aligned summit later that month in Havana agreed to explore the possibility of obtaining, in that meeting's formal declarations, a "positive reference to implementation of [the 1987 General Assembly resolution]."[91]

Prodded by delegations from Peru and India, the foreign ministers at the Havana summit indeed "affirmed their support for the early submission of an amendment proposal with a view to convening a conference as the earliest possible date. . . ."[92] Members of PGA in Mexico, Peru and Venezuela contacted other members of their parliaments, and their foreign ministries, urging them to authorize a Conference call.[93] The Mexican government began to inch toward allowing Garcia Robles to sign a letter calling for a Conference, but it continued to hedge; on June 23, Foreign Minister Sepulveda wrote to Grimsson that "it would be advisable to proceed with certain precautions" but that he did favor the initiation of "a consulting process not only with the sponsoring countries [of the United Nations Resolution] but also with other countries that consider this appropriate, with the objective of ascertaining the degree of support" that the Conference call could obtain.[94] Armed with this degree of authority, the words of the Havana statement, and the argument that the world had now waited fruitlessly for a CTB for a quarter of a century, Garcia Robles became confident that he could make further progress on the sidelines of the Conference on Disarmament during its July session in Geneva. Throughout that month, he held meetings with ambassadors, always late in the day after the Mexican mission had closed, a tactic that precluded sending reports to Mexico City until the following day, after other countries' agreements had been obtained. The fact that the August 5 anniversary of the PTBT was only days away forced foreign ministries to make the decisions that they had for so long avoided and helped him to achieve his goal.[95]

Success

On August 5, the six countries that had been represented at the May luncheon meeting wrote letters to the foreign ministers of the three depositary governments, formally submitting their governments' proposal to amend the Treaty by prohibiting nuclear test explosions in all environments, and a request that the proposal be circulated to all parties.[96] The text that they proposed was identical to the one that Professor Chayes had drafted for PGA years earlier. In order to reduce concern about the effect of tampering with a treaty that enjoyed the support of nearly every country in the world, the only changed proposed in the actual text of the treaty was the addition of one sentence providing that "Protocols annexed to this Treaty are an integral part of the Treaty." The six sponsoring countries simultaneously offered two protocols, however. The first banned all tests of nuclear weapons (and nuclear explosions allegedly for peaceful purposes). The second was a place-holder for much more complex verification proposals that would be drafted by experts retained by PGA and submitted by the sponsoring governments at a later time.[97] Because the main stumbling block to the success of the Conference would be the U.S. government's likely resistance to the amendment, PGA held its press conference to announce the Conference call not in Geneva or New York, but in Washington, and the principal speakers were two Senators and two Representatives.[98]

Although PGA leaders were euphoric that some action had finally been taken, they could only have been disappointed by the response of the American press to the action of the six sponsors and to the press conference. The New York Times gave the story five short paragraphs which appeared in only one of the paper's editions[99]; the nation's other major papers didn't carry the news at all.[100]

While PGA's diplomatic initiative was finally getting launched, a grass roots effort to press the United States and other governments toward a test ban was also emerging. Not since the PTBT had been signed in 1963 had the traditional peace groups, or any other significant political action groups, focused on the test ban issue. During the CTB negotiations of the 1970s, the Carter administration's efforts took place in a vacuum; virtually no organized public support existed to back up the government's attempts to halt testing. In the early 1980s, the nuclear "freeze" movement usually included a test ban in its much larger agenda, but adherents of the movement differed significantly on what was to be "frozen," the test ban was often lumped together indiscriminately with halts in research and development, and little attention was devoted to verification. From the old peace organizations and from newer environmental protection and arms control groups, however, a new coalition was formed.

In January, 1988, Physicians for Social Responsibility (the U.S. affiliate of Dr. Lown's IPPNW), the Natural Resources Defense Council, and several other organizations held a three-day test ban conference at Las Vegas, near the Nevada Test Site.[101] At the conference, on behalf of PGA, Tovish called for the creation of an international campaign to press for a CTB.[102] Within two months, IPPNW, the Council for a Livable World, and more than twenty other groups organized an international committee, which soon spawned the U.S. CTB Coalition. The Coalition attempted to coordinate, through joint planning, its member organizations' CTB activities. From its inception, the coalition functioned effectively, through its meetings and newsletters, as an information clearinghouse for groups with agendas as diverse as test site protests, national legislation, and advancing the amendment conference, but also from the very beginning, Coalition members divided sharply on some difficult issues of strategy. For example, in its second month of operation, the Coalition was unable to take a stance on the bill again pending in Congress to cut off funds for tests over one kiloton if the Soviet Union also suspended such testing and allowed verification; some member groups could not take a position that appeared to endorse low-level testing.[103]

While the Coalition built up its organizational membership, sought foundation funds, and debated protest, media, and legislative strategy, PGA concentrated on increasing the number of countries requesting an amendment conference from the initial six to the 39 that would be needed to meet the PTBT's criterion—a third of the parties—for forcing the depositaries to call the meeting. It hoped to obtain the necessary requests within three months; in fact, the effort would take nearly three times as long.[104] In September, at a meeting of 95 non-aligned countries (51 of which were represented by their foreign ministers), it had its first opportunity to shore up support; the event was successful, with the foreign ministers stating that they "welcomed and supported" the action that had been taken the previous month.[105] By a stroke of good fortune, PGA's international credibility was enhanced two weeks later when the government of Iceland fell and in the new coalition, Grimsson became Minister of Finance.[106] On the other hand, the long-term prospects for a successful amendment conference effort were diminished by the fact that although the Democratic Party's nominee for President advocated a CTB during both televised debates with his opponent,[107] his opponent led in the polls all fall and ultimately won the election. While it seemed possible that George Bush would eventually alter the Reagan administration's policy on CTB, the likelihood of a significant change in the outlook of the U.S. government certainly dropped with the declining fortunes of the Dukakis-Bentsen ticket.

To force the depositaries to call the Conference, PGA needed to recruit 33 more requesting countries. It began by contacting the UN ambassadors of all likely prospects. PGA's letters—which were usually forwarded to the ambassadors' home capitals for decision—were followed up by phone calls, visits, and in some cases, by further contacts from the Mexican or other supportive delegations.[108] In many instances, the UN Ambassadors who were very familiar with the issue after several General Assembly resolutions recommended that their foreign ministers join the bandwagon.[109] By the end of the General Assembly's session in December, a total of 30 countries had signed requests to convene a Conference.[110]

Three countries were especially important to PGA's effort to recruit co-requestors. India and Pakistan were "near-nuclear" countries, each thought to have small atomic arsenals, and neither a signatory to the Non-Proliferation Treaty. If either or both could be persuaded to call for the PTBT amendment conference, their actions could add significantly to the credibility of the effort, for these were among the handful of countries about which the world was most worried. Their participation could help to demonstrate to the United States, whose government really did worry about proliferation, that a CTB was considered important by countries from which the American government wanted additional arms control.

Early in February, 1989, Kennedy Graham, a former New Zealand diplomat who had taken over from Nicholas Dunlop as Secretary-General of PGA, met with Shaukat Umer, Pakistan's Deputy Representative to the UN. His reaction was that a Pakistani request for the Conference might be a good idea, and he agreed to follow it up.[111] At about the same time, Maxime Faille, a Canadian member of the PGA staff, made the rounds of disarmament experts who were attending the semi-annual meeting of the Conference on Disarmament in Geneva. His meetings with diplomats there included one with Rakesh Sood of India, who took a strong interest in the project. Faille gave him literature and a list of countries that had already called for the conference, and Sood promised to consult with others on his disarmament delegation.[112]

The Soviet Union presented the third special case. PGA did not seek or expect a request for the Conference from Moscow, but it did want the Soviets to continue to support the Conference publicly (as it had in the United Nations); to prevent the other depositaries from dragging their feet once 39 countries had filed requests; and to support the CTB amendment in the Conference itself. For these purposes Grimsson and ter Beek flew to Moscow, where they met with Anatoly Lukyanov, Vice President of the Supreme Soviet, Anatoly Dobrynin, Gorbachev's principal foreign policy advisor, and several other senior Soviet officials. The Soviets were impressed that PGA had been able to move its project from the conceptual stage to the point at which a new international event was near fruition, and their continuing commitment to a CTB was evident, but they seemed reluctant to take any public leadership role with respect to the amendment conference for fear of triggering a negative counter-reaction from the United States. In particular, the Soviet leaders did not agree to PGA's proposal that the Amendment Conference should at least begin before the Fourth NPT Review Conference scheduled for August, 1990. PGA made the point that having some progress on the CTB issue before the NPT Review Conference could produce, from the NPT meeting itself, an endorsement of the amendment effort and formal encouragement to complete the process. While the Soviets appreciated the political logic of this strategy, they would not commit to propose such a schedule to their fellow depositaries.[113]

Grimsson's trip to Moscow nearly coincided with events in the Soviet Union that would eventually become of great significance to Soviet testing policy. In February, two nuclear tests at the Semipalatinsk Test Site in Kazakhstan vented radioactive and toxic materials into the atmosphere. At the time, the Kazakh poet Olzhas Suleimenov was campaigning for a seat in the Congress of People's Deputies in the Soviet Union's first relatively open elections. Suleimenov used a scheduled campaign speech on local television to call for a mass meeting, and two days later, five thousand people showed up and adopted a resolution calling for the test site to be closed. Inspired by the protests that for years had been held at the United States' test site, the crowd formed a group that called itself "Nevada," later broadened to "Nevada-Semipalatinsk." Suleimenov was easily elected to the Congress of People's Deputies, was selected by that body to become a member of the Supreme Soviet, and there became the leader of a movement to halt nuclear testing. Within months, he had wrested from the Soviet leadership a commitment to cancel eleven of the 18 tests that it had scheduled for the year.[114]

But while the Soviet leadership's resolve to seek a negotiated end to nuclear tests could only be strengthened by the internal pressure building near its main test site, Gorbachev and his advisors felt themselves unable to make progress on the issue at a pace faster than George Bush, the new American President, was willing to accept. The Soviets had already tried to pressure the Americans by a unilateral moratorium lasting a year and a half, but the American government had not stopped testing, and the moratorium had not produced substantial protests against continued American tests either in the United States or elsewhere in the world. A second moratorium would have risked a clash with the Soviet military, at a time when the economic health of the Soviet Union was beginning to deteriorate, for no clear gain. Indeed, from the perspective of Soviet decision-makers, a new unilateral halt could only have cheered hard-line American policy-makers. Accordingly, the Soviets had had little choice but to accept the United States' proposal to spend a period of years negotiating further arrangements to verify the 1974 Threshold Test Ban Treaty, as a "first step" toward further test ban limitations, even though a former U.S. Deputy Assistant Secretary of Defense had conceded that Pentagon policy makers were using the verification talks to delay having to discuss a CTB.[115] The Soviet government reluctantly concluded that "we can't proceed on [a CTB] when we have no popular support in the West."[116]

Soviet equivocation did not materially affect the response of other countries. In January and February, additional requests to convene a Conference were sent to the depositaries by several governments, including the government of India, and Tovish colored in more areas on a map on his office wall. By the end of March, only one more request was needed. Five days later, PGA learned of two more requests, and Pakistan, not wanting to appear less interested than India in nuclear arms control, made its request shortly thereafter.[117] The United States, the Soviet Union, and Britain were now legally bound to participate in a conference call. But as PGA officials suspected, the game of political hardball was just beginning.

Notes

1. William Hinton, *Fanshen: A Documentary of Revolution in a Chinese Village* (New York: Vintage Books, 1966).

2. The account of Tovish's life before he became associated with Parliamentarians for Global Action is based on a telephone interview with him, June 27, 1990. In 1983, Parliamentarians for Global Action was called Parliamentarians for World Order (PWO). It changed its name in 1986 to Parliamentarians Global Action for Disarmament, Development and World Reform. Executive Committee Minutes, Jan. 10, 1986. This name was shortened in 1990 to Parliamentarians for Global Action. To avoid confusion, this book refers to the organization only by its current name.

3. Minutes of the first meeting of the Provisional Committee of PWO, Nov. 23, 1977.

4. PWO Minutes, Dec. 6–7, 1980.

5. Grimsson's early history is based on an interview in New York City, June 3, 1990.

6. PWO Minutes, Nov. 9, 1983.

7. Grimsson interview, June 3, 1990.

8. PWO minutes, Nov. 9, 1983.

9. Telephone interview with Aaron Tovish, Sept. 5, 1991.

10. Don Obderdorfer, "U.S., Soviets Urged to Break Arms Deadlock," *Washington Post* May 22, 1984, p. A1.

11. Rone Tempest, "India Summit Calls for Ban on Space Arms," *Los Angeles Times* Jan. 29, 1985, p. 5, col. 3; Edward Cody, "Six Countries Urge U.S. to Join Soviet Test Ban; Leaders Offer to Help Monitor Agreement," *Washington Post* Aug. 8, 1986, p. A 25; Bengt Ljung, "U.N. Nuclear Disarmament Verification System Urged," United Press International dispatch Jan. 21, 1988.

12. Frank von Hippel, "Arms Control Physics: The New Soviet Connection," *Physics Today* November, 1989, pp. 39–42. For discussions of the nature and significance of the NRDC project, see Glenn Garelik, "The Grounds for a Test Ban Treaty," *Discover Magazine* June 1987, p. 50; Michael Duffy, "Public Squabbles, Private Deal," *Time* July 14, 1986, p. 25; Robert Cowen, "Amassing Data To Help Monitor Nuclear Tests," *Christian Science Monitor,* July 16, 1986, p. 4. For an analysis of the United States' government's reaction to the project, see Philip G. Schrag, *Listening for the Bomb: A Study in Nuclear Arms Control Verification Policy* (Boulder: Westview Press, 1989).

13. Grimsson Interview, June 3, 1990.

14. Through the contacts maintained by PGA's secretariat in New York, its members could get expert analyses of fast-breaking events faster than it could obtain them by making inquiries through their own ministries, giving members an advantage over their rivals in internal parliamentary debates and negotiations. Interview with Aaron Tovish, in New York City, Dec. 21, 1989.

15. Grimsson interview, June 3, 1990.

16. Francis Clines, "Reagan Denounces Ideology of Soviet as 'Focus of Evil'," *New York Times* March 9, 1983, p. A1.

17. Bernard Lown, address to Fourth World Congress of International Physicians for the Prevention of Nuclear War, June 4, 1984. The Soviet Union was so skittish about this subject that at the request of his Soviet co-president, Lown gave his talk only in the morning plenary of the Congress, when other Soviet officials would not be present.

18. Interview with Dr. Bernard Lown in Chestnut Hill, Mass., April 14, 1990.

19. Treaty on the Non-Proliferation of Nuclear Weapons, Art. VIII, reprinted in *U.S. Arms Control and Disarmament Agency, Arms Control and Disarmament Agreements* (Washington: U.S. Arms Control and Disarmament Agency, 6th ed. 1990), pp. 98–102.

20. Treaty Banning Nuclear Weapon Tests in the Atmosphere, in Outer Space, and Under Water, Art. II. The entire Treaty is reproduced in Appendix A.

21. Amendments to the Non-Proliferation Treaty also require approval of "all nuclear-weapon States Party to the Treaty and all other Parties which, on the date the amendment is circulated, are members of the Board of Governors of the International Atomic Energy Agency."

22. Interview with Aaron Tovish, in New York City, Dec. 21, 1989.

23. Olivia Ward, "Bill Epstein's 43-year mission to the U.N.," *Toronto Star* May 21, 1989, p. D1.

24. Interview with Aaron Tovish, Dec. 21, 1989.

25. Treaty for the Prohibition of Nuclear Weapons in Latin America (1967), reprinted *U.S. Arms Control and Disarmament Agency, Arms Control and Disarmament Agreements* (Washington: U.S. Arms Control and Disarmament Agency, 6th ed. 1990), pp. 68–86.

26. "Salute to Garcia-Robles," *Disarmament Times* December, 1989, p. 1.

27. Interview with William Epstein, in New York City, June 30, 1990.

28. Aaron Tovish, "From Limited to Comprehensive: Amending the Limited Test Ban Treaty," and Aaron Tovish, "Strategy to Convene a Successful Multilateral Conference for a Comprehensive Test Ban Treaty," (unpublished, undated drafts, apparently written in early November, 1984). See Letter to Glenn Seaborg from Aaron Tovish, Oct. 30, 1984 (referring to the "memorandum" Tovish was then drawing up on procedure for activating the amendment procedure, which he expected to be ready in "mid-November"). See also Christopher Paine, Memorandum: Suggested Action Proposals for FCPI New Delhi Summit (Dec., 1984).

29. Grimsson interview, June 3, 1990.

30. PGA, Chronology of Events Leading up to Activation of Partial Test Ban Treaty (PTBT) Amendment Conference (undated, but apparently September, 1988).

31. See Letter to Hon. Rajiv Gandhi, Prime Minister of India, from Olafur Grimsson, May 31, 1985. Even before the summit, Congressman Tom Downey, a member of the PGA board, broached the idea to representatives of four of the leaders at a preparatory meeting in Athens.

32. Letter to Olafur Grimsson from George Ball, Abram Chayes, Harlan Cleveland, John Kenneth Galbraith, Roswell Gilpatric, W. Averell Harriman, Carl Kaysen, Arthur Schlesinger, Jr., Herbert Scoville, Jr., Glenn Seaborg, and Jerome Wiesner (April, 1985).

33. Letter to Hon. Rajiv Gandhi, Prime Minister of India, from Olafur Grimsson, May 31, 1985; Letter to Hon. Jose Sarney, President of Brazil, from Olafur Grimsson, July 2, 1985.

34. Minutes of PGA Executive Council Meeting, April 19, 1985.

35. *Ibid.* Argentina had signed but not ratified the Partial Test Ban Treaty. PGA believes that its ratification in 1986 came about as a result of its bringing this omission to the attention of the head of Argentina's new civilian government, Raul Alfonsin. Grimsson interview, June 3, 1990.

36. Grimsson interview, June 3, 1990.

37. Walter Pincus, "U.S. Bars Nuclear Test-Ban Talks Until Stockpiles are Reduced," *Washington Post* Nov. 21, 1985 (refusal to negotiate); Amendment 3262 to S. 2723, Omnibus Defense Authorization, *Congressional Record* 98th Cong., 2nd Sess, June 20, 1984, p. 17410.

38. Minutes of PGA Executive Council Meeting, Sept. 15–16, 1985.

39. Grimsson interview, June 3, 1990.

40. Gharekhan later told Grimsson about Gandhi's expectations in that meeting. Grimsson interview, June 3, 1990.

41. William Epstein, "A Critical Time for Nuclear Nonproliferation," *Scientific American* August, 1985, pp. 33, 37–38.

42. Grimsson interview, June 3, 1990.

43. PGA Executive Committee Minutes, Sept. 15–16, 1985. The three potential nuclear powers were Brazil, Argentina and India. Grimsson did not try to obtain the attendance of his own country, because in Iceland, he had to defer to foreign ministry procedures and could not be as free-wheeling as he could in other countries. Grimsson interview, June 3, 1990.

44. Grimsson interview, June 3, 1990. Tovish's recollection differs; he believes that everyone knew in advance that Garcia Robles would chair the meeting. Telephone interview with Aaron Tovish, Sept. 5, 1991.

45. Interview with Aaron Tovish in New York City, Dec. 21, 1989.

46. Grimsson interview, June 3, 1990.

47. Jozef Goldblat, "Will the NPT Survive?" *Bulletin of the Atomic Scientists* January, 1986, pp. 35, 37.

48. Stephen Weeks, "World Nuclear Conference Faces Showdown Over Nuclear Tests," *Reuters* September 18, 1985; William Epstein, "Reviewing the Non-proliferation Treaty," Background Paper No. 4, Canadian Institute for International Peace and Security (March, 1986).

49. PGA Executive Committee Minutes, October 27, 1985.

50. A/40/80B (Dec. 12, 1985).

51. A/40/PV.113. After this vote, the United States Department of State included the Mexican initiative as an example of Mexican opposition to US policy in a diplomatic inquiry as to why Mexico voted so often against the United States in the General Assembly. The Mexican Foreign Ministry replied that Mexico's voting record had remained consistent over many years, while the American position had changed considerably, a response that accurately characterized, among other matters, the situation with respect to the CTB issue. Minutes of PGA Executive Committee, Jan. 10, 1986, p. 5.

52. Minutes of PGA Executive Committee, Jan. 10, 1986, p. 5.

53. The details of this trip are drawn from the Grimsson interview, June 3, 1990.

54. Don Oberdorfer, "Leaders of Six Nations Urge A-Test Ban Before Summit," *Washington Post,* March 11, 1986, p. A7.

55. Flora Lewis, "Foreign Affairs: Why Not a Test Ban?" *New York Times* January 24, 1986, p. A27; Gary Lee, "Soviet Union Extends Ban on Nuclear Arms Testing," *Washington Post* March 14, 1986, p. 1.

56. For a good description of the very successful monitoring project, see Garelik, p. 50.

57. Lee, p. 1.

58. Minutes, PGA Executive Committee, June 7, 1986, p. 2.

59. Aaron Tovish, reporting to PGA, Minutes of the PGA Executive Committee, June 7, 1986, p. 9.

60. Minutes of PGA Executive Committee, Sept. 12–13, 1986, p. 10.

61. *Ibid.*

62. Grimsson had spoken to the International Pugwash Conference in Belgrade, and the Pugwash Council had adopted a statement supporting the Amendment Conference idea. Statement of the Pugwash Council, Budapest, September, 1986.

63. H.R. 4428, National Defense Authorization Act for FY 1987, *Congressional Record* 99th Cong., 2nd Sess., August 15, 1986, p. 22050, (passed by a vote of 255–152–24).

64. *Threshold Test Ban and Peaceful Nuclear Explosions Treaties,* Exec. Rept. 100–1, Report of the Committee on Foreign Relations, Feb. 27, 1987, p. 7.

65. Letter to Dr. Olafur Grimsson from Senators Paul Simon, Edward Kennedy, Howard Metzenbaum, Spark Matsunaga, Tom Harkin, Carl Levin, Quentin Burdick, Bennett Johnston, William Proxmire, Patrick Leahy, and Frank Lautenberg, Sept. 12, 1986.

66. Resolution of the European Parliament, 11 Dec. 1986. The vote was 92–55.

67. A/RES/41/46B, Dec. 3, 1986.

68. Robert Lindsey, "438 Protesters are Arrested at Nevada Nuclear Test Site," *New York Times* February 6, 1987, p. A8.

69. Interview with Dr. Bernard Lown in Chestnut Hill, Massachusetts, April 14, 1990 (details of Lown's conversation with Dobrynin and Gorbachev's note).

70. "Soviet Union Resumes Nuclear Tests; Blames Move on U.S.," *Reuters* February 26, 1987.

71. Parliamentarians for Global Action, Chronology of Events Leading Up to Activation of Partial Test Ban Treaty (PTBT) Amendment Procedure (undated), p. 3.

72. Letter to foreign ministers from Olafur Grimsson, June 19, 1987.

73. Letter to Olafur Grimsson from L. Tindemans, Foreign Minister of Belgium, July 22, 1987.

74. Letter to Olafur Grimsson from Foreign Affairs Minister Tadashi Kuranari, July 22, 1987.

75. Letter to Olafur Grimsson from v. Butler, Disarmament Division, Auswartiges Amt, Aug. 27, 1987.

76. Minutes of the Executive Committee of Parliamentarians for Global Action, May 8–9, 1987, p. 8.

77. Interview with Aaron Tovish in New York City, June 3, 1990.

78. Interview with Aaron Tovish in New York City, June 3, 1990.

79. Grimsson interview, June 3, 1990.

80. Grimsson interview, June 3, 1990.

81. See, e.g., "Group Seeks to Widen Nuclear Test Ban Treaty," *International Herald Tribune* Aug. 6, 1987.

82. Official Records of the General Assembly, 42d Session, p. 62 (Resolution 42/26 B) (Nov. 30, 1987) (text); A/42/PV.84 (vote). The negative votes were those of the U.S., the United Kingdom, and France.

83. "Joint Statement on Schultz–Shevardnadze Meeting," *Summary of World Broadcasts* September 19, 1987, part 1.

84. The agreement was signed at the summit between Presidents Bush and Gorbachev in Washington, in May, 1990.

85. Minutes of PGA Executive Committee, Jan. 22–23, 1988.

86. Minutes of PGA Executive Committee Meeting, March 18–19, 1988. Tovish recalls demanding that the project be given one more chance. Afterwards, "everyone at the meeting pulled me aside, saying that it was time to recognize that there simply wouldn't be any follow-through by the non-aligned countries and as a result, the conference would never take place." Telephone interview with Aaron Tovish, Sept. 5, 1991.

87. The Commission is a forum in which all UN members, not only those in the Conference on Disarmament, meet to discuss disarmament issues; it is an arena for debate, but not for negotiation or other action.

88. Letter to Amb. Alfonso Garcia Robles from Olafur Grimsson, April, 1988.

89. "Working Luncheon on Implementation of Resolution A/42/26B," (PGA document, May, 1988).

90. Parliamentarians for Global Action, "A New Road to a Comprehensive Test Ban: Guide to an Amendment Conference, April, 1989 Supplement," p. 1; "Summary of working luncheon agreement" (PGA document, May, 1988).

91. *Ibid.*

92. A/S-15/27, Paragraph 20 (June 3, 1988).

93. Minutes, PGA International Council, June 3, 1988.

94. Letter to Olafur Grimsson from Foreign Minister Bernardo Sepulveda Amor, June 23, 1988.

95. Interview with Aaron Tovish in New York City, June 3, 1990.

96. Five ambassadors to the Conference on Disarmament signed a single letter to each depositary government; the Venezuelan Foreign Minister wrote separately. Parliamentarians for Global Action, "A New Road to a Comprehensive Test Ban: Guide to an Amendment Conference, April, 1989 Supplement," p. 1.

97. The text of the Amendments that were eventually drafted with PGA's help and submitted by six proposing governments appears in Appendix B.

98. The Congressional speakers were Senators Tom Harkin and Paul Simon and Representatives George Brown and Tom Downey. Paul Warnke, who had served as President Carter's ambassador to the CTB talks in 1978, also spoke. See Parliamentarians for Global Action, "A New Road," p. 2.

99. "U.N. Urged to Enact Total Nuclear Test Ban," Aug. 5, 1988, p. 5 (national edition). The *Times* story was not bylined, and it contained several errors, including the headline's incorrect statement that the United Nations (as opposed to the Treaty parties) was being urged to take action.

100. A handful carried opinion columns describing the event. See William Epstein and Glenn Seaborg, "An Amended Nuclear Pact Holds Hope of Total Ban," *Los Angeles Times* Aug. 5, 1988, sec. 2, p. 7; Gwynne Dyer, "How a nuclear test ban might really happen," *Cleveland Plain Dealer,* Aug. 9, 1988.

101. Showing off the craters and facilities of the Site to the leadership of the movement that was trying to shut it down, the U.S. Department of Energy gave one of its regular ten-hour guided tours to two bus loads of conferees. See Philip Schrag, "Seeing Ground Zero in Nevada," *New York Times* March 12, 1989, Sec. 5, p. 8.

102. Parliamentarians for Global Action, Chronology of Events Leading up to Activation of Partial Test Ban Treaty (PTBT) Amendment Procedure, p. 4 (undated, but apparently September, 1988).

103. International Comprehensive Test Ban Campaign, Minutes, April 20, 1988, p. 2. In 1988, for the third consecutive year, the House passed such a bill as an amendment to the annual defense authorization but abandoned it in a House-Senate conference. H.R. 4264, Sec. 936 (100th Cong., 2d Sess.); see Conference Rpt. 100–989 to H.R. 4481 (Sept. 28, 1988).

104. Olafur Grimsson, quoted from August 5, 1988, press conference, in *The Arms Control Reporter,* Chronology 1988 (entry for 5 August) (hope for 39 signatures by the end of October); Parliamentarians for Global Action, "A New Road to a Comprehensive Test Ban, p. 3 April, 1989, Supplement," p. 3. (39th and 40th signatures were announced April 5, 1989).

105. Final Document of the Non-aligned Foreign Ministers' Conference, Nicosia, Cyprus, Paragraph 31 (Sept. 11, 1988).

106. New Icelandic Government Formed, Xinhua General Overseas News Service, Sept. 28, 1988.

107. Transcript of the Presidential Debate, Part II of II, *Washington Post,* Sept. 26, 1988, p. A18; "The Presidential Debate," *New York Times,* Oct. 14, 1988, p. 14.

108. The letter to H.E. Dr. Filipe Hector Paolillo, Uruguay's ambassador, from Aaron Tovish, dated March 7, 1989, was typical of PGA's requests; it reported on progress toward the goal of 39 signatories, reiterated the value of the Conference, recited the General Assembly resolutions, and encouraged the ambassador "to cable your Government in order to obtain authorization to send a letter of request to each Depositary Government."

109. See fax transmission to Mexican Ambassador Miguel Marin-Bosch from Aaron Tovish, Nov. 8, 1988.

110. Parliamentarians for Global Action," A New Road to a Comprehensive Test Ban, April, 1989 Supplement," p. 2. The General Assembly passed a fourth resolution supporting the amendment conference. A/RES/43/63B (December 22, 1988).

111. Note to Aaron Tovish from Kennedy Graham (undated but apparently early 1989).

112. Maxime Faille, Trip Report (undated, but referring to meetings in January and February, 1989).

113. Parliamentarians for Global Action, "Delegation to Moscow," *Global Action Update,* p. 3 (April, 1989); Summary of Discussions between Parliamentarians Global Action and Soviet Leaders (March 9–10, 1989) (meeting in Moscow); Tovish, "Partial Test Ban Treaty amendment effort: Status and some thoughts on strategy," (informal paper, Sept. 22, 1989) (argument for holding at least the first session of the Amendment Conference before the NPT Review Conference).

114. Peter Zheutlin, "Nevada, U.S.S.R.," *Bulletin of the Atomic Scientists* March, 1990, p. 10; "Soviet Group Demands End to nuclear Testing," *Boston Globe* March 25, 1989, p. 3; Michael Gordon, "Soviets Cut Back Nuclear Testing As Hazards Become a Local Issue," *New York Times* July 8, 1989, p. A3.

115. Frank Gaffney, Jr., "Test Ban Would Be Real Tremor to U.S. Security," *Defense News* September 5, 1988, p. 35 (Mr. Gaffney was Deputy Assistant Secretary of Defense for International Security Policy during the Reagan administration).

116. The statement was made by Soviet foreign minister Edouard Shevardnadze to Bernard Lown, during a meeting in Moscow in April, 1989. Interview with Dr. Bernard Lown in Chestnut Hill, Massachusetts, April 14, 1990. For an illustration of opposition to a second unilateral test moratorium within the Soviet government, see V. Mikhaylov (Deputy Minister of Nuclear Power Generation and the Nuclear Industry), "Why should the country's nuclear test sites remain silent?" *Pravda* Oct. 24, 1990.

117. PGA celebrated at a reception in Washington, attended by the Indian ambassador to the United States and several American legislators including Senator Edward M. Kennedy and Senate Foreign Relations Committee chairman Claiborne Pell.

3

The Year of Skirmishes

Political events result from some combination of planning and fortuity. Aaron Tovish and his colleagues at Parliamentarians for Global Action had planned with care the steps necessary to force the convening of an amendment conference. By a stroke of good luck, their efforts took years longer than they had anticipated and had succeeded just as a new American President was formulating his foreign policy. Still better luck would have placed in the White House any of several Democratic candidates who favored a CTB.[1] As events unfolded, however, George Bush had won the Presidency, and no Republican President since Dwight D. Eisenhower had championed the test ban issue.

PGA's Evolving Strategy

Approaching his work as a veteran of the peace movement, Tovish had originally thought about the conference as a tactic to put pressure on the Reagan administration by embarrassing it. He had imagined that PGA could fairly quickly line up the requests to call the conference, that it would be held soon thereafter, and that the United States would vote against the overwhelming majority of states, as it so often did in the United Nations. This vote, however, would be more visible, because it would not be buried in an avalanche of other international resolutions. When the United States and Britain voted against the rest of the world in the more highly visible amendment conference, there could be an international counter-reaction, and perhaps even a domestic backlash in the 1986 Congressional elections.

Two years later, it was obvious to Tovish that he had been naive. Other countries didn't mind putting the United States on the spot in the General Assembly; a major function of that body, after all, was to serve as an official pollster of governments. By contrast, creating a new international institution was a very serious step, one that would be warranted, in the view of many non-aligned nations, only if real progress toward a policy objective could be achieved. The fact that Ronald Reagan would leave the American Presidency early in 1989 provided that possibility. The amendment conference could become a stage on which the new American leader could change the direction of U.S. policy on this issue. Its pendency on the international calendar would provoke a review of US policy by the new administration. Even if the resulting change were not a multilateral amendment of the PTBT, but only a reopening of tripartite CTB negotiations as a counter to the multilateral effort, PGA's initiative would be successful. By 1989, therefore, Tovish had refocussed his objectives. The existence of the Conference having been assured, he sought to develop a strategy for making it into an effective international institution rather than a one-shot public relations event.[2]

Numerous obstacles lay in the way. First, although the effort to initiate the amendment conference project had given PGA a choice of many countries in which to work, any change in U.S. policy would have to focus on a small number of decision-makers in Washington, some of whom were holdovers from the Reagan years and others of whom were just being appointed. Second, the institutional forces arrayed against such a change, in the weapons laboratories and the career bureaucracy, remained formidable. Third, the test ban question had been virtually invisible in American public debate since the Carter years, and even then it had been overshadowed by strategic arms limitation issues. Fourth, although PGA had been able to direct the amendment conference effort to this point, more of the leadership would now pass to the nations that had asked for the meeting; as the representatives of a non-governmental organization, Tovish and Grimsson might be invited to consult privately or even to attend some caucuses, but it would be improper for them even to be present at most intergovernmental meetings.

PGA and its allies were not without some assets, however. First, they continued to enjoy the support and confidence of forty nations, and particularly of the six original sponsors of the Conference. Second, further limitations on testing—if not a complete CTB—were favored by many members of the U.S. Congress, including a majority of House members. Third, the Soviet government's support of a CTB was unwavering, although as a tactical matter, it had elected to proceed at the pace set by the United States. Fourth, many officials in Western governments also favored a CTB, although they had shown through United Nations abstentions that they were not inclined to support either the United States or the non-aligned countries in a symbolic showdown. In addition, the peace groups in the United States and other countries, acting through the US CTB Coalition and related organizations, were beginning to devote more attention to the test ban issue (inspired, in part, by the success of the effort to call the Amendment Conference). But in early 1989, it was too early to tell whether they would ever have the resources or the public support to have any real political impact on a Republican administration.

For more than a year, as the amendment conference moved closer to reality, PGA and other supporters of a CTB worked on three fronts simultaneously. PGA continued its contacts with the sponsoring nations. Supportive members of Congress, working together with peace and religious groups, tried to build political support within Congress and to change the Bush administration's outlook. Peace organizations, led by the Coalition, also tried to build grass-roots support through membership and media activities.

PGA's first move was to organize a "caucus of amendment conference requesters," and to offer them some suggestions for making the conference meaningful. It suggested that the conference be preceded by "a single preparatory meeting, open to all parties," that the conference should open in the Spring of 1990, that both the preparatory meeting and the conference should be held at UN headquarters, and that the conference be "open-ended" rather than terminate after a single session.[3]

Each of these procedural issues was significant. It had become customary for major international arms control conferences to be preceded by a preparatory meeting at which issues such as structure, rules of procedure and agenda were determined, obviating the need for senior diplomats to use limited conference time for those functions and relegating to less visible preliminary events the potentially fractious divisions over procedural matters. Nevertheless, the depositaries might try to minimize the importance of the conference by refusing to hold a preparatory meeting, or by taking the position that they themselves could decide the organizational questions.

Opening the conference in the Spring of 1990 was politically important. The 4th Review Conference under the Non-Proliferation Treaty—and the last before that agreement came up for extension in 1995—would open in August, 1990. The United States and Britain would be under considerably more pressure to take moderate positions before the Review Conference than afterward, because hostility to a CTB expressed at the amendment conference could provoke claims at the Review Conference that the nuclear weapons states were not living up to their disarmament commitments under the NPT; American and British opposition to progress on a test ban might even prevent the Review Conference from reaching consensus on a final statement, as had happened in 1980. Or, as PGA put it, "as the 1990 Review Conference approaches, the nuclear powers will be under pressure to demonstrate their good faith in seeking a test ban [and with] the cooperation of all the participants, the amendment conference could strengthen immeasurably the non-proliferation regime and facilitate a positive outcome to the 1990 Review."[4]

Holding the conference in New York was also of tactical significance. The only two obvious venues were Geneva, where the multilateral Conference on Disarmament held its semi-annual sessions, and at United Nations headquarters in New York. PGA preferred New York in part because although 35 PTBT parties had disarmament staffs in Geneva, 80 others, all of whom were represented in New York, did not. But PGA also preferred a New York venue because of the "much wider media coverage" that was likely there.[5]

PGA's leaders believed that making the Conference a continuing institution rather than a one-time political event was "extremely important," arguing that "to expect any forum to reach agreement . . . in a single session would be totally unrealistic. It is thus essential that the amendment conference be able to hold as many sessions as are required to negotiate all aspects of an agreement."[6] This stated view reflected reality, because a CTB would have to include complicated verification provisions that would take a long time to explain to policy-makers, and it would be longer still before all countries would agree to realistic verification on their territory. But in addition, an open-ended conference was essential to PGA because it would continue to keep the issue alive and to apply pressure to the U.S. and Britain, pressure that could only grow as the 1995 date for a vote to extend the NPT approached.[7] Furthermore, an open-ended strategy was necessary to persuade skeptical countries that there existed a scenario under which practical results could eventually emerge from the effort.

PGA hoped that the six original requestors of the conference would convene a meeting of all 41 petitioning countries, so that they could jointly urge these procedural steps, either to the depositaries or to the United Nations General Assembly. A UN resolution in the fall dealing with procedural issues could help to strengthen the hands of the requestors in bargaining with the depositaries, just as previous resolutions had helped to legitimate the conference call. At the moment of its greatest success, however, the movement was struck by a leadership crisis.[8] No country seemed willing to call meetings or to press for a common front on the procedural questions. Mexico, in particular, was playing a much smaller role than it had. President Miguel de la Madrid had left office, and Garcia-Robles had retired. PGA had frequently inquired whether the new government of President Carlos Salinas de Gortari would continue its role in the project, and it had not received any encouragement.

Fortunately, Sylvia Hernandez, a former President of PGA, had left the Mexican Senate and had become one of the most senior officials of the governing party in Mexico. She arranged for Grimsson, now the Finance Minister of Iceland, to meet with Salinas. In Mexico City, Grimsson recounted for Salinas how forty countries had asked for the conference as a result of an initiative by Mexico, one that had been favored by officials, whom Grimsson named, who continued to hold office under Salinas. If it did not follow through, Mexico would be abandoning these 40 countries, including two countries that were becoming nuclear weapon states, India and Pakistan. Salinas committed his government to following up the effort.[9] Within days, Mexico chaired a strategy meeting, at UN headquarters, of all requesting countries.[10] A major objective of this and subsequent meetings was to agree on procedural objectives and to develop a plan through which the authority of the General Assembly could be brought to bear to support them.

Meanwhile, members of Congress who supported further restrictions on testing pressed their case with the new American administration. In May, 1989, when it had become clear that the amendment conference would be called, twenty-three senators and a hundred and forty two House members wrote to President Bush, warning that "a decision to veto [a CTB] amendment could have serious consequences for our moral and diplomatic standing in the world, as well as for the survival of the non-proliferation regime." The legislators recommended that the new President avoid such a juncture by proposing to the Soviet Union a "mutual, verified phase-out of nuclear weapons tests leading to conclusion of a comprehensive test ban treaty."[11] They advocated that both nations be given a limited period to conduct an agreed quota of tests for the purpose of verifying the reliability and safety of their stockpiles, followed by a second pre-CTB period during which they would lower the size and numbers of their tests and install in-country seismic monitoring systems.[12]

The grassroots U.S. CTB Coalition hired Dr. Carolyn Cottom, a veteran CTB activist, as its Executive Director, and it continued to try to put the testing issue on the American political map. But its successes continued to be confined to convincing other organizations to align themselves with the issue, rather than taking the issue to a wide audience. By the end of 1989, the Coalition would include 59 national organizations,[13] but the test ban issue received only very scattered media coverage.

The Bush Administration's Policy

Despite these international and domestic activities, when the Bush administration was able, after several months of reviewing its policy,[14] to take action on test ban issues, it chose to continue unchanged the policies that the Reagan administration had put into place. In particular, it determined to continue to resist further limits on testing, and to concentrate, instead, on extracting from the Soviet Union further concessions with respect to verification of the 1974 Threshold Test Ban Treaty.[15]

Ironically, just as the Bush administration decided not to alter the stance of the United States government, the test ban issue began to become a more urgent one for the Soviet Union. Suleimenov's campaign against testing at Semipalatinsk had acquired greater political significance as the Soviet government faced increasing hostility from its outlying republics such as Kazakhstan. In June, the Soviet Prime Minister announced that the Soviets planned to reduce the number and size of tests at Semipalatinsk, and for the first half of 1989, the number of Soviet tests fell by half, compared with the same period of 1988.[16] Shortly thereafter, the Supreme Soviet addressed an appeal to the U.S. Congress, noting that some of its members were taking "vigorous steps in the sphere of internal policy toward curtailing the Soviet nuclear test program," calling for new CTB negotiations, "welcoming" the idea of amending the PTBT, and asking for a meeting of Soviet and American members of parliament to discuss the testing issue.[17]

Soviet calls for a CTB were met, as usual, by the American government's insistence that the Soviet Union first agree to additional verification for the 1974 Treaty, and that it accept the American proposals for such verification. The Soviet government had little choice but to agree, in order to clear this roadblock to further limits on testing. In August, it accepted the American demand to use a direct measurement device known as "CORRTEX" to determine the yields of most of the underground tests permitted by that treaty, insisting only that the yields also be measured by seismometry.[18] Pentagon officials resisted this Soviet condition, even though it called for still more verification, because seismometry, unlike CORRTEX, could also prove useful for verifying further restrictions on testing, such as a one-kiloton threshold; they did not want a demonstration that could establish the verifiability of a low-yield ban.[19] But a State Department official's prediction that "it's hard not to take yes for an answer" proved to be correct.[20]

Mexico's New Resolution

Meanwhile, progress toward convening the amendment conference had slowed. Six months after receiving the necessary number of requests, the depositary governments had held a meeting among themselves,[21] but they had not begun to consult the requestors about a date and place. PGA's leadership did not doubt that the depositaries would eventually convene the conference, because the requirement that they do so, in text of the PTBT, was clear. But the delay put pressure on PGA's strategy of holding the conference before the NPT Review Conference, the probability of which PGA began to rank as "less than even."[22] Rumors began to circulate of the depositaries' intention to call for the conference to be held after the NPT Review Conference had concluded.

Mexican Ambassador Miguel Marin-Bosch (left), with Aaron Tovish, executive director, Parliamentarians for Global Action (photograph by Nina Tovish).

Garcia-Robles was, at this time, on the verge of retirement.[23] Miguel Marin-Bosch, a diplomat who had served as deputy head of the Mexican Mission to the United Nations, was in the process of succeeding him as Mexico's leading disarmament diplomat. As Garcia-Robles' biographer, Marin had already begun to acquire his mantle, and his technical expertise with respect to disarmament issues earned him the respect of his colleagues. To put pressure on the depositaries, Marin drafted and introduced a General Assembly resolution along the lines that the caucus of requesting states had discussed. It called for a preparatory meeting in January, 1990, and an "initial two-to-three week session in May/June."[24] He also arranged for a meeting open to all PTBT parties, held at United Nations headquarters on November 8. At the meeting, he sought consensus on holding the conference in New York, and on convening it before the NPT Review, but his efforts were unavailing.[25] The depositaries chose not to attend, but nine NATO countries spoke in favor of a 1991 meeting, expressing their fear that a failed amendment conference before the NPT Review Conference would "have adverse effects on the Review,"[26] The meeting broke up without resolving either the date or place of the conference, but the countries present at the meeting asked Ambassador Nabil El Araby of Egypt, who had chaired it, to try to work out agreement between the requesting countries and the depositaries.[27]

Lines of battle were quickly being drawn over the issues of the opening date, the venue of the conference, how the meeting would be financed, and how long it might last. In response to Marin's introduction of the draft United Nations resolution, the depositaries had immediately announced in the United Nations their plan to convene the conference in Geneva, for "a period of up to two weeks" beginning in January, 1991.[28] Marin's subsequent efforts to negotiate the time and place, and thereby to head off formal invitations by the depositaries to a conference at a time and place of their choice, were unavailing. One day after the meeting of the ambassadors in New York, and despite the arrangement to have El Araby attempt to find common ground, the United States publicly committed itself not only to torpedoing any amendment, but also to hard positions on all of the critical procedural issues. In a Senate Foreign Relations Committee hearing on the amendment conference, the Bush administration announced that "we have consulted with the other Depositaries and have agreed that the conference should take place in Geneva, opening on January 8, 1991. . . . Within a few days, each Depositary will be issuing diplomatic notes [inviting the parties at that place and time]."[29]

The Bush administration also drew lines in the sand on the duration, costs, and inevitable outcome of the conference. It announced its opposition to a conference lasting more than two weeks, and to holding more than one session. It announced that it would not pay more than 14% of the costs of the conference, although it pays 25% of the costs of the United Nations and a higher share of the cost of Non-Proliferation Treaty reviews. It declared that it would not participate in drafting an amendment, and that if the amendment came to a vote, it would vote in opposition. "In making our position clear," it added, "we hope that other parties will be dissuaded from any further attempts to pursue their interest in a CTB by using the . . . amendment process."[30]

The United States government's decision to pre-announce that it would veto a CTB amendment had not been a subject of Presidential or cabinet-level policy-making. It "had been established that a CTB was only a long-term goal, so our position on the Amendment Conference was a given. It flowed automatically [and was discussed only] at the Deputy Assistant Secretaries' level. . . . It was always a given that the U.S. would exercise its veto."[31] For all practical purposes, however, the decision had the same effect as if it had been made by the President himself.

The American determination to veto an Amendment was hardly surprising, but the U.S. government's related announcements regarding the procedural questions distressed officials of the countries that had requested the conference. "We saw it as a strategy to minimize publicity and the effectiveness of publicity, and to limit participation," said one.[32]

Marin's response was to mobilize as many countries as possible against the depositaries' effort to dictate the modalities of the conference. Seeking the widest possible support, he modified his resolution to accommodate the depositaries' desire that the conference not produce a failure on the eve of the NPT review. As amended, his resolution called for a preparatory meeting in New York at the end of May, 1990, a one-week session of the conference immediately thereafter, and a "second substantive" session in New York in January, 1991. This bifurcation would ensure that no vote would be taken until after the NPT Review Conference had been held. To put the world on record against the United States' effort to curtail the conference by withholding funding, Marin added a paragraph calling on the parties to share the costs of the conference "on the basis of the present scale of assessments of the United Nations."[33]

The depositaries pre-empted the United Nations. The day before Marin's resolution was scheduled to be voted on in the pertinent United Nations committee, the depositaries issued their formal invitations to all parties to attend an amendment conference in Geneva in January, 1991.[34] The Committee nevertheless took up the resolution and sent it forward with a positive recommendation to the floor of the General Assembly. The vote was 108 to 2, with only the United States and Great Britain opposed. Despite its having sent out notices for a 1991 meeting in Geneva, the Soviet Union supported the Mexican resolution. Twenty-one countries abstained, including most NATO members.[35] Shortly thereafter, the resolution was approved by the General Assembly, this time by a vote of 127 to 2, with 22 abstentions.[36]

As 1989 came to a close, neither side could claim either the moral authority to determine the conference arrangements or a victory in the procedural skirmishes that had taken place. The depositaries arguably had a legal right to determine, without the consent of the majority, when and where an amendment conference would take place, and how it would be paid for, and the United Nations was technically irrelevant, since the PTBT was an agreement of its member parties; some parties were not UN members, and some UN members were not parties. On the other hand, while it was relatively easy for the United States and Britain to ignore the expressed desires of the world community as to testing itself, it was hard for their diplomats to argue that they had such a significant stake in a time or venue that the non-aligned countries should be ignored. Furthermore, the total isolation of the United States and Britain, as a result of the defection of the Soviet Union on the resolution and the abstention of their Western allies, was a factor weighing in favor of compromise.

Caucuses and Chitchatting

At this point, Marin requested a meeting between the six original requesting states and the three depositaries. The United States counter-proposed a meeting open to all parties, probably because it did not want to seem to agree that the six originators had any special claim of authority. Marin was happy to go along with the American suggestion, both because the United States' representatives would be more constrained to be reasonable before a larger audience and because the margin against the Anglo-American position would be greater in the larger group. Before the meeting, Marin learned that the principal U.S. diplomat working on the PTBT amendment conference would be Mary Elizabeth Hoinkes, the Deputy General Counsel of the U.S. Arms Control and Disarmament Agency. He called her and told her that although he had suggested the meeting, he did not want to chair it; he proposed, and she agreed, that he would turn the chair over to Yasushi Akashi, the Undersecretary for Disarmament Affairs of the United Nations. In the meeting, however, when he attempted to do so, the British representative objected, on the ground that the United Nations Secretariat had no legitimate role in a meeting of treaty parties, and both the Americans and the Soviets agreed. Marin stood his ground, saying that a neutral chair did not imply recognition of United Nations authority over treaty matters, and Akashi did chair the session. Unfortunately, the meeting had been called on such short notice that most delegations were unable to address the date and venue issues; all they could do was agree to hold a second meeting on January 22, ten days later.[37]

Between the two meetings, several caucuses occurred. The six originators met with Akashi to urge him to appoint a United Nations official as the UN's representative to the conference; such an official could, more easily than any parties, draft an agenda for the conference, prepare proposed rules of procedure, and suggest a structure for the event. The depositaries also met with him and urged him not to make such an appointment, and he determined, in view of the controversy, to hold off. Then representatives of about 55 non-aligned PTBT parties met to work out their strategy for meeting with the depositaries.[38]

The second meeting, however, was anticlimactic. Delegates from 75 countries attended, and by general agreement, Edmond Jayasinghe, the Sri Lankan delegate, chaired it. With respect to the main issues of date and place, the American and British representatives claimed that they were not prepared for a discussion, because they had not had a sufficient opportunity for consultations among the depositary governments; the British delegate claimed that his government's expert on these issues was in Geneva, preparing for the Conference on Disarmament session that was about to begin. They said that their representatives in Geneva would consult with one another there, and they agreed to meet the non-aligned countries again in New York, two weeks later. The Soviet delegate was even more evasive, claiming that he was at the meeting in his "personal capacity" and had no instructions from Moscow.[39] Meanwhile, the depositaries refused to agree to ask the Secretary-General to appoint a representative to begin organizing the conference.[40] Many of the delegates were deeply disappointed by the unwillingness of the depositaries to cooperate in reaching agreement on procedural arrangements for the conference. Furthermore, the delay that they were forcing was in fact making it less likely that the conference could be held before the NPT review. But Jayasinghe concluded that the atmosphere of the meeting was sufficiently constructive that by doing a "round of chitchatting," particularly with representatives of Western European countries that could press the U.S. and U.K. to compromise, he could eventually get something worked out.[41]

Further American Retreats

Not all of the delegates shared Jayashinghe's optimism, because the United States and Britain seemed to be hardening their stances. Just after the January 22 meeting with the depositaries, delegates read in their morning newspapers (or in clippings faxed to them by PGA) that now that the bilateral talks on a new Threshold Test Ban Treaty verification protocol were on the verge of producing agreement, the United States had decided to renege on President Reagan's 1986 commitment to follow negotiation of the protocol by immediately instituting negotiations on further testing limitations.[42] The press reported that the Bush administration had decided to delay such negotiations for an indefinite period, although the change in policy was "certain to anger arms control advocates and perhaps Moscow."[43] The administration claimed that the purpose of the delay was "to have a period in which to observe the implementation of the protocols in order to give both sides experience with these new verification methods."[44] But officials confided in reporters that the real reason for the policy change was that the Defense Department "is opposed to the new nuclear testing constraints expected to result from the talks [once they resumed]. . . . The decision to defer the negotiations indefinitely, rather than repudiate them outright, resulted from compromise with other agencies."[45]

As predicted, the administration's about-face provoked calls for Congressional intervention[46] and criticism from the Soviet Union, which noted

that these "actions by the US side" were "contrary to the existing understanding" and that bilateral negotiations with the United States were only
"one of the means" for achieving a CTB, another being "the proposal . . .
to amend" the PTBT.[47] Gorbachev personally reaffirmed the Soviet Union's
"readiness at any time to end nuclear tests completely and forever if the
USA will also do the same."[48]

Nevertheless, the move disrupted and divided arms control advocates,
who had to give priority to reacting to the administration's retreat in
bilateral negotiations as well as its failure to move forward in a multinational forum. Test ban advocates in the U.S. House of Representatives sent
a letter to the Secretary of State calling for resumption of the step-by-step
process of negotiating lower thresholds and quotas of nuclear tests, but
Tovish advised the U.S. CTB Coalition not to support the letter because it
contemplated a gradual phase-out of testing rather than an immediate
halt.[49] He believed that there was no point to seeking an early compromise
of the CTB issue, when the American administration showed no sign of
being interested in any further restrictions on testing. After a month of
internal negotiations, the Coalition was able to agree to write its own letter,
expressing the hope that the superpowers would "agree to a date certain
to reopen substantive talks to *end* all nuclear testing."[50]

The American policy change did not make Jayasinghe's "chitchatting"
any easier, but the American government began to yield very slightly on
the procedural arrangements for the conference. When the treaty parties
met again in an informal session on February 12, the Western countries
agreed that a preparatory conference could be held in New York, although
the United States continued to argue that the conference itself should be
held in Geneva the following January. This proposal divided the non-
aligned countries. Some wanted to continue to negotiate; others wanted to
try to convene the conference themselves, in New York, during the spring.
Still others considered a compromise in which the conference would be
held in New York but would be delayed until January. Many of them
resented being pushed around by the depositaries, but they feared that
nothing constructive could come out of a confrontational conference, or
one that they called and the depositaries boycotted. Tovish privately advised
certain delegates to be firm on the location of the conference because the
depositaries could not effectively insist on a Geneva venue. If they insisted
unilaterally on convening the event there, the non-aligned could use their
majority control over all issues (other than adoption of an amendment
itself) to move the meeting to New York. But disappointed by the depositaries' proposals and uncertain of their own course, the non-aligned
countries could agree only that the dialogue should continue.[51]

Within a few days after this meeting, the Bush administration threw
two more buckets of ice water on the prospects for a test ban. First the

President's national security advisor replied to the members of Congress who had protested the Bush administration's increasingly negative attitude toward negotiated test restrictions. His letter ignored most of the legislators' arguments for a phase-out and said that "the Administration cannot endorse a ban, as you suggest, as a 1995–2000 goal. A testing ban must be viewed in the context of a time when we do not need to depend on nuclear deterrence to ensure international security. . . ."[52] Second, the Secretary of Energy signed a devastatingly negative report to Congress on the prospects for developing an arsenal of nuclear weapons based on designs that would not need testing.

This report had been required by a law passed in 1988 at the behest of CTB advocates such as Representative Edward Markey.[53] In the statute, Congress had required the Secretary of Energy to establish and support a program "to assure that the United States is in a position to maintain the reliability, safety and continued deterrent effect of its stockpile . . . in the event that a . . . comprehensive ban on nuclear testing is negotiated" and to make annual progress reports to Congress. The components of this program were to include "vigorous . . . stockpile inspection and nonexplosive testing . . . [and plans] to assure that the specific materials . . . needed for remanufacture . . . are available . . . if [remanufacture become necessary] in order to satisfy reliability and safety requirements."[54]

Although the pro-CTB sponsors of the law intended to propel the United States toward a weapons management regime that could be consistent with a test ban, the law gave the Department of Energy a possible argument for more rather than less testing, at least in the short run. If current nuclear weapon designs had not been created with a possible CTB in mind (and they had not, because the weapons laboratories had never taken seriously the government's stated commitment, from 1957 to 1982, to a negotiated CTB), it might be necessary to design, develop and deploy a whole generation of new types of nuclear weapons that would not decay or otherwise deteriorate, and require remanufacture, over very long periods of time. A new design might be needed for every delivery system in the arsenal, and each of them might require numerous nuclear tests. In its first annual report, the Secretary of Energy exploited this paradox to an extent that the law's authors could never have imagined. He noted that even if designs for weapons could be developed that were less sensitive to aging or to slight changes in materials, "the entire stockpile would have to be rebuilt." He said that "at least 10 years will be required to have any significant success in evaluating the capability to maintain and modernize the U.S. deterrent under further testing constraints." In other words, until the year 2000, the Department couldn't even analyze whether the Congressional objective was feasible, much less achieve it. But "the Department has initiated the development of a 10-year plan that will lay out a program of activities, goals and objectives that will allow us to evaluate whether [the Congressional goal] would be possible." Furthermore, the Department could already predict what the ten-year study would show: "When the investigation is complete, some level of nuclear testing will likely be required to maintain a credible nuclear deterrent."[55]

Thus the atmosphere deteriorated as the PTBT delegates continued to grope their way toward some agreement on when and where to convene the conference. Two weeks and many caucuses later, all parties had agreed that a preparatory conference would be held at the end of May, but the non-aligned countries were on the verge of abandoning hope of convening the actual conference in June, as called for by the United Nations resolution. They had no support for their plan among Western nations and no way of forcing the depositaries to accede to their calendar. They also took seriously the likelihood that, in the end, they would have to agree that, in exchange for a preparatory meeting in New York, they would have to agree to allow the conference itself to go forward in Geneva. The essential problem was on the surface a legal one—the fact that the Treaty granted exclusive authority to the depositary countries to convene the parties, which prevented the non-aligned, until convened, from exercising their majority power. At root, though, the problem was really political. Delegates from a majority of parties might have tried to call the conference itself, at a time and place of their choice, putting more pressure on the United States to avoid a scene before the NPT Review. Although this course was privately favored by some of the representatives in New York, who were becoming increasingly frustrated by the United States' rigidity, they could not have obtained support from their capitals for such a confrontational stance.[56]

The Procedural Compromises

By the end of February, though, two subtle shifts by the United States and Britain began to produce some movement. First, the depositaries took it upon themselves to write to the Secretary-General of the United Nations, requesting his assistance in coordination. The non-aligned had long wanted the machinery of the United Nations to begin to move forward, so this news was welcomed. Second, the American delegates began to absent themselves from the meetings of diplomats, which had become an almost daily affair, and they hinted that it would be easier for the American government to accept arrangements on which all the other countries (including the British) had agreed. No one spelled out the reasons for the sudden absence of Americans, but it seemed as if the American delegates would have an easier time persuading the most anti-CTB agencies in Washington to accept a *fait accompli* than to obtain their agreement to any arrangements favored by the non-aligned.[57]

On February 26 through 28, after many conversations including the conference proposers, U.S. allies in Europe and Asia, and the British representative, the Australian delegate circulated two drafts of a "Non-paper" listing six options for conference arrangements. A "non-paper," in diplomatic parlance, is a document which actually says "non-paper" on it, enabling the drafter to float a trial balloon having no official status. Non-papers are sometimes authorized by senior foreign ministry officials, although those officials may want to leave other countries guessing about whether the diplomat who circulated the paper had authority from her capital. The options in the non-paper included, in addition to the original proposals of Mexico and the depositaries, such possibilities as holding a week long preparatory conference in May with a "short opening session" in September or December; a two-week preparatory conference in June and a two week January conference, both in New York; and an "organizational session" in May followed by a "substantive session" in January.[58]

The non-paper was worked over by the delegates during those three days, in meetings chaired by Jayasinghe; this work resulted in the creation of three additional options that were circulated at a meeting the following day. These included holding an "Organisation of the Conference" in May; a "session for the organisation of the Conference" in May; and a "preliminary meeting" in May "to address organisational aspects of the Conference."[59] Increasingly, the options on which the delegates focussed all contemplated that the conference would be held in New York but delayed until January, and that some sort of preliminary event, variously described, would be held in New York before the NPT Review. The differences among the variations in the nomenclature of the preliminary event may seem trivial, but the diplomats believed that what was at stake was the issue of what could legitimately be achieved by that meeting. Everyone agreed that the preliminary event could discuss the agenda and procedures for the conference, but could representatives who attended it also make speeches about test ban policy itself? If the preliminary event were really the "short opening session" of the Conference itself, it seemed obvious that they could, whereas if the preliminary event was limited to addressing "organisational aspects" they might be barred from doing so. The other proposed formulations left this question somewhat ambiguous.

After nearly four full days of discussions, the diplomats settled on still another ambiguous description, which Jayasinghe had drafted. They agreed "to hold in New York the Conference from 7–18 January 1991 preceded by a Meeting for the organisation of the Conference from 29 May to 8 June 1990."[60] The non-aligned had obtained their preferred location for the conference, but they had to some extent conceded on dates, in that the conference would not begin until after the NPT review. On the other hand, the "Meeting" would take place before the NPT review, and it was not designated a "preparatory" conference; therefore, substantive policy statements could be in order. Nevertheless, with its specification of the task of the Meeting, this formulation did point away from substantive work at that session, although the non-aligned delegates successfully insisted that the word Meeting be capitalized to enhance the status of the event and to further distinguish it from a traditional, procedural preparatory conference. The British and Soviet delegates said that they would accept this compromise if the American government (which was still absent from these procedural negotiations) would do so, and the following week, as expected, the American representative agreed to it as well.[61]

The skirmishes were far from over, however. All that had been determined were the date, place and name of the Meeting. At the next negotiating session, the United States delegation was back at the table, represented not by Ms. Hoinkes but by Laura Clerici, a more junior diplomat attached to the United States' Mission to the United Nations in New York. Backed by the British on all but the last point, Clerici insisted that the Meeting should produce no official summary records of its proceedings, that ambassadorial credentials should not be required of delegates, that non-governmental peace organizations should be excluded, that all other observers (such as the press) should also be excluded, and that all governments should equally share the costs of the gathering.[62]

These proposals were entirely consistent with the United States' desire to downplay the significance of the Meeting, to reduce the likelihood that it would attract publicity, and, in the case of the cost-sharing proposal, to reduce the likelihood of widespread participation (because the United States would be paying only about 1% of the cost rather than 25%, as it did with respect to the United Nations, or even 14%, the figure Ms. Bailey had mentioned in her Senate testimony). For example, a requirement that delegates be designated as ambassadors would require countries to send higher-level officials to the Meeting, and it would give the Meeting greater prominence in news media around the world. The Clerici proposals would, in essence, recapture for the Meeting the attributes of a preparatory conference (which traditionally did not require ambassadors and did not permit observers) despite the decision to call the event by another name.

On the night of March 23, the day after Clerici announced her proposals, several of the non-aligned leaders agreed to leak word widely that at the following meeting, the non-aligned countries would be angry with the American and British delegations for backtracking on what they regarded as a consensus decision to have more than a preparatory conference. The purpose of the leak was to encourage the United States to back down and to agree that the Meeting would enjoy a higher status. Nevertheless, Clerici incensed the non-aligned leaders by focusing on the issue of costs and restating her view that all of the countries should pay equal shares. William

Epstein, the United Nations official who had been consulting with Parliamentarians for Global Action, called Hoinkes to find out whether this unprecedented proposal was really United States policy. Hoinkes reassured him that "it's not our last position."[63] Within days, the clamor against the United States' proposal had become much greater, and non-aligned countries were threatening to leave the question of costs unresolved until the Meeting convened on May 29, and to argue the issue of cost-sharing in public. At a lunch with Mexican delegates, Hoinkes partly backed down, agreeing that the United States would pay 12 1/2% of the cost, half of what it would have to pay under the United Nations scale. When this offer was repeated in the multilateral consultations, the non-aligned countries rejected it, but the issue was not one on which they could launch an effective protest.[64] Nevertheless, the fact that the Meeting and Conference had now been set for a specific time and place did give them some additional bargaining power, because now a disagreement with the depositaries did not run the risk of delaying the conference indefinitely. As a result, they were able to propose that Jayasinghe chair the Meeting. The depositaries did not oppose this proposal.[65]

During April and May, most of the remaining issues were also resolved through compromise. Ambassadorial credentials were not required for the Meeting, but a summary record would be made and non-governmental organizations were permitted to observe. The agenda of the Meeting would include time for general remarks, enabling countries the opportunity to put their views on nuclear testing on record before the NPT Review, but without any possibility of bringing an amendment to a vote before that conference. The question of the United States' share of the costs of the Meeting and conference was not among the issues that were compromised. The American government's unwillingness to pay its customary share of the costs of a conference, simply because it did not like the agenda, continued to rankle many delegates, in part because accepting the lesser United States share for this Meeting could set what they regarded as a very bad precedent for future conferences or negotiations under other international agreements.

Activists and Legislators

From March through May, while the diplomats were wrangling over procedural arrangements, other CTB advocates were struggling, with little apparent success, to popularize the issue. Taking advantage of having organized networks of city-based local coalitions over the previous two years, the U.S. CTB Coalition launched a campaign that it called "Cities Talk Back," a play on the CTB acronym. The idea was that in 1990, it would mobilize whatever grass roots support it had to brief members of

Congress about the PTBT amendment conference and to raise funds for a media campaign including "TV spots, media appearances by experts, airing of test ban videos, op eds by experts, letters-to-the-editor, and signature ads." During the conference, the "culmination of the campaign will be city-based actions around the world . . . . City council and state legislature resolutions, and statements by mayors, governors, and community leaders will be communicated to President Bush."[66] An early goal of this strategy was to obtain a favorable vote by the National Governors Association on a resolution, introduced by Oregon Governor Neil Goldschmidt, calling on the three leaders of the depositary states "to actively participate in the [amendment conference] and work toward an end to testing worldwide."[67] This effort failed when the resolution died in committee because it was a "foreign policy matter."[68] But essentially the same objective was achieved when the U.S. Conference of Mayors voted to hold a special meeting in New York, on the day before the PTBT Amendment Conference, to discuss "The Budget, CTB, and the Cities" and to help focus public attention on the test ban issue.[69]

The effort to mount a media campaign floundered as funds, never plentiful, became scarce.[70] The Coalition never had money to produce even one television spot, much less to purchase time in which to show it. On the eve of the Bush-Gorbachev summit in May, at which the new Threshold Test Ban verification protocol would be signed, it spent $2000 to send press materials to newspapers and columnists all over the country. Although these materials represented what the Coalition thought was an unconventional slant on the Threshold Test Ban—that only a CTB would represent real progress on arms control—Coalition members later "bemoaned" the fact that not a single paper used the information.[71]

The Coalition also tried to impress the U.S. government with the amount of citizen interest in a CTB by sending its U.N. ambassador, Thomas Pickering, a large number of telegrams and mailgrams on the eve of the Meeting of the PTBT parties. Its goal was to generate at least 5000 such messages, but it was able to produce only 3000. Nevertheless, it was able to report that Pickering's office was "very impressed by the deluge."[72]

Soviet and American activists participated jointly in a further effort to rally public interest in the test ban issue. Olzhas Suleimenov, who had so quickly travelled the distance from poet to anti-testing activist to member of the Supreme Soviet, organized an "International Citizens Congress for a Nuclear Test Ban," which International Physicians for the Prevention of Nuclear War co-sponsored. This four-day meeting, uniting Soviet and American test ban advocates, as well as activists from numerous other countries, would include speeches and panels in Alma Ata, Kazakhstan; a visit to a village thirty miles from the Semipalatinsk test site; conversations with villagers exposed to radioactive fallout; participation in a mass public demonstration against testing; and dedication of a monument to atomic bomb victims.[73] About 200 Americans made the trip to Alma Ata, but like the other activities in which Coalition members engaged, the International Citizens Congress was ignored by the American press.

In the United States Congress, CTB supporters had two plans. The first was to pass a resolution urging the President to proceed with the next phase of testing reductions, notwithstanding the "pause" that the administration had announced in January, and offering some general words of support for the amendment conference. In April, Senate Foreign Relations Committee Chairman Claiborne Pell introduced such a measure; it would have resolved that the President should tell the Soviet Union of a U.S. desire to "identify and agree upon a definite timetable for the early achievement" of a CTB and "pursue negotiations in good faith" in the amendment conference.[74] At about the same time that this resolution was introduced, twenty-two senators wrote to the President, complaining that the "pause" violated commitments that the administration had made to Congress; Senator Edward M. Kennedy, who had organized the group, said that American security interests in non-proliferation were "being undermined by the narrow concerns of the weapons bureaucrats."[75]

The second Congressional plan was to cut funds from the portion of the Department of Energy's budget devoted to research, development and testing of nuclear weapons, putting indirect pressure on the Department to cut the number of American tests. As a result of the pressure from Suleimenov and his followers in Kazakhstan, the annual number of Soviet tests had already fallen drastically, from 23 in 1987 and 17 in 1988 to only 7 in 1989, and the Soviets had not tested at all in the early months of 1990.[76] Furthermore, the Soviets announced in early March that the Semipalatinsk site would be closed within three years and all testing would thereafter be conducted at the much more inhospitable Arctic site of Novaya Zemlya island;[77] just three weeks later, a Soviet Prime Minister told the Supreme Soviet that testing at Semipalatinsk would be ended for the time being.[78] Budget-cutting had a real chance, since it united liberals who favored a CTB with moderates seeking deficit reduction or peace dividends from the end of U.S.-Soviet arms competition. Senator Kennedy would have liked to cut the amount of funds available for testing by about 25%, but he doubted that such a large cut could pass the House. By late spring, an amendment by Representative Peter DeFazio to cut the research, development and testing budget by 5% seemed to be the only possibility for successful action.[79] In any event, neither the Pell resolution nor the budget-cutting amendments would come up on the House or Senate floors before summer.

Aaron Tovish's own contribution to the effort to increase public consciousness of the test ban issue was to organize a three-country media event involving members of parliaments. Through members of PGA, he circulated in parliaments in more than sixty countries an open letter calling on the heads of state of the three depositaries to address the amendment conference in person, suspend testing during the conference, and work to achieve a CTB amendment.[80] PGA hoped to obtain 2000 signatures from legislators. Then, on the eve of the Meeting at the end of May, two legislators from the U.S., Britain, and the Soviet Union would travel to each of the three capitals to try to present copies of the letter, and the 2000 signatures, to the three heads of state. At each stop, they would hold a press conference and seek meetings with members of parliament.[81] PGA's plan for pre-Meeting publicity collapsed in mid-April, however, when Presidents Bush and Gorbachev scheduled a summit on May 30, making it impossible to see either of them, or to get any press attention, just before the Meeting. The three-capital tour had to be postponed until the fall.

These largely unreported activities of CTB proponents contrasted sharply with another CTB-related event, a week before the Meeting, that made front page news across the country. After digging for more than a year, Washington Post reporter R. Jeffrey Smith discovered that the Department of Energy had found a safety problem in the W-79 short-range nuclear artillery shells deployed in Europe. New computer calculations, confirmed by nuclear testing, showed that this weapon could detonate accidentally if struck by a bullet or by shrapnel from a conventional explosive. Some of the shells had been returned to Texas for the installation of additional steel plating. More importantly, the discovery had led to a review of the safety of the W88 warhead in the new Trident II submarine-launched missiles, and the Secretary of Energy said that he "wouldn't feel comfortable until the whole stockpile," as opposed to only 35% of it, used Insensitive High Explosive rather than highly volatile chemicals in their nuclear detonators.[82] Although Smith did not mention it, any wholesale redesign of stockpiled weapons to incorporate Insensitive High Explosive could well require years of additional nuclear testing. In addition, Smith found that the weapons designers had packed the cores of the nation's nuclear artillery shells with extra plutonium to reduce the amount of high explosive and therefore their overall weight, putting them "right on the edge of safety by virtue of their design alone."[83] This design decision, too, might eventually be reversed, leading to military requirements for new artillery shells with safer designs and new nuclear tests. Indeed, the directors of the two nuclear weapons design laboratories lost no time in writing to the Secretary of Energy that "nuclear testing continues to be crucial to meeting nuclear weapons requirements. This fact has been dramatically underscored in the past two years with the events surrounding the W79 artillery shell and the questions raised about the W88 Trident II warhead."[84]

In the last week of May, the story about unsafe warheads was breaking, the Coalition was showering telegrams on Pickering, Suleimenov's International Congress was convening, and Mikhail Gorbachev was on his way to Washington to meet George Bush and to sign the protocol that would bring the Threshold Test Ban Treaty into effect sixteen years after it had been signed. In New York, the delegates to the Meeting were still arguing about costs. On May 18, they had settled every issue but that one, agreeing that Jayasinghe would preside over the Meeting, and that Sohrab Kheradi of the UN Secretariat would be the Secretary General.[85] But the United States still would not offer more than about half of what it would have been obligated to pay under the UN Scale. Apparently to needle the United States' delegate, Marin suggested that the United States pay no assessment at all, that all others pick up its share according to the UN Scale, and that the US attend the event "as a guest of the Conference."[86] That meeting ended with continued deadlock.

A week later, the Parties had their final showdown on the issue of financing. The United States continued to refuse to pay more than 12.5%. The non-aligned countries could have refused to budge as well, kicking the decision of costs over to the Meeting itself. The Meeting, in turn, could by majority vote have imposed the U.N. Scale of Dues on itself, but this risked some possibility that the U.S. would have refused to participate or simply refused to contribute more than 12.5%, leaving the Conference is a fiscal quandary. The non-aligned countries backed down, perhaps because the actual amount of the estimated shortfall was a relatively small amount—less than $ 100,000—a serious annoyance (because delegates would have to explain it to their foreign ministries at home) and a dreadful precedent,[87] but not worth the risk of jeopardizing the Conference.[88] In the final pre-Meeting agreement, the Parties agreed that the depositaries would be given a combined assessment of one-third of the costs of the conference (diplomatically masking the size of the U.S. share)[89] and that all other participants would make up the U.S. shortfall by making "voluntary" contributions in proportion to their shares under the U.N. Scale, but that the arrangement would not constitute a precedent for any future conferences with respect to which a wealthy nation chose not to pay what others thought should be its share.[90] Since some delegates had to confirm this arrangement with their capitals, the Parties agreed to meet again briefly, a few minutes before the Meeting officially began, to ascertain whether any hitch had developed.

The Opening Session of the Meeting was delayed for 40 minutes while this last unofficial meeting of the Parties took place. Jayasinghe asked whether any delegation was unable to pay its "voluntary" share, and none responded. This final administrative detail apparently resolved, the Meeting could at last take place.

Notes

1. Gov. Michael Dukakis, who won the Democratic nomination in 1988, called for a CTB in both of his televised debates with Vice-President Bush. See Chapter 2, note 107. Representative Richard Gephardt and Senator Paul Simon, two other Democratic candidates, were also outspoken CTB advocates, and Simon was a PGA member.

2. Interview with Aaron Tovish, in New York City, March 24, 1990.

3. Memorandum to participants in the caucus of amendment conference requesters from Parliamentarians for Global Action, May 22, 1989.

4. Parliamentarians for Global Action, "A Partial Test Ban Treaty Amendment Conference: Ten Questions and Answers" (1989).

5. Parliamentarians for Global Action, *A New Road to a Comprehensive Test Ban* 14–15 (1988).

6. Memorandum to participants in the caucus of amendment conference requesters from Parliamentarians for Global Action, May 22, 1989.

7. "Just by existing, the Conference exerts pressure, and this is a political exercise in exerting pressure. . . . To bring [the worldwide CTB constituency together, you need a forum. You need the show to go on and you need to tie it to the closing phases of the Non-Proliferation Treaty." Interview with Olafur Grimsson in New York City, June 3, 1990.

8. Letter to Foreign Minister Ali Alatas of Indonesia from William Epstein, July 12, 1989.

9. Grimsson interview, June 3, 1990; letter to President Carlos Salinas de Gortari from Olafur Grimsson, Aug. 4, 1989.

10. Memorandum to Heads of Missions from Parliamentarians for Global Action (undated) (including agenda for meeting to be chaired by Mexico on August 15, 1989).

11. A few months earlier, twenty-five American experts on test ban policy, most of whom favored at least some further restraints on testing, had recommended that in view of the strong political opposition to an immediate CTB, the President who would be elected in 1988 should agree with Soviet leaders to a bilateral phaseout of testing. The Belmont Conference on Nuclear Test Ban Policy (David A. Koplow and Philip G. Schrag, Rapporteurs), "Phasing Out Nuclear Weapons Tests," *Stanford Journal of International Law,* v. 26, p. 205 (1989). Copies of the report had been sent to the new administration and to members of the pertinent Congressional committees.

12. Letter to President George Bush from Senator Claiborne Pell, *et al.,* May 11, 1989.

13. International Comprehensive Test Ban Campaign, *Comprehensive Test Ban News* Jan. 25, 1990, p. 4.

14. In May, 1989, John King, Deputy Assistant Director of the Arms Control and Disarmament Agency, told Kennedy Graham, PGA's Secretary-General, that "it may be quite a while" before the U.S. Government decided its policy with respect to the Amendment Conference. King made it clear, however, that while the administration had yet to make decisions about the time, place, and other arrange-

ments for the Conference, "everybody knows what will happen at the end of [it]". Kennedy Graham, notes of Meeting with John King, May 2, 1989.

15. On May 11, 1989, the United States and the Soviet Union announced the resumption of negotiations to develop a new verification protocol, providing for more intrusive measures to determine whether tests exceeded the 150 kt limit of that Treaty. President Bush repeated what had become the Reagan administration's litany on the subject, saying that he opposed a CTB "until the United States no longer depends on nuclear deterrence." The Bush administration even decided not to modify the severe verification demands that the Reagan administration had made in the talks on verification, demands that had led to stalemate. R. Jeffrey Smith, "Superpowers to Resume A-Test Talks," *Washington Post* May 12, 1989, p. A30.

16. Michael Gordon, "Soviets Cut Back Nuclear Testing as Hazards Become a Local Issue," *New York Times* July 8, 1989.

17. Appeal by the USSR Supreme Soviet to the United States Congress, Aug. 1, 1989.

18. R. Jeffrey Smith, "Monitoring of High-Yield Blasts Offered," *Washington Post* Aug. 12, 1989, p. A13.

19. *Ibid.*; R. Jeffrey Smith, "Nuclear Test Proposal Splits U.S. Officials," *Washington Post* Sept. 14, 1989.

20. *Ibid.* The agreement to use both CORRTEX and seismic monitoring of yields was incorporated into the Protocol to the Treaty Between the United States of America and the Union of Soviet Socialist Republics on the Limitation of Underground Nuclear Weapon Tests, and it entered into force, after ratification by the two governments, in December, 1990.

21. A/C.1/44/PV.41 (Nov. 17, 1989) (Statement of United Kingdom Ambassador Ian Kenyon).

22. Minutes of Executive Committee Meeting of Parliamentarians for Global Action, July 21–22, 1989.

23. "Salute to Garcia-Robles," *Disarmament Times,* December, 1989, p. 1.

24. Draft resolution A/C.1/44/L.25, discussed by Ambassador Marin during the First Committee's deliberations, A/C.1/44/PV.26, p. 12 (Nov. 2, 1989) and A/C.1/44/PV.40, p. 6 (Nov. 17, 1989). For the formal history of the resolution, see A/44/773, p. 2.

25. A/C.1/44/PV.40, p. 6 (Nov. 17, 1989).

26. "Amendment Conference for CTB: When, Where?" *Disarmament Times* Nov., 1989, p. 1.

27. *Ibid.*

28. Statement of Amb. Ian Kenyon of the United Kingdom, A/C.1/44/PV.26, p. 16 (Nov. 17, 1989).

29. *Hearings Before the Senate Foreign Relations Committee on Nuclear Test Ban Issues,* 101st Cong., 1st Sess., Nov. 9, 1989 (testimony of Dr. Kathleen C. Bailey, Assistant Director, U.S. Arms Control and Disarmament Agency).

30. *Ibid.*

31. Interview with Mary Elizabeth Hoinkes, chair of the interagency working group for Amendment Conference issues, in Washington, D.C., March 21, 1990.

32. Interview with Edmond Jayasinghe, Deputy Permanent Representative of Sri Lanka to the United Nations, in New York City, Jan. 15, 1990.

33. A/C.1/44/PV.40, p. 7 (Nov. 17, 1989); A/C.1/44/L.25/Rev.1; A/44/773, p. 3 (Dec. 5, 1989).

34. A/C.1/44/PV.41, p. 46 (Nov. 17, 1989).

35. A/C.1/44/PV.41, p. 54 (Nov. 17, 1989).

36. A/44/PV.81, p. 16 (Dec. 15, 1989) (provisional transcript issued Dec. 28, 1989).

37. Interview with Aaron Tovish (who learned these details from several participants) in New York City, Jan. 15, 1990.

38. Telephone interview with Aaron Tovish (who had interviewed two non-aligned delegates), Jan. 23, 1990.

39. Telephone interview with Edmond Jayasinghe, Deputy Permanent Representative of Sri Lanka to the United Nations, Jan. 23, 1990.

40. Telephone interview with Aaron Tovish (who had interviewed two non-aligned delegates), Jan. 23, 1990.

41. Telephone interview with Edmond Jayasinghe, Deputy Permanent Representative of Sri Lanka to the United Nations, Jan. 23, 1990.

42. E.g., R. Jeffrey Smith, "Breaking Pledge, U.S. to Defer Underground Nuclear Tests," *Washington Post* Jan. 24, 1990, p. 24, c. 1. The United States government had said that once the Threshold Test Ban Treaty had been ratified, the U.S. and the U.S.S.R. "would *immediately* engage in negotiations on ways to implement a step-by-step parallel program—in association with a program to reduce and ultimately eliminate all nuclear weapons—of limiting and ultimately ending nuclear testing," U.S. Department of State, Requirements for US Nuclear Testing, *Gist,* June, 1987 (emphasis added), and that after ratification, the United States would *"immediately* propose" such negotiations. "The Relationship Between Progress in Other Areas of Arms Control and More Stringent Limitations on Nuclear Testing," A Report by the President to the Congress, Aug. 26, 1988 (transmitted by letter to Speaker Jim Wright from President Ronald Reagan, Sept. 8, 1988) (emphasis added).

43. Warren Strobel, "U.S. delays talks on underground nuclear tests," *Washington Times* Jan. 22, 1990, p. A9.

44. State Department briefing, Jan. 24, 1990.

45. R. Jeffrey Smith, "Breaking Pledge, U.S. to Defer Underground Nuclear Test Talks," *Washington Post* January 24, 1990, p. 24, c. 1.

46. "Oh, never mind about that Reagan promise," *Atlanta Constitution,* Feb. 3, 1990, p. A20 (editorial).

47. Ministry of Foreign Affairs briefing, MFA Press Center, Moscow, Jan. 30, 1990.

48. British Broadcasting Corp., Summary of World Broadcasts, "Gorbachev's Address to Global Forum on Environmental Protection," Jan. 23, 1990.

49. Minutes, U.S. CTB Coalition, Feb. 5, 1990, p. 3.

50. Letter to Secretary of State James Baker from Carolyn Cottom, Coordinator, U.S. CTB Coalition (March 1, 1990).

51. Telephone interview with Aaron Tovish, Feb. 13, 1990.

52. Letter to Representative Dante Fascell from Brent Scowcroft, Feb. 20, 1990, reprinted at *Congressional Record* p. S 13761 (Sept. 25, 1990).

53. National Defense Authorization Act, Fiscal Year 1989, Public Law No. 100–456, September 29, 1988, Sec. 1436.

54. *Ibid.*

55. Department of Energy, *Annual Report to Congress, vol. I, Program Status of Preparations for Further Limitations on Nuclear Testing,* at pp. 16–18 (December, 1989) (unclassified version), (transmitted by letter to Senator Sam Nunn from Secretary of Energy James D. Watkins, Feb. 22, 1990)

56. Telephone interview with Aaron Tovish, Feb. 27, 1990.

57. Telephone interview with Aaron Tovish, March 2, 1990.

58. "PTBT" Amendment Conference: Alternative Options: Non:Paper:Revision 2 (Feb. 28, 1990).

59. "PTBT Amendment Conference: Alternative Options: Non:Paper:Summary" (March 1, 1990).

60. Report of the Chairman to the Meeting of the States Parties Held on 1 March 1990 on the Informal Consultations of the Parties Held on 27–28 February and 1 March 1990.

61. Telephone interview with Aaron Tovish, March 2, 1990.

62. Interview with William Epstein in New York City, March 24, 1990.

63. Telephone interview with William Epstein, March 30, 1990.

64. *Ibid.*

65. Telephone interview with Aaron Tovish, April 16, 1990.

66. International Comprehensive Test Ban Campaign, "A Strategy for Ending Nuclear Weapons Testing" (undated but apparently January, 1990).

67. International Comprehensive Test Ban Campaign, *Comprehensive Test Ban News* Jan. 25, 1990.

68. U.S. Comprehensive Test Ban Coalition, *Comprehensive Test Ban News* Apr. 2, 1990.

69. U.S. Comprehensive Test Ban Coalition, *Comprehensive Test Ban News* June 27, 1990; Resolutions of the United States Conference of Mayors, 58th Annual Conference (1990). This plan reportedly was approved by the mayors because they were angered by reports, conveyed to their annual meeting by House Ways and Means Committee Chair Dan Rostenkowski, that the end of the cold war would not produce a "peace dividend" for the cities. *Ibid.*

70. See Laurie Goodstein, "Anti-War Movement Suffers Peace Deficit," *Washington Post* June 3, 1990, p. A3, col. 1 ("[As a result of decreased fear of nuclear war,] a few groups, especially those focused on defeating particular weapon systems, have folded. Others face shrinking budgets and staff cutbacks as fund-raising grows more difficult").

71. U.S. Comprehensive Test Ban Coalition, *Comprehensive Test Ban News* May 14, 1990; Minutes, June 15, 1990.

72. U.S. Comprehensive Test Ban Coalition, *Comprehensive Test Ban News* May 14, 1990 and June 27, 1990.

73. International Physicians for the Prevention of Nuclear War and Nevada Semipalatinsk Movement, brochure for International Citizens Congress (undated, but distributed in March, 1990).

74. S.J. Res. 287 (101st Cong., 2d Sess.), introduced Apr. 5, 1990.

75. Senator Edward M. Kennedy, Press Release, April 8, 1990.

76. "Forty-Five Years of Nuclear Testing," *Arms Control Today,* November, 1990, pp. 6–7.

77. R. Jeffrey Smith, "Soviets to Close Major Site of Underground Atomic Tests," *Washington Post* March 10, 1990, p. A1, col. 1.

78. Arms Control Reporter, Comprehensive Test Ban, 608.B.195 (28 March, 1990 (citing Helsinki domestic radio, March 28, 1990). The Soviet Union conducted no tests at Semipalatinsk, and only one at Novaya Zemlya, in 1990.

79. U.S. Comprehensive Test Ban Coalition, Minutes, June 15, 1990.

80. International Parliamentary Open Letter, attached to Parliamentarians for Global Action, Global Action Test Ban Bulletin, March, 1990.

81. *Ibid.*

82. R. Jeffrey Smith, "Defective Nuclear Shells Raise Safety Concerns," *Washington Post* May 23, 1990, p. A1, col. 1; R. Jeffrey Smith, "New Explosive Key to Safety," *Washington Post* May 23, 1990, p. A18, col. 3.

83. R. Jeffrey Smith, "Computer Model Flagged Problem," *Washington Post* May 23, 1990, P. A18, col. 1.

84. Letter to Secretary James Watkins from John H. Nuckolls, Director of the Lawrence Livermore National Laboratory, and Siegfried S. Hecker, Director of the Los Alamos National Laboratory, quoted in *Congressional Record* p. H 7796 (Sept. 18, 1990). For an evaluation by a CTB advocate of the need to continue to test nuclear weapons as a result of these safety concerns, see Mark, "Do We Need Nuclear Testing?" *Arms Control Today* November, 1990, pp. 12–17.

85. "Test Ban Meeting All Set, U.S. Wants to Cut Its Own Cost," *Disarmament Times* v. XIII, No. 2 (May, 1990).

86. *Ibid.* In an interview, Marin added, "One hundred and seventeen of the 118 parties to the Treaty have instructions to stick to the U.N. scale of assessments, so all of these acrobatics are because one country does not want to pay its assessed share." "CTB is Part of NPT (interview with Miguel Marin-Bosch)," *Disarmament Times* v. XIII, No. 2 (May, 1990).

87. Well into the Meeting, some delegations were still fuming. A week after the meeting began, the Indian ambassador said, "we remain convinced that the UN Scale of Assessment, for all delegations, without exception, is the only basis for the sharing of costs of our conference. If we have agreed to join some extraordinary arrangements evolved for meeting the shortfall arising from a less-than-universal adherence to the UN Scale of Assessment, it is on the understanding that they would not be necessitated again." Amb. C. R. Gharekhan, June 4, 1990.

88. The UN Secretariat estimated the cost of supporting the Conference (including the Meeting) at $ 870,400. For this sum, it would prepare records of the events in all official languages, provide staff assistance at the sessions, pay consultants to develop the background papers mandated by the Meeting, and prepare an information kit in French and English. PTBT/CONF/M/4 (May 30, 1990). The U.N. Secretariat's estimate of the shortfall was 9.701% of this total, or $84,437. See PTBT/CONF/M/4/Add.1 (June 7, 1990).

89. By contrast, the same depositaries had paid an aggregate of 55% of the costs of the Third Review Conference of the Non-Proliferation Treaty, the objectives of which they fully supported. See NPT/CONF.III/41, App., Sept. 9, 1985.

90. Statement by the President concerning the decision on the arrangements for meeting the costs of the Meeting and the Conference, May 29, 1990.

4

The Meeting

Opening Session

In Conference Room 4, one of the large rooms ordinarily used by committees of the General Assembly, the delegates gathered for the Opening Session of the organizational Meeting. They sat in six concentric semicircles around a raised dais, each semicircle containing about thirty delegations. With one minor exception, this first assembly exactly followed the script that had been so carefully negotiated in the informal consultations. Indeed, before the session began, the Secretariat distributed written texts with the exact words that Akashi and Jayasinghe would use to guide the Meeting to confirm the decisions that had been made behind closed doors.[1] Despite the scripted nature of the event, however, and in sharp contrast to most hearings and floor debates in the United States Congress, about two-thirds of the delegations were in attendance during both the opening session and the formal speeches, and when xeroxed copies of the delegates' prepared speeches were distributed by the Secretariat (usually at the beginning or end of such a speech), delegates crowded around the distributor to obtain copies while they were still available. For some delegates, cabling their fellow delegates' remarks back to their foreign ministries may have been a way to impress on officials back home how much world-wide support existed for a CTB.

In his opening statement, Under-Secretary-General Akashi pointed out that even in 1963, the Eighteen Nation Disarmament Committee had termed CTB negotiations "long overdue." No disarmament issue, he said, had attracted so much persistent effort as the CTB question; "it has been the object of more General Assembly resolutions than any other item on nuclear disarmament." He reiterated the view of the Secretary-General that "no single multilateral agreement could have a greater effect on limiting the further refinement of nuclear weapons" and that a CTB was the "litmus test of the real willingness to pursue nuclear disarmament."[2] But continuing to quote the Secretary-General, he also hinted that a gradual phaseout of testing might be the best way to achieve a test ban: "significant additional restrictions on nuclear testing . . . leading *progressively* to a complete halt [along with quantitative cuts in weaponry] offer the best way to release the world from the fearful possibility of nuclear war."[3] Akashi then noted that "it is my understanding that it is indeed the wish of States Parties" that Jayasinghe be elected President of the Meeting, and that in the absence of any objection, Jayasinghe would be elected.

Taking the rostrum, Jayasinghe delivered his own opening address. The Conference in January, he said, would be among "the most important gatherings in the field of arms limitation and disarmament that will take place this decade." He noted the "divergences of viewpoints" on a CTB but claimed (perhaps optimistically) that the delegates shared a "fundamental agreement that the proposed objective—the achievement of a comprehensive test ban—is one worthy of all our consideration and efforts."[4] Turning to organizational matters, Jayasinghe noted that "following prior consultations" the Bulgarian and Australian delegates had been agreed upon as Vice-presidents of the Meeting, and Kheradi would be Secretary-General; without discussion, they were declared chosen.[5] Within minutes, and also by a process of unanimous consent, the Meeting adopted the rules of procedure and the agenda that had been hammered out in the months of informal consultations.

The agenda was skeletal. It provided for seven half-days of "general exchange" of views, or open-ended substantive or procedural speeches. (In fact, so few delegations wanted to speak that three of the seven half-days of speeches were eventually canceled). It also specified three items to be resolved under the heading of "organization of the Conference:" its provisional agenda, its draft rules of procedure, and the background documents that would be prepared for it.

With respect to the first two items, no documents were circulated. But the six nations that had initiated the Conference call now distributed a list of eleven types of issue papers that they wanted the Secretariat to prepare. These included studies of the implications of a test ban for the development of new weapons systems (including space-based systems), the relationship of a CTB to proliferation, and verification problems.[6] Although similar studies of at least some of these matters had been done by independent scholars,[7] research authored by the Secretariat would have a more neutral source and would therefore be easier for some delegations to draw upon.[8] The request for eleven different types of background papers was, in fact, a bargaining ploy. They knew that many delegates would not read more than one substantial background paper, and what they really wanted was for the Secretariat to prepare a single document, of perhaps a hundred pages, that would actually be read by delegates whose background on the test ban issue was not already extensive. But they expected the U.S. and the U.K. to oppose the preparation of any official background papers whatever, so they asked for eleven documents in order to end up with one. "It's ridiculous," a junior member of a non-aligned delegation said. "You have to play games like children."[9]

Only at the end of the opening session was there any departure from the script, providing a refreshing suggestion that at least occasionally, diplomacy can take place in the open. The last item on the day's agenda was formal confirmation of the agreements that had been reached on financing the U.S. shortfall. Jayasinghe announced his "understanding that all delegations who intend to participate will accept their share of the voluntary contributions."[10] His script called for him to say that "I take it that delegations are in agreement on the financial arrangements" and that "it is so decided."[11] In fact, however, Jayasinghe put the question affirmatively, asking whether all delegations agreed.

The delegate from India asked for the floor and expressed a reservation. "A voluntary contribution is a *voluntary* contribution," he said, "and my delegation will take its decision in due course."

Apparently not wanting to create dissension, Jayasinghe replied that "it's our informal understanding that each party will take its decision on voluntary contributions."

But the combination of the Indian delegate's reservation and Jayasinghe's possible endorsement prompted the Canadian delegate to speak. "It was our understanding that the purpose of the informal meeting just before this one was to find out if each delegation had instructions and could indicate that it was prepared to pay," she said. "No delegation indicated that it had not received such instructions. It is on that basis that my delegation came to this meeting."[12]

Jayasinghe tried to bridge the gap between the two delegations. He asked whether the Meeting could adopt the agreement on cost-sharing, along with the informal understanding that each participating state would make a voluntary contribution to cover the shortfall. But the Indian delegate objected to "adopting" what was only an "informal" understanding, and the Canadian delegate agreed that it should not be formalized. "But his earlier statement *contradicted* the informal understanding," she complained.

Jayasinghe's diplomatic skills enabled him to cut short what could have become a contentious problem. The purpose of the morning's off-the-record gathering, he said, was to find out whether any delegates had any observations contrary to the arrangements worked out at the previous meeting. There were none. Therefore, he asked, "on that basis" could the Meeting adopt the cost-sharing agreement? There being no objection, he declared the matter decided. Jayasinghe had defused the controversy, without requiring either the Indian delegate to pledge payment or the Meeting to adopt any formal statement incorporating the understanding about voluntary payments. While it was possible that the issue would recur (if the Indian government decided, after all, not to pay the additional assessment), the session could close without further controversy.

Policy Statements

During the next several days, 27 delegations, primarily from the non-aligned group, spoke in the general debate, and most of them addressed the substance of a comprehensive test ban.[13] In recognition of its role as the primary moving force behind the Conference, Mexico was afforded the honor of leading the debate, and Marin-Bosch delivered what most delegates thought was simultaneously the most scholarly and the most militant address made at the Meeting.

Marin's Address

Marin began with a survey of past views and actions on CTB, but while his summary was ostensibly an historical survey, few if any delegates could fail to note that he was also twitting the British and American delegations for their recalcitrant positions on the CTB by quoting their former leaders to them. On August 27, 1962, he recalled, President Kennedy and Prime Minister Macmillan had said that they "cannot emphasize too strongly the urgency we attach to the problem of ending all nuclear testing once and for all." In that same year, the British delegate to the Eighteen Nation Disarmament Committee identified CTB negotiation as one of the principal reasons for the very establishment of that body: "We have all of us been sent here to negotiate agreements acceptable . . . to the whole world community . . . on nuclear weapon tests. . . . I do not believe that there is one of us who would disagree with what the representative of Mexico said, namely that nuclear weapons testing is 'the most serious form of rearmament.'" The American negotiator had said, in 1962, that "if we do not stop testing altogether, we may stop human progress altogether."[14]

Marin then reminded the delegates that historically, the surface explanation for the nuclear weapons states' failure to negotiate a CTB was verification, although perhaps the real reason was "the tempting dream of obtaining, by further nuclear tests, some military advantage or an important lead from possible discoveries in that field." To strip away at least the surface disagreements, he suggested that in the Amendment Conference, the United States and Britain could "put forward their CTB verification requirements" and "hear the USSR's opinion in that regard." This portion of his text hinted that perhaps under Gorbachev, the Soviet Union would simply accept any reasonable verification requirements that the West might demand, reducing the number of issues ostensibly separating the parties or perhaps forcing the United States to admit the extent to which its opposition to a CTB was based on a desire for continued innovation, a claim that the non-aligned states could more easily decry than one based on the technicalities of seismic identification.[15]

Turning to the present gathering, Marin put on the public record his government's dissatisfaction with the way the depositary governments had called the Conference. They should not have "arrogated to themselves the right to decide how, when and where" to hold it.

Finally, he observed that "twenty-seven years of patience" was enough. In 1963, a British negotiator had said that the PTBT was a "significant first step," but "what history has recorded over the last twenty-seven years is an unbridled nuclear arms race." Further, where the Western countries had once argued in favor of a test ban that it would "stop the development and improvement of nuclear arsenals," now they brazenly claim that this very feature makes a CTB undesirable—they want to test to ensure that their nuclear weapons are "up to date." But, he warned, the willingness of the nuclear weapon states to amend the PTBT would be a key element in the willingness of other countries to extend the NPT in 1995.

Other Statements

Other delegations echoed many of Marin's points, but several themes in particular were stressed repeatedly:

The Relevance of the End of the Cold War. Several delegates expressed their countries' belief that sooner or later, the nuclear weapons states would be compelled to recognize that new political alignments would inevitably alter military doctrines; as a result, their perceived need for testing nuclear weapons would evaporate. "Disarmament negotiations of the past were tempered by the cold war atmosphere," noted Amb. James B. Moultrie of the Bahamas.[16] "The climate of distrust and suspicion appears to have changed," agreed another delegate.[17] One ambassador, engaging in what may have been wishful thinking, analogized popular influence on arms control to the popular revolutions in Eastern Europe in 1989: "[in] Eastern Europe . . . old ideological and military hostilities are breaking down. . . . In a situation where the people have virtually taken disarmament into their own hands and dictate the pace of changes affecting their destiny, the political leaders could only face reality and take the cue that the era of nuclear deterrence is effectively over."[18]

The Importance of a CTB for Non-Proliferation. Delegates reiterated their countries' views that progress toward a CTB was central to preventing proliferation. "There cannot be an effective or successful non-proliferation regime, unless a comprehensive test ban of nuclear weapons is achieved."[19] "There are several who are actually a screwdriver's turn away from a nuclear capability. Under the moral pressures of a CTB, they will hopefully be deterred from making that decision."[20] These formal statements on behalf of nations may have been of genuine political importance. It had become commonplace for officials in Washington who opposed a CTB to discount its non-proliferation value. While other governments may not be able to speak authoritatively about the importance of stockpile reliability or the necessity of testing to maintain it, they are a primary source of knowledge about what deters countries from seeking a nuclear weapons capability. Their "moral pressure" argument is strikingly similar to the view of Christopher Paine, that testing helps to perpetuate a "global norm" in which the possession and brandishing of nuclear weapons is equated with power, and that a test ban will create a new global norm in which possession of nuclear weapons is, at best, an evil with which a few states are tainted.[21]

The Link Between a CTB and the NPT. The link between a CTB and the NPT was expressed both positively and (as Marin had done) negatively. Nepal asserted that "failure [to end testing] would entail serious consequences for continued viability of the NPT beyond 1995."[22] Kenya hoped that a CTB would be a reality before 1995, "the year when we the majority, the non-nuclear parties, will have an absolute right and equality with the nuclear parties to determine the future of the Non-Proliferation Treaty."[23] Even Pakistan, which was not a party to the NPT, quoted the warning from the Belgrade statement of the non-aligned states.[24]

Qualitative Limits on the Arms Race. A few countries discussed the importance of a CTB in terms of slowing the qualitative arms race. It would, said the Nigerian delegate, be the "only effective bulwark" against "the development of irreversible third-generation nuclear weapons systems."[25] Pakistan believed that a CTB would "make it difficult, if not impossible, for the [nuclear powers] to develop new designs of nuclear weapons and would also place constraints on the modification of existing weapon designs."[26] India termed nuclear testing "the principal engine of the nuclear arms race" and a CTB a matter of the "highest priority."[27]

Disappointment with the Nuclear Powers. A large number of countries took advantage of the Meeting to express their dismay with the apparent lack of interest of the nuclear weapons states in completing their work as promised in 1963 and 1968. "While non-nuclear weapon states have lived up to their part of the bargain [of the Non-Proliferation Treaty], the nuclear weapon states still have to fulfill theirs."[28] "To the utter disappointment of the international community no serious attempt has been made to start these negotiations."[29] "Neither its reaffirmation [as a major goal] nor the protracted debates at [all three NPT review conferences] have made any impact."[30] Two aspects of the disappointment were particularly apparent. First, some countries were scornful of the Threshold Test Ban Treaty, regarding it almost as a step backward, in that it would "legitimize" tests under 150 kilotons[31] and "suit the particular strategic interests of the nuclear powers."[32] Second, some delegations cited the impasse over a mandate for the Conference on Disarmament as further evidence of the unwillingness of the nuclear powers to move at all in the direction of negotiating further limits on testing.[33]

The Significance of the Amendment Conference. Some delegations highlighted the role that the Conference would play in the long history of test ban negotiations: it is an "historic occasion where for the first time the Parties to a major multilateral arms control agreement . . . could participate in the negotiations for the banning of nuclear weapon tests."[34]

The Conference as a Lever. Several delegates hoped that the Amendment Conference, while not an optimal forum for progress toward a CTB, might force the West to open CTB negotiations elsewhere, particularly in the Conference on Disarmament. This view was stated by Romania,[35] but it was supported with surprising vigor by Western countries.[36]

The Desirability of a New Moratorium. A few delegations used their general remarks to call upon the nuclear weapon states to initiate a moratorium on testing for the duration of the Conference.[37]

In the general debate, no delegation spoke out in opposition either to the idea of a comprehensive test ban or to the use of a PTBT Amendment Conference as a vehicle for considering the idea. The closest that anyone came to this position was the statement of the British delegate that "the position of my Government on the question of a comprehensive test ban is well known."[38] The United States delegate did not speak, and the Soviet Union's delegate supported the proposed Amendment.[39]

Markers

Although negotiation of the procedural arrangements for the Conference was scheduled for closed sessions, a few delegations elected to use their public remarks to state their positions on these issues, perhaps on the theory that locking themselves in publicly on some of these questions would increase their bargaining power at a later time.[40] Five procedural issues were addressed in the public sessions:

Committees of the Amendment Conference

In its statement (immediately following Marin's opening salvo), Sri Lanka called for the creation of at least three "Committees/Working Groups," to work on "verification, peaceful nuclear explosions, and universal adherence."[41] The next day, the Philippines supported exactly the same committees, going a step further by suggesting that they be formed in time so that each could prepare a progress report "for submission to the

January, 1991 session;"[42] under this proposal, the Meeting itself would probably have to constitute the Committees so that work could take place between June and January. The Philippines also asked that the Conference be empowered to establish "additional committees . . . as the need arises." Consistent with the Anglo-American strategy of creating a minimalist Conference, and one that would not actually write any agreements, the British delegate argued that "there will be no need for complex committee structures or machinery for drafting. Thus we see a Plenary which might occasionally constitute itself as a Committee of the Whole under the same chairmanship but no other committees open to the full membership of the Conference."[43] Australia took a middle position, calling for one committee that would look at "three crucial issues: verification, scope, and compliance."[44] Although more work could be accomplished by three committees acting simultaneously, the Australian position was attractive to some of the non-aligned countries, because "small delegations" would not be able to staff several committees at once.[45] Mexico, whose leading role gave its views special force, eventually supported a single committee of the whole, chaired by the President of the Conference, which would consider all three of the areas that Sri Lanka had identified.[46]

Duration

The Sri Lankan delegate adverted, rather obliquely, to the need for some mechanism for keeping the Conference in being for a period of years to continue to exert pressure on the Western states. It wanted the Conference to address "other ways and means that would ensure a definite time frame and continuity until an agreement regarding a CTB is reached by consensus [and] preliminary consideration [of such ideas] at this stage."[47] The Philippine delegate referred, more directly, to the Conference "possibly continuing [after 1991] in the subsequent two years until it is resolved."[48] Mexico became the only delegation to take the floor for a second time, and Amb. Marin added his voice to discussion of the duration issue:

> We are ready to work for as long as it takes to achieve [a permanent solution]. It is not a matter of going to the Conference in January to examine mechanically the draft amendment, vote on it and, if it is not approved, forget the issue. The two weeks we have set aside perhaps will not be enough. We must therefore be prepared to go on with the work until we reach the goal we have set.[49]

Decision-Making

On the key question of how decisions—other than the ultimate decision on adopting amendments to the Treaty—would be made, the Philippine delegate proposed that "in the absence of a consensus, decisions should be taken by a simple majority of those present and voting." Mindful that UN resolutions on testing had been characterized by numerous abstentions by the NATO allies of the U.S. and U.K., he sought to avoid having such abstentions count against a working majority: "abstentions should not be considered as voting."[50]

Background Documents

Responding to the written call by the six requesting countries for eleven background papers, the British delegate took a fairly hard—some might say patronizing—line on preparation of background documents by the Secretariat. Since the task of the Conference was "simple" and should be carried out "without fuss," the British did "not therefore see any need for the elaboration of a long list of Background documents" such as that called for by the six original requesting countries. "If some delegations need guidance as to the history of the issue I am sure we can point them to several excellent existing papers," he said.[51] The Philippines took the opposite view, urging that the Secretariat prepare "several" background papers (on seven topics),[52] and the New Zealand delegation staked out a middle position, arguing that a balance of "cost against utility" was needed. "Purely factual" papers, it said, could be prepared "without too much difficulty," but "some others" would "involve considerable efforts and deftness on the part of the Secretariat in adequately reflecting, and balancing, the different views involved. This could be a lengthy and difficult exercise."[53] This issue was eventually resolved by agreement to compromise by calling on the Secretariat to produce "a brief background document" covering the eleven topics (slightly rephrased) but "drawing on, so far as possible, relevant existing documentation."[54]

Participation

In view of concerns by non-governmental organizations that, to reduce the visibility of the Conference, the U.S. and U.K. would attempt to prevent them from speaking (or perhaps even observing), a few delegations put on record their support for allowing such groups to participate.[55] The Soviet Union heightened the concerns of the peace groups by stating flatly that non-governmental organizations "should not have some sort of a special status of participation."[56]

Negotiations over Procedure

The real procedural decision-making of the Meeting, like the pre-Meeting procedural wrangling, was done in closed session.[57] The first issue was the question of the agenda of the Conference. The six countries that had originally requested the Conference had circulated a draft agenda with routine items such as "programme of work," "general debate," and "consideration of the Amendments to the Treaty."[58] The only contentious matter in this proposal turned out to be its first item, the "Opening of the Conference by the Secretary-General of the United Nations." The United States and Britain wanted the Conference to be opened by Jayasinghe, who would merely read a message from the Secretary-General. Both symbolic and psychological issues were at stake in this disagreement. The personal participation of the Secretary-General would "send a message" to each foreign ministry about the importance of this Conference; further, his presence would ensure that, at least for the opening day, nearly every country would be present and would be represented by a diplomat with the rank of Ambassador.[59] Some of the nonaligned countries claimed that this was a closed issue—that it had been arranged, in a "gentlemen's agreement" on April 27, that the Secretary-General would open the meeting with a speech. Others said that with the Conference taking place in "the UN's house," it was only proper that the Secretary General be asked to open it. When the Canadian and Spanish delegations said that they, too, recalled the "gentleman's agreement" and some of the Western nations also said that they would prefer the Secretary-General to address the Conference, it became clear that the U.K. and U.S. would have to retreat.[60] They did retreat, but it took them until the following day to do so because "they can't reverse themselves in a single day."[61]

The most important questions concerned rules of procedure for the Amendment Conference. The United Nations Legal Department proposed (as had the New Zealand delegation) that the Conference develop rules based on those used by the Third Review Conference of the Seabed Treaty.[62] Most of these rules were uncontroversial; for example, despite its public speech, the U.K. did not strenuously oppose Mexico's proposal that the Conference establish a Committee of the Whole. But a few areas proved contentious.

Decision-Making

As a result of the compromises made in pre-meeting negotiations, the Rules of the Meeting provided only that "[e]very effort will be made to adopt decisions of the Meeting by consensus;"[63] nothing at all was said about voting, although it was informally understood that voting would resolve any impasses. The non-aligned countries believed that something explicit had to be said about voting in the rules for the Conference itself, so that they could use their working majority on all issues except adoption of an Amendment to the Treaty (to which the veto provisions of the Treaty would apply), and they had extracted from the West an agreement that the "consensus" formula expressed in the rules of the Meeting would not be carried over into the Conference.[64] Of course, when the issue of the voting rules for the Conference arose, a Western country could claim that the Meeting was barred, by the absence of a rule authorizing any voting, from adopting rules of the Conference by anything but consensus, but the non-aligned countries were confident that they could put that issue to a vote and prevail.

The Seabed Treaty Review Conference Rules authorized voting, but they pointed very strongly away from that decision-making mechanism. They specified that matters of procedure would be decided by a majority of representatives present and voting, but that as to matters of substance, "every effort should be made to reach agreement . . . by means of consensus. There should be no voting on such matters until *all efforts* to achieve consensus have been exhausted."[65] Furthermore, under those Rules, the desires of the majority could be further impeded by built-in delays (which could be of real significance toward the end of the event) and by a two-thirds rule for substantive matters:

> If, notwithstanding the best efforts of delegates to achieve consensus, a matter of substance comes up for voting, the President shall defer the vote for 48 hours and during this period of deferment shall make every effort with the assistance [of the Conference leadership] to facilitate the achievement of general agreement and shall report to the Conference prior to the end of the period. [If consensus is not possible,] voting shall take place and decisions shall be taken by a two-thirds majority of those present and voting, provided that such majority shall include at least a majority of the States participating in the Conference.[66]

Some delegations believed that while this procedure might be suitable for a Seabeds Treaty Review Conference at which no issues were expected to be at all contentious,[67] it too strongly pointed away from resolving knotty issues by counting delegations' votes. For example, if amendments to the text of the proposed CTB or verification protocols were suggested, they would surely be considered "substantive," and the Seabed Treaty Review Conference rules would give the Western delegations undue voting strength. Furthermore, what would happen under the clause calling for a 48-hour delay if an important issue arose during what had been scheduled as the last 48 hours of the Conference?

Mexico therefore proposed an alternative. First the Rules of the Conference should specify the delegates' right to resolve issues by voting, and all decisions other than the approval of amendments to the Treaty could be taken by a simple majority of those present and voting. A subsequent sentence in the Mexican draft rule provided that "nevertheless, every effort should be made to adopt decisions by consensus."[68] The order in which the voting and the consensus paragraphs appeared was crucial, Mexico believed, because if a search for consensus were phrased "as a precondition, they will never let us vote."[69]

The Canadian delegation countered with a draft combining the requirement for depositary agreement for Amendments with the Seabed Treaty procedures for other decisions. Under the Canadian draft, the "every effort" clause would come before the voting rules; procedural issues could be decided by a simple majority; a 48-hour delay would be built in before voting; a two-thirds majority would be required for substantive decisions; and, as in the Seabed Treaty procedures, if there were a disagreement about whether a matter was procedural or substantive, the Chair of the Conference would decide that question subject to an appeal to the Conference, with a simple majority required to sustain the appeal.[70]

Neither the non-aligned countries nor the United States was satisfied with the Canadian position. The non-aligned could tolerate putting the search for consensus literally ahead of the right to vote, because the order in which these items appeared was more psychological than legal. But the 48-hour delay was intolerable in a Conference with time-bounded sessions, and the two-thirds rule threatened the non-aligned countries' control over the Conference. By counting the countries that had come to the Meeting, they found that only about 70 nations of the 118 Treaty Parties had actually sent delegates. In the General Assembly vote in December, two countries had voted "no" and 22 Western nations had abstained. Furthermore, the Soviet bloc of perhaps seven votes (including the Byelorussian and Ukrainian SSRs, which, as UN members, were also Treaty Parties) might well vote with the United States and Great Britain on issues other than the ultimate adoption of an Amendment.[71] If the same countries participated in the Conference that had attended the Meeting, the non-aligned group could count on only 39 of the 70 votes, a majority but not two-thirds. Furthermore, the Western delegations were large enough so that each of them could keep someone on the floor of the Conference at all times, whereas some of the non-aligned countries might not always be present.

The problem that the two-thirds rule for substantive issues created was somewhat reduced by the Canadian proposal for resolving whether issues were substantive or procedural. With their majority, the non-aligned countries were in a position to elect the Chair of the Conference, and they had a likely candidate in Ali Alatas, the Foreign Minister of Indonesia. Alatas came from one of the six requesting states, knew the test ban issue, and had been the first person to support Garcia Robles' request for a United Nations resolution in support of the amendment conference concept. As a prominent figure in world affairs, he was probably not a person to whom the Western countries could easily object. It would be hard for a Western country to propose a person with a rank below Foreign Minister to counter a Foreign Minister, and few countries acceptable to both the West and the non-aligned would be willing to commit their Foreign Ministers to two weeks in New York to chair the Conference. As a result, the non-aligned could hope that at least as to ambiguous issues, they would be able, by dint of rulings from the Chair or, if necessary, a majority vote, to resolve issues by a majority rather than two-thirds even under the Canadian proposal.

The most important issue that might be considered of an ambiguous character, at least by some delegations, was the question of recessing the Conference to a subsequent year. The United States delegation, which had attended carefully to the speech in open session in which Mexico had called for stretching out the process, believed that by allowing the Conference to determine, by a simple majority, that an issue was "procedural," Canada was turning control over the Conference (including the recess issue) to the non-aligned bloc. Furthermore, the U.S. delegation feared that whatever rules were established, a majority of the Conference, or perhaps two-thirds, might be able to change the rules themselves; since the United States could not be certain of Soviet bloc support, it might not be able, even under a two-thirds rule for amending the rules, to prevent them from being altered. As a result, the American delegate could be heard remonstrating with the Canadian delegate during a recess. In addition, the American delegate proposed that no Conference decision adopted by consensus, including the rules of procedure themselves, should be subject to change except on the same consensual basis.

The compromise that emerged from bargaining was close to the Canadian proposal. It accepted the precedence of the search for consensus over voting; accepted the distinction between procedural and substantive issues (the latter to be decided by two-thirds); allowed the Chair and the body to decide which issues were procedural. But it scrapped the 48-hour waiting period.[72] One delegate suggested that this compromise was accepted because since no one could predict with certainty just how many countries would participate, who would control how many votes, how the Chair would rule on ambiguous issues, or how the Conference would feel about appealing rulings of the Chair, the compromise was "dangerous for everybody, a balance of terror." With respect to amending the rules themselves, the American delegation became more and more insistent, as the days of negotiation unfolded, on making them impossible to amend without American consent. As a result, the non-aligned delegates suspected that somewhere in the twelve pages of single-spaced rules there lay a trap, some rule or absence of a rule that they would eventually regret, and they stalked the corridors asking each other whether they could find it. Nobody could figure out why the Americans cared so much to make the rules virtually unamendable; consequently they had no basis for taking issue with the United States delegation. They accepted the United States proposal for amending the rules only by consensus, hoping that they would not later kick themselves for having done so.[73]

Duration

As noted, all countries' delegates were keenly aware that the most important procedural issue was whether the Conference would end (with or without a vote on an Amendment) in January, 1991, or whether it would become an ongoing international institution as PGA had planned. No one expected the United States and Britain to reverse themselves and permit negotiation of any sort of amendment. But by the same token, many nonaligned states did not want the Conference to end without putting continuing pressure on the American and British governments, and they hoped to continue the Conference in some way past January—either minimally, by having a second session in 1992 or 1993, with at least one further session on the eve of the NPT extension meeting in 1995, or more ambitiously, by having continuing committee work take place between sessions as well. They therefore wanted rules or other understandings that would explicitly allow a majority to vote for a recess of the Conference to a later time (despite the depositaries having convened the Conference for a period to end January 18). But this issue would be so contentious as to be incapable of resolution until it had to be resolved, at the Conference itself. As one delegate said, "the climate is too difficult to raise hard issues now. Every small thing is so difficult, like the issue of who will open the meeting. We will just have to let the important issues go until the Conference itself."

Legally, two different aspects of the emerging rules of procedure were implicated. First, one of the Seabed Treaty Review Conference Rules gave highest precedence to a motion to "suspend the meeting".[74] This rule was accepted without discussion or controversy by delegates to the Meeting on the first day that the rules were discussed. But what did it mean to suspend the Conference? Would a suspension have to be limited to a period of time within the period for which the Conference had been called by the depositary governments, or could it be suspended for a year or two? Second, whether or not the "suspension" rule was the pertinent text to be interpreted, by what mechanism could the Conference decide to continue itself beyond 1991? The voting rules for the Conference would probably be determinative, which is why so much attention was given, on all sides, to the Canadian proposal for deciding whether issues required majority or super-majority voting.

On another level, however, the issue of duration was not primarily a legal one at all, but an economic one. Most delegations believed that the

Conference would probably be another fruitless exercise in the long test-ban history; given the probability that George Bush would be President of the United States through 1996, they were loathe to expend the financial and human resources necessary for multiple head-bashings. The fact that the United States had refused to pay its UN-scale share of the expenses of the Secretariat compounded their cost, and the still-implicit threat that the United States and Britain might boycott any future sessions altogether, requiring other countries to make up the full amount of their considerable shares of the costs, discouraged some delegations from considering additional sessions. For delegations in the leadership, such as Mexico and Sri Lanka, the small amounts of money that additional sessions would require were well spent, but the leaders of the non-aligned group were not certain that the troops would follow.

The issue of continuing the Conference after 1991 was so sensitive that it was barely mentioned, even in closed session. When the Canadian delegate said, in arguing for her proposal to distinguish between procedural and substantive questions, that it should be made clear that a decision to make the Conference an ongoing event should be "substantive" (and therefore require a two-thirds vote), not a single delegation responded, as though she had burped at a tea party.

Participation by Non-Governmental Organizations

The Seabeds Treaty Review Conference rules provided that non-governmental organizations could attend plenary meetings and receive copies of Conference records, but those rules did not permit non-governmental groups to speak to the Conference.[75] Most non-aligned countries wanted to permit non-governmental organizations both to attend the Conference and to address it; according them this privilege would not only recognize their role in creating the Conference but, more important, could increase the publicity that the Conference received, because each such organization would have its own press release and its own press contacts. Furthermore, some of the organizations might be able to have nationally or internationally prominent persons as their spokespersons. The United States and United Kingdom were opposed to opening the Conference to non-governmental groups, and particularly to speeches by members of such groups, but the non-aligned countries could cite a significant precedent; non-governmental organizations had been allowed two particular periods in which to address the Third Special Session on Disarmament of the United Nations General Assembly.[76] In view of this precedent, the Western countries did not strenuously attempt to prevent non-governmental organizations from speaking, but they made a slight show of opposition and they tried to give the addresses of non-governmental representatives as little status and visibility as possible. The New Zealand delegate said in closed session that certain international officials such as the Director-General of the International Atomic Energy Agency should be permitted to address the Conference, and that although presentational rights would be afforded to these officials that "would not be the case for other observers." But the New Zealand delegation retreated in the face of protests from the non-aligned countries, and it was agreed that although non-governmental organizations would not be able to address the Conference or its committee of the whole, they would be allowed to address an "informal" meeting of the conference; simultaneous translation would be made available, but their speeches would not be included in the official printed records of the Conference.[77]

Openness

It was a foregone conclusion that the formal sessions of the Conference would be open for the public and the press to observe, but much of the real argument among nations could be relegated to meetings of the Committee of the Whole, with only the ultimate resolutions of issues revealed in open session. Many delegates anticipated that in order to avoid public controversy (and therefore news), the depositary states would try to keep as much of the Conference as possible closed to the public and press. Furthermore, the Seabeds Treaty Review Conference Rules provided that all committee meetings would be "held in private,"[78] although the main committee at the Third NPT Review Conference had been open.[79] On June 1, a caucus of the nonaligned states determined to try to open the entire Conference to public scrutiny, a position that Yugoslavia advocated on behalf of these countries in a closed session of the Meeting later that day. This issue was resolve by compromise, with meetings of the Committee of the Whole to be public unless the Conference voted to close them, and meetings of any working groups established by the Conference to be held in private.[80]

Byplay at the Fringes

Another, still more trivial level of diplomatic activity took place at the fringes of the Meeting, as the Western delegations missed no opportunity to seal the Meeting off, to the extent possible, from the outside world. Having done what they could to limit what the delegates themselves could accomplish, the Western group sought to prevent what they would regard as excessive involvement by non-governmental organizations or the press.

The first incident involved a young Canadian, Maxime Faille, who had once worked for Parliamentarians for Global Action. A few months before the Meeting, he had left PGA to join the staff of the disarmament department of the United Nations Secretariat. Because he was familiar with nuclear testing issues and the background of the Amendment Conference, his new employer had assigned him to a junior staff position on the Secretariat of the Meeting. When the Canadian delegation to the Meeting heard about this assignment, it protested to the Secretariat, claiming that Faille's links to Canadian non-governmental organizations compromised his neutrality. Although the United Nations Secretariat is independent of any nation, it bowed to the Canadian protest and assigned Faille to other duties.

An appeal to the delegates from the international test ban conference in Alma Ata was the subject of a second incident. Three days before the Meeting convened, the physicians and peace activists who were meeting in Alma Ata passed a resolution addressed to the delegates at the Amendment Conference. It said that continued nuclear testing would produce new generations of more sophisticated weapons systems and encourage prolif- eration, and that "only a comprehensive test ban will demonstrate that the nuclear powers intend to keep their part of the non-proliferation bargain." The Alma Ata conferees promised to "spare no effort in the coming months to galvanize the support of people everywhere for your efforts."[81]

Aaron Tovish faxed a copy of this statement from Alma Ata to his office in New York, where it was typed onto PGA letterhead. On the second day of the Meeting, a PGA staff member left a stack of copies on a table in the Conference Room, next to the entrance door, a table already on which copies of the latest issue of the Disarmament Times (published by the Non- governmental Organization Committee on Disarmament, Inc.) were al- ready piled. The United States delegation objected to this placement of unofficial material on a table within the official Room,[82] and as a result, a member of the UN Secretariat staff directed that the papers be removed.

The next morning, the Alma Ata appeal was back on the same table. As the Meeting progressed, it was then possible to observe a minor drama superimposed on the formal speeches. While the Peruvian Ambassador was speaking, a member of the U.S. delegation approached a Secretariat staff member and whispered something to her in the back of the room. The staff member sought out the woman observing the Meeting for PGA and remonstrated that she had previously told her that PGA could not put an unofficial statement on the table. The PGA representative replied that she had not put it on the table; the Mexican delegation had done so. That was different, the Secretariat staffer conceded. The Secretariat staffer ex- plained the situation to the U.S. delegation, but this did not end the protest. During the address by the Philippine ambassador, the staffer could be seen ascending the podium where she spoke quietly with Sohrab Kheradi, the Secretary-General of the Meeting. A few moments later, during the New Zealand ambassador's statement, the staff member went to the literature table and took one copy of the Alma Ata statement to Kheradi, who read it. Shortly thereafter, the staffer was observed conferring with the Mexican delegation, and then mounting the podium again for another talk with Kheradi, who this time conferred with Jayasinghe and then spoke again to the staffer. Finally, the staffer talked once more with the U.S. delegation, and that ended the matter: the leaflets remained on the table. What had happened was that Mexico had let it be known that if the U.S. pressed its objection, the Mexican ambassador would immediately raise the issue to be resolved by a vote of the Meeting.

The resolution of incidents like these could not have any impact on the outcome of the meeting. But whether a former PGA employee could participate in a minor staff capacity and whether leaflets could appear on a table were important to some delegations because they tested the limits of the Conference symbolically. For the moment, there were few other battles to fight; these were the only ones in which Canada, Mexico or the U.S. could demonstrate their control of the Conference machinery.

Public Relations

Since the Amendment Conference was set in motion primarily to put some pressure on the United States government, if only to open bilateral or multilateral CTB negotiations elsewhere, PGA hoped that the Meeting would attract some publicity. Of course the Conference itself would be a better news focus, but one of the concessions that the non-aligned countries had extracted from the U.S. and U.K. was that the Meeting could include opening statements of policy, and several delegations were quite willing to oblige with speeches from which quotations could be taken.

Nevertheless, the Meeting received virtually no publicity. It may have been doomed from the start, it terms of its publicity value, by the fact that it appeared to be only an organizational or procedural event, despite the successful effort by non-aligned countries not to denominate it a Preparatory Conference. But in addition, a Bush-Gorbachev summit meeting, originally planned for later in the summer, was advanced so that it would be completed before Gorbachev had to prepare for and attend a Communist Party Congress. Gorbachev arrived in the United States just as the Meeting of the Parties was getting under way, and his visit preoccupied the foreign policy reporters and filled the pages of American newspapers.

The summit also derailed the main publicity event that PGA had planned. Early in the spring, it had begun to circulate, in parliaments all over the world, a petition calling on the leaders of the U.S., U.K., and U.S.S.R. to end nuclear testing. It had planned to collect hundreds or thousands of signatures from members of many legislatures, and then, with much public fanfare, have a delegation of American, British and Soviet members of Parliament carry copies of these parliamentary petitions to President Gorbachev, Prime Minister Thatcher, and President Bush, and finally to the Secretary General of the United Nations at the Meeting. But just as Aaron Tovish had lined up a group of members of Congress willing to travel to Moscow in late May with the parliamentarians' petition, Gorbachev announced that he would be coming to see President Bush at that time, requiring PGA to postpone the visit to three capitals until a later time.

A more modest version of the parliamentary visits was arranged. Five members of Congress, two members of the British parliament, and two members of the Supreme Soviet agreed to participate in a day of activities at the Meeting in New York. They would spend two hours at PGA headquarters planning strategy; observe the Meeting and greet delegates on the floor; hold a press conference; have a lunch with a large number of delegates; visit the Secretary-General of the United Nations; talk with the Ambassadors to the Conference of each of the three nuclear weapons states; and conclude with a City Hall reception hosted by the Mayor of New York City.[83] The visit would have two purposes: it would be a focus for news stories about the Meeting, and it would demonstrate to the delegates that their deliberations were being followed by at least some members of each of the three represented parliaments, and that they had some degree of support in those bodies.

The visit failed in its first purpose, but it may have succeeded, to some degree, in its second. The publicity value of the event was diminished by several factors. The most interesting Soviet participant, Olzhas Suleimenov, was unable, at the last moment to receive permission to leave the Soviet Union, the result of sparse attendance at meetings of Supreme Soviet committees and a consequent freeze on travel by their members until after Gorbachev had returned home and reported on the summit. Suleimenov was able to participate in the PGA strategy meeting by telephone, and Giorgi Arbatov, Director of the Soviet Union's US-Canada Institute, attended the reception, but Arbatov was a familiar figure to United States reporters and, in contrast to Suleimenov, an establishment official. In addition, the press conference was sparsely attended in a dingy lounge used by U.N. correspondents, and the Mayor had to attend the New York State Democratic Convention in Albany and was unable to return in time to greet the ambassadors and parliamentarians at his reception.

On the other hand, many of the delegates were visibly impressed by the presence of five members of Congress,[84] and by the strongly supportive statements they made at the luncheon. They were surprised that a fairly prominent Conservative M.P. was in attendance,[85] and they were electrified by George Foulkes, a Labour Party spokesman on foreign affairs, who told them that in view of the polls, which were at the time predicting a Labour victory in the next general election, he looked forward to returning to the Conference after 1992 as a Minister of Her Majesty's Government. In a meeting with few prospects of real progress, the possibility that within two years the British government might switch from one that aligned itself with the U.S. to one that actively pressed for a CTB came as a breath of hope.

Closing Session

The Closing Session of the Meeting was intended to be ceremonial; the delegates would confirm the decisions to which they had agreed in the closed negotiations, and they would make numerous statements of mutual gratitude for their cooperation in working everything out without voting. But a last-minute hitch developed, causing the Session, originally scheduled for 3:00 PM, to be postponed for an hour and a half while the delegates caucused in private.

The problem was that the UN Secretariat had written, in its draft of the Report of the Meeting that the delegates would adopt, that "at their meeting on 8 March [the Parties] decided to hold the Amendment Conference in New York from 7–18 January 1991." This may have been a correct statement of history,[86] but Mexico and certain other non-aligned countries were alarmed at the recitation of this implicitly consensual "decision" in a formal document, because along with the Report of the Meeting they would that day be adopting the Rule, insisted on by the American delegate, that "decisions adopted by consensus may not be reconsidered unless the Conference reaches a consensus." Was this the trap that the American delegate had set? Would she later claim that the March 8 decision on a January 18 closing date having been reached consensually, the Conference could not agree, over an American objection, to hold a subsequent session?

This issue went to the heart of the strategy that PGA and the non-aligned nations had planned. Something had to be done to protect the record. Several non-aligned delegates spoke among themselves and developed a plan, which they did not reveal in advance to the Americans or British.[87] As soon as the rules of procedure were adopted, a member of the Mexican delegation took the floor and said, aware (the Closing Session being an open meeting) that her remarks would be recorded in the official summary record, that "we understand that the Rules of Procedure just adopted are applicable only to the Amendment Conference and only deal with decisions made in that Conference." The Indonesian delegate added that "my delegation supports the views just stated by Mexico." No other delegation spoke to the subject.[88]

Did the U.S. delegation really plan to try to apply the rule against reconsideration retroactively to the March 8 decision on the duration of the Conference? It seems unlikely, in view of Ms. Hoinkes' response to an inquiry by the author immediately after the Meeting ended. Asked what the United States' attitude was toward Mexico's remarks on reconsideration, she replied that the U.S. fully agreed with them; "nothing the Conference does is precedential for any other conference or negotiation."[89] Her response demonstrates that she interpreted the Mexican comment in reference only to *prospective* application, and she probably would not have put this gloss on it if she had been working for days on a way to apply the rule against reconsideration retrospectively.

The final remarks in the meeting were, as planned, an exchange of congratulations among delegates in which they remarked on how well they had worked together. But the incident of the Mexican statement demonstrated how much conflict and distrust lay just below the diplomatically sanded surface.

Notes

1. Election of the President of the Meeting; Brief for the President of the Meeting, both distributed May 29, 1990.

2. Opening Remarks by Mr. Yasushi Akashi, Under-Secretary-General of the United Nations for Disarmament Affairs (May 29, 1990).

3. *Ibid.* (emphasis added), quoting the Secretary-General's report on the work of the Organization to the 44th session of the General Assembly.

4. Statement by Amb. Edmond Jayasinghe, May 29, 1990.

5. The only consequence of the election of the Vice-presidents—apart from reminding everyone that cold war blocs had not yet disappeared from view—appeared to be that a Secretariat staff member placed a little plaque with the words "Vice President" in front of each of them.

6. PTBT/CONF/M/6, May 25, 1990.

7. For example, on the relationship between testing and the development of new weapons, see Steve Fetter, *Toward a Comprehensive Test Ban* (Cambridge: Ballinger, 1988).

8. A delegate explained to the author that the Secretariat could not only draw upon but actually reproduce certain studies by others. Circulation by the Secretariat, with a United Nations document number, would not necessarily increase the probative value of a study, but it would make it easier to cite by delegations to the Conference because, among other things, it would be equally accessible to all delegations.

9. Interview, June 6, 1990.

10. Statement by the President concerning the decision on the arrangements for meeting the costs of the Meeting and the Conference (May 29, 1990).

11. *Ibid.*

12. One can only speculate on the nature of the implication in this statement that if India would not pay an increased share, Canada would take the extreme step of boycotting the Meeting. Was a threat to walk out a standard ploy by which

Canada—or other Western countries with minority voting power—exercised power in the informal consultations? Was Canada speaking only for itself, or was there a hint that it spoke, as well, for its neighbor and close ally, the United States?

13. Countries addressing the Meeting were Sri Lanka, Nigeria, Bangla Desh, the United Kingdom, Peru, the Philippines, New Zealand, Brazil, Yugoslavia, the Byelorussian SSR, Colombia, the Ukrainian SSR, Tanzania, the Bahamas, Indonesia, Canada, the U.S.S.R., Sweden, Pakistan, India, Mexico, Nepal, Romania, Australia, Venezuela and Kenya. The continental Western European countries were conspicuous by their silence.

14. Statement by Ambassador Miguel Marin-Bosch, May 30, 1990, quoting ENDC/PV.75.

15. Marin subsequently circulated a draft resolution calling on the nuclear weapons states that were party to the treaty to distribute their views on verification before the January Conference. Draft decision circulated by Mexico, June 1, 1990. This proposal eventually became a resolution of the Conference. PTBT/CONF/1, July 18, 1990.

16. June 1, 1990.

17. Amb. Nana S. Sutresna of Indonesia, June 1, 1990.

18. Amb. E. A. Azikiwe of Nigeria, May 30, 1990. The claim that people were exercising new power and affecting governmental nuclear arms policies was not entirely fanciful; a popular movement in the Soviet Union had already extracted from Soviet leaders a promise to close that country's principal nuclear weapons test site within three years.

19. Amb. E. A. Azikiwe of Nigeria, May 30, 1990.

20. Ambassador Iftekhar Ahmed Chowdhury of Bangla Desh, May 30, 1990.

21. Paine's argument to this effect at the Belmont Conference is reflected at Belmont Conference on Nuclear Test Ban Policy (David A. Koplow and Philip G. Schrag, Rapporteurs), "Phasing Out Nuclear Weapons Tests," *Stanford Journal of International Law* vol. 26, No. 1 (1989), pp. 221–22.

22. Amb. Jai P. Rana, June 4, 1990.

23. Amb. Michael Okeyo, June 4, 1990. Amb. Okeyo even wondered aloud how, if the nuclear weapons states wanted to continue perfecting their weapons through testing, they could convince the non-nuclear states "and other recent nuclear weapon states that the PTBT is in our interest." This veiled reference to possible disintegration of the PTBT as well as the NPT was not remarked on by any other delegation.

24. A CTB "is absolutely essential for the preservation of the non-proliferation regime embodied in the Non-Proliferation Treaty." Amb. Nasim Ahmed, June 4, 1990.

25. Amb. E. A. Azikiwe, May 30, 1990. "The Bahamas supports a CTBT because of its potential to prevent the development and deployment of new nuclear weapon systems." James B. Moultrie, June 1, 1990.

26. Amb. Nasim Ahmed, June 4, 1990.

27. Amb. C. R. Gharekhan, June 4, 1990.

28. Amb. Sedfrey A. Ordonez of the Philippines, May 31, 1990.

29. Amb. Daya Perera of Sri Lanka, May 30, 1990.

30. Amb. Nana S. Sutresna of Indonesia, June 1, 1990.

31. Amb. Daya Perera of Sri Lanka, May 30, 1990.

32. Amb. Nana S. Sutresna of Indonesia, June 1, 1990. This charge was accurate, in that the United States had suggested the 150 kt limit not because of verification thresholds but to ensure that it could continue to test certain designs of warheads in its strategic stockpile. *Threshold Test Ban and Peaceful Nuclear Explosion Treaties, Hearings Before the Senate Committee on Foreign Relations and the Subcommittee on Arms Control, Oceans and International Environment,* 95th Cong., 1st Sess., August 3, 1977, p. 49 (testimony of Vice Admiral Patrick J. Hannifin, Director, Joint Staff Organization, Joint Chiefs of Staff).

33. Amb. Dragoslave Pejic of Yugoslavia, May 31, 1990, noting the inability of the Conference on Disarmament to agree on the mandate within which "to at least discuss, let alone negotiate" a CTB "despite the very flexible position" of the non-aligned group in the Geneva body. In more restrained terms, Amb. Don MacKay of New Zealand noted that "regrettably" the Conference on Disarmament had "failed" to provide a forum for discussion. May 31, 1990.

34. Amb. Daya Perera of Sri Lanka, May 30, 1990.

35. Amb. Nicolae Micu, June 4, 1990.

36. Amb. Peggy Mason of Canada, June 4, 1990; Amb. Jill Courtney of Australia, June 4, 1990 (the Conference should "try to stimulate the launching of substantive work" in the Geneva Conference.)

37. Amb. Miguel Marin-Bosch of Mexico, May 30, 1990; Amb. Sedfrey Ordonez of the Philippines, May 31, 1990; Amb. Jose Angelo Lasso of Ecuador, June 4, 1990.

38. Amb. Ian Kenyon of Great Britain, May 30, 1990.

39. The Soviet Union's readiness to amend the treaty and convert it into a CTB was subsequently reiterated personally by President Mikhail Gorbachev. United Nations Press Release DC/2334, January 7, 1991.

40. Another function of the public statements, particularly the very specific statements by Mexico, may have been to signal potential allies of what positions the speakers wanted others to take. The non-aligned countries, and even sub-groups such as the Arab countries, held several closed caucuses during the Meeting, but attendance at those meetings was not always universal. In addition, most delegations distributed copies of their formal speeches so that they could be studied by other delegations and reported accurately to foreign ministries around the world.

41. Amb. Daya Perera, May 30, 1990.

42. Amb. Sedfrey A. Ordonez, May 31, 1990.

43. Amb. Ian Kenyon, May 30, 1990.

44. Amb. Jill Courtney, June 4, 1990. She did not explain what she meant by "scope," and particularly whether she meant to raise the potentially divisive issue of whether a CTB would bar experiments with nuclear energy involving sudden releases of atomic power in the sub-ton range.

45. Amb. Jai P. Rana of Nepal, June 4, 1990.

46. Amb. Miguel Marin-Bosch, June 4, 1990. The Sri Lankan and Philippine calls for three committees were not part of a bargaining strategy and were not worked out with Mexico in advance or negotiated in a caucus of the non-aligned; Mexico genuinely disagreed with those other countries.

47. Amb. Daya Perera, May 30, 1990.
48. Amb. Sedfrey Ordonez, May 31, 1990.
49. June 4, 1990.
50. *Ibid.*
51. Amb. Ian Kenyon, May 30, 1990.
52. Amb. Sedfrey Ordonez, May 31, 1990.
53. Amb. Don MacKay, May 31, 1990. Australia expressed similar opinions, suggesting a "reference list to assist delegations and a supplementary document prepared to cover any outstanding issues."
54. PTBT/CONF/M/12, June 7, 1990.
55. Amb. Miguel Marin-Bosch of Mexico, June 4, 1990; Amb. Jai P. Rana of Nepal, June 4, 1990; Amb. Jill Courtney of Australia, June 4, 1990.
56. Statement by E. N. Golovko, as reported in Press Release No. 78 of the Soviet Mission to the United Nations, June 5, 1990.
57. Because of the mutual desire of national governments to keep real negotiating secret, the public sometimes fails to appreciate how grueling and frustrating diplomacy can be. An Australian diplomat commented on the Meeting, "Looking at the documents, one gets no idea of the protracted disputes which preceded them. However, the discussions and then negotiations were some of the most difficult I have experienced." *Arms Control Reporter,* Limited Test Ban Treaty Chronology 1990, p. 601.B.25 (1990).
58. PTBT/CONF/M/8, May 31, 1990.
59. Interview with a United Nations official, June 1, 1990.
60. Interview with a non-aligned delegate, June 1, 1990. The U.K. and U.S. delegates may have been unaware of the "gentlemen's agreement" because their delegations were represented by lower-level officers on the day it was reached, and although these officials undoubtedly wrote up memoranda of the negotiations for their superiors, so many minor decisions were being reached that it might have been hard for the senior diplomats to keep track of all of them.
61. Interview with a non-aligned delegate, June 1, 1990.
62. These rules are found in Rules of Procedure for the Third Review Conference of the Parties to the Treaty on the Prohibition of the Emplacement of Nuclear Weapons and Other Weapons of Mass Destruction on the Seabed and the Ocean Floor and in the Subsoil Thereof, SBT/CONF.III/5, Sept. 20, 1989 (hereafter referred to as Seabed Treaty Review Conference Rules).
63. PTBT/CONF/M/2, Rule 2.
64. Interview with a delegate, May 31, 1990.
65. Seabed Treaty Review Conference Rule 28.
66. *Ibid.*
67. On the lack of controversy at the Third Seabed Treaty Review Conference, see Sergio Duarte, "The Third Review Conference of the Sea-Bed Treaty—A Panorama," *Disarmament* v. XIII, No. 2, pp. 257, 258–59 (1990).
68. Draft Rules of Procedure for the PTBT Amendment Conference: Decision Making (Draft of Mexico, June 4, 1990.)
69. Interview with a member of the Mexican delegation, June 4, 1990.
70. Adoption of Decisions (Canadian draft, June 5, 1990).

71. In June, 1990, just a few months after the revolutions in Eastern Europe, few realized that most of the "Soviet bloc" had already vanished. Not until the General Assembly met a mew months later did it become clear that the former allies of the U.S.S.R. would now generally vote with the West.

72. PTBT/CONF/M/11, Rule 28, June 8, 1990.

73. The decision was embodied in PTBT/CONF/M/11, Rule 29, June 8, 1990. In fact, the United States position, that no decision adopted by consensus should be subject to reconsideration except by consensus, had precedential roots not only in the Seabed Treaty Review Conference Rules but also in the Rules of Procedure of the Third NPT Review Conference. NPT/CONF.III/41, Rule 27.

74. Seabed Treaty Review Conference Rule 23 (a). In parliamentary terms, a motion with highest precedence is one that can be made at any time, even while another motion (e.g., a motion to adjourn the Conference permanently) is on the floor.

75. Seabed Treaty Review Conference Rule 42.

76. See A/S-15/PV.1, May 31, 1988 and A/S-15/PV.5, June 2, 1988.

77. PTBT/CONF/1, decision 5, July 18, 1990.

78. Seabed Treaty Review Conference Rule 42.

79. NPT/CONF. III/41, Rule 43.

80. PTBT/CONF/M/11, Rule 43, June 8, 1990. As a practical matter, this outcome was closer to the Western position than to what the non-aligned sought, because any significant bargaining could be relegated to a "working group." On the other hand, information leaked quickly and easily from all of the closed meetings. See Chapter 6.

81. Appeal to the Participants in the Test Ban Treaty Amendment Conference from the Participants in the International Citizens Congress for a Nuclear Test Ban, Alma Ata, U.S.S.R., May 26, 1990.

82. Interview with a member of the Mexican delegation, May 31, 1990.

83. Press release, Parliamentarians for Global Action, June 4, 1990.

84. The Representatives who attended were Democrats Bob Carr, Lane Evans, Edward Markey, and Martin Sabo, and Republican Bill Green.

85. This was Bowen Wells, a member of the Foreign Affairs Select Committee of Parliament and the chair of the All-Party Group on the United Nations.

86. Aaron Tovish believes that it was not correct and that the Parties decided only the place, leaving standing the previous decision by the depositaries as to the date. Interview with Aaron Tovish, June 8, 1990.

87. Interview with a member of the Mexican delegation, June 8, 1990.

88. PTBT/CONF/M/SR.13, p. 6, June 21, 1990.

89. Interview with Mary Elizabeth Hoinkes, June 8, 1990.

5

Intermission

International Politics

The road from the Meeting to the Conference detoured through Geneva. In August and September, many of the same nuclear diplomats, including Marin-Bosch for Mexico and Hoinkes for the United States, would reassemble for the Fourth NPT Review Conference. Five years earlier, the third such Conference had divided, as usual, over the CTB issue, but the parties had agreed to disagree, stating in the Final Document their differing views on the test ban question.[1] Few predicted that this Review Conference would be any more contentious.[2] Between 1985 and 1990, the nuclear weapons states had achieved considerable progress on arms control (including the Intermediate Nuclear Forces Treaty). The liberalization of the Soviet Union and the demise of the Warsaw Pact had promised reduced superpower tension in the period ahead, and although the U.S. and the U.K. were still dug in on the substance of the CTB issue, the Meeting had proceeded with some resentment over the financial issue but otherwise without much rancor.

The first two weeks of the three week Review Conference were devoted primarily to formal speeches.[3] On the fourth day, however, the group of non-aligned states introduced a draft resolution that called upon the nuclear weapon parties to the treaty to undertake a dozen new arms control measures to show greater progress toward fulfilling their obligations under the treaty; the first new commitments in the list were "an immediate moratorium on all nuclear testing," full "support" for the Amendment Conference, and the announcement at that Conference of their intention "to pursue negotiations in good faith with a view to achieving a comprehensive nuclear test ban treaty prior to 1995."[4] In an accompanying statement, they recognized the "positive elements and effects" of recent disarmament agreements, but they complained that "the modernization and qualitative improvement of nuclear weapons systems continue unabated."[5] To underscore the link between the CTB issue and a substantial extension of the NPT, the states that had originally called for the Amendment Conference (except Peru, because a Peruvian was chairing the Review Conference) introduced a resolution stating that a CTB would "strengthen the [NPT] and facilitate its extension for a significant period beyond 1995."[6] With ten other countries, they introduced still another resolution calling for a committee to meet as soon as the fall of 1991, to begin to prepare for the 1995 conference that would determine for how long the NPT would continue.[7] Although the resolutions did not say so explicitly, Marin argued that the NPT should not be given a long extension in 1995 unless a CTB had been agreed to.[8]

During the Conference, Marin and his allies compromised on many of these proposals. They dropped, for example, the call for a new testing moratorium. But a Department of Energy member of the United States delegation revealed that "the U.S. position on CTB is inflexible," and Hoinkes (acting as legal advisor to the U.S. delegation) said that not only was testing needed for safety and reliability but that the United States might need new types of nuclear weapons in an environment in which it had negotiated away much of its existing arsenal.[9]

Although the disagreement about testing seemed difficult if not impossible to resolve, the delegates made progress on other aspects of nonproliferation. As the conference went into its final week, they were on the verge of agreeing that suppliers of nuclear products to countries that had not joined the NPT (such as Pakistan and India) should require them to submit to international inspection of all of their peaceful nuclear facilities, not only those in which the exported products would be used. This so-called "full-scope" safeguards rule was already in effect for exports to NPT parties, who had become annoyed that some countries, such as Britain, Belgium, and Italy, made fewer demands of NPT holdouts than of NPT parties. In addition, Nigeria was seeking to begin a process that would lead to a treaty under which the nuclear powers would agree not to threaten or use nuclear weapons against countries that had signed the NPT or the treaty creating a nuclear-free zone in Latin America. The United States had made such a promise but had resisted a treaty commitment to that effect. For the first time, a U.S. delegation appeared to have authority to agree to a conference that would write a non-use agreement. Furthermore, the conferees appeared to be close to agreement on language that would call for the nuclear weapon states to separate all of their weapons and non-weapons nuclear production facilities, so that international inspectors could visit and examine all of their purportedly peaceful installations.[10]

All of these measures, including some statement about a comprehensive test ban, would by tradition come together in a Final Document which, under the rules of the Review Conference, would have to be approved by consensus—that is, unanimously. A drafting committee, chaired by the Swedish delegate, began to try to meld the proposals that had been put forward on each topic, but with respect to the draft resolutions on CTB, that task seemed virtually impossible. For example, the Chairman proposed for the Conference to say that a CTB would make "the single most important" contribution toward strengthening non-proliferation. The United States wanted to change "the single most" to "an," while Sri Lanka, though in other ways content with the Chairman's language, wanted to add that "continuation of testing would put the future of the NPT beyond 1995 in doubt."[11] Where the Chairman would have "invite[d]" all Parties to give the Amendment Conference "their fullest support," the United States would have wanted only to invite them to "contribute constructively," and Mexico, alluding to the strategy of keeping the amendment conference going until 1995, would have called for the delegates to continue working "through as many sessions as necessary to conclude successfully their work."[12]

The Conference was scheduled to end on Friday, September 14. Late that day, with 95% of the text of a Final Document resolved,[13] the Chairman of the drafting committee proposed what he hoped would be a final compromise on the CTB question. "The Conference further recognized that the discontinuance of nuclear testing would play a central role in the future of the NPT well beyond 1995," his draft read. "The Conference also stressed the significant importance placed upon negotiations, multilateral and bilateral, during the next five years, to conclude a comprehensive test ban treaty. [The Conference urges to Conference on Disarmament to return to this topic] with an appropriate mandate."[14] Mexico and the other members of the non-aligned group were willing to drop their threat of putting the future of the NPT in doubt, as well as their demand for reference to multiple sessions of the amendment conference. They were even willing to accept the Chairman's language.[15] But the United States was not willing to do so. The U.S. and Britain insisted on adding an additional sentence: "The Conference notes the joint commitment of the United States and the Soviet Union to proceed with the step-by-step negotiations on further intermediate limitations on nuclear testing, leading to the ultimate objective of the complete cessation of nuclear testing as part of an effective disarmament process."[16]

This addition was unacceptable to several non-aligned countries; it asked them to recognize with some degree of approval not only a negotiation whose main achievement had been postponement of any progress since 1974 on the test ban issue, but also the principle of further intermediate limitations (such as a 75 or 50 kt threshold) that were inconsistent with a CTB. Furthermore, the placement of this sentence just after the diluted warning about 1995 might imply that some further ratcheting down of the threshold levels might be sufficient to assuage the concerns that nations would then otherwise express.

Some non-aligned delegates believed that they could accept the United States' sentence, provided that it were moved elsewhere in the Document, away from the mention of 1995. But the United States refused to consider moving the sentence, and Felix Calderon, a member of the Peruvian delegation, insisted that the offending sentence should not appear anywhere in the document. Night had fallen, but a two hour recess followed, with much caucusing and lobbying.[17] The United States refused to move or alter the sentence; even with the proposed addition, the language was, according to a U.S. delegate, "right on the outer fringe of what we could accept [under our instructions from Washington]" and (apparently during the recess) it had been rejected by the Pentagon.[18] The non-aligned group would not agree to the American sentence as proposed, so the U.S. delegation did not have to face the problem of what it would have done if its proposal had been accepted by the other countries.

Again the Review Conference was at an impasse. At 3:30 in the morning, the President of the Conference, Osvaldo de Rivero of Peru, proposed a final take-it-or-leave it plan, similar in approach to the compromise to which the Third Review Conference had turned, five years earlier. It would have expressed the "regret" of the Conference that it could not agree on text regarding the disarmament commitments of the nuclear powers, and it attempted to summarize the contrasting views of the two camps. Marin did not find the summary acceptable, however, for while it noted that some countries believed that "the continued testing of nuclear weapons . . . would put the future of the Treaty beyond 1995 in grave doubt," it did not otherwise refer to the importance of making efforts to negotiate a CTB *agreement,* and it did not call for CTB discussions to resume in the Conference on Disarmament.[19] At 5:30 A.M., he objected to the text, bringing the Review Conference to a close without a Final Document.[20]

Ten years earlier, the Second NPT Review Conference had also failed to reach consensus on a final document, and neither event resulted in tangible, immediate harm.[21] But this collapse was more serious, for three reasons. First, this was the last Review Conference before consideration of the treaty's extension in 1995, and the atmosphere was far from optimal. Second, the Review Conference could have begun to establish ground rules for the 1995 meeting, such as when preparatory conferences would begin to work, but the confrontational atmosphere prevented effective work on that subject.[22] Finally, failure to agree on a Final Document sunk near-agreement on the several ways to strengthen the Treaty on which consensus had nearly been achieved, such as convening a conference to negotiate a non-use treaty. With respect to that issue, for example, "the final agreed language was not made public and the United States may now feel relieved of any obligation to help organize the conference the Nigerians and others want."[23]

At the same time, however, the failure at Geneva seemed to increase the importance of the PTBT Amendment Conference. If anyone had doubted it before, the primacy afforded to a test ban by at least an important bloc of non-aligned states was now clear. "Deadlock Threatens Future of Nuclear Treaty," the New York Times reported, noting that "third world countries insisted on a total nuclear test ban within five years".[24] Furthermore, the fact that the United States had thus far blocked the Conference on Disarmament from discussing a CTB at its meeting scheduled for late January left the Amendment Conference, in early January, as the only forum in which the issue could even be raised, much less negotiated.

Domestic Politics

American peace groups had hoped to use the period between the end of the summer and the beginning of the Amendment Conference to build support in Congress and in the public generally. Two events made this effort more difficult than ever.

To the extent that Congress was willing to focus on the test ban issue at all, it was preoccupied with ratification of the Threshold Test Ban Treaty, which finally had been submitted to the Senate for advice and consent after Presidents Bush and Gorbachev had signed the verification protocol at the end of June.[25] In addition, Iraq's invasion of Kuwait on August 2 reopened the question of whether the United States should really plan major cuts in its military budget.[26]

The day before his bill to cut 5% from the research, development and testing budget was scheduled to be voted on in the House, Representative DeFazio withdrew it, reportedly because many representatives had water projects in the same Energy and Water Appropriations Bill that included nuclear testing funds, and these representatives feared retribution by the chairman of the Energy and Water Subcommittee, who was thought to oppose the DeFazio amendment.[27] On the other hand, Representative Doug Bosco introduced a resolution, similar to the one that Senator Pell had offered in the Senate, urging the President to resume bilateral talks for the "early achievement" of a verifiable CTB and to express his willingness to pursue negotiations in good faith in the Amendment Conference; he then offered his resolution as a non-binding "sense of Congress" amendment to the annual defense authorization bill.[28] Unlike the one-kiloton threshold bills that the House had passed in earlier years, the Bosco amendment did not have "teeth," but Congressional enactment of a low-threshold bill in a year in which the Senate was approving a 150-kt Threshold Treaty was a political impossibility. At least the Bosco amendment gave the Coalition a focus for action that was somewhat more practical than several projects that had been undertaken by its constituent organizations, such as the Women's International League for Peace and Freedom's effort to persuade thousands of Americans to "send a rinsed, dried and crushed egg shell" to the President with the message, "Don't crush our hopes for the future . . . support the Comprehensive Test Ban Treaty."[29]

Coalition member organizations made a serious effort to support the Bosco amendment by having members in their districts contact local members of Congress to urge support. When Bosco took the floor of the House to speak for his proposal, he was armed with a new argument. He cited Iraq's invasion of Kuwait, and its past efforts to obtain nuclear weapons, as evidence that the United States needed to work harder to prevent proliferation, and he reminded his colleagues that "just last week the [NPT Review Conference] broke down over the single issue of the U.S. refusal to negotiate [a CTB]."[30] The amendment was opposed by the ranking Republican on an Armed Services Committee panel looking into the safety of nuclear weapon designs, on the ground that more testing might be needed to improve weapon safety.[31] Nevertheless, it passed the House by a vote of 234–182.[32]

In the Senate, the situation was more complicated. When the PTBT was approved in 1963, the Joint Chiefs of Staff had extracted, as the price of their support, a series of "safeguards," such as a pledge that a program of underground testing would continue, and a promise that the laboratories would be maintained.[33] Now, by analogy, the Administration wanted a new series of "safeguards" to accompany the Threshold Test Ban Treaty, including a statement by the Senate that "to ensure the preservation of a viable deterrent," testing should continue within the bounds permitted by the new Treaty and the laboratories should be maintained. Senator Pell also wanted to pass a resolution like the one he had introduced earlier in the year, referring positively to a CTB. Accordingly, the resolutions of ratification reported to the Senate, and approved by it, included somewhat inconsistent declarations through which the Senate both supported continued testing and stated that the United States "shares a special responsibility with the Soviet Union to continue the bilateral Nuclear Testing Talks to achieve further limitations on nuclear testing, including the achievement of a verifiable comprehensive test ban."[34] The Senate conferees working on the defense authorization bill insisted on going no further than these words, and they refused to accept the Bosco amendment's call for "early achievement" of a CTB or to refer explicitly to the Amendment Conference. The House conferees yielded, and the Senate's language was left to express the sense of Congress.[35]

Even this very small degree of success in obtaining an official statement of the desirability of a CTB was somewhat remarkable, given the fragile health of the Coalition. After three years of operation, it continued to have only a single full-time staff member; four months before the Amendment

Conference was to convene, the Coalition was unable to meet its current payroll.[36] Nevertheless, it pressed forward, pleading for contributions and planning for rallies and media events to highlight the Amendment Conference.[37]

It faced major obstacles, though, in its effort to enhance press coverage of the conference. The failure of the press to cover the Meeting in May and June might be explained away on the ground that the Meeting was procedural, but even the NPT Review Conference had been poorly reported in the American press. The Washington Post, for example, hadn't covered it at all, and the New York Times had relied on a Reuters wire service dispatch. Furthermore, the United Nations Security Council had set January 15, during the Amendment Conference, as the deadline after which force could be used against Iraq if it did not withdraw from Kuwait; at the very least, the world would be watching Washington and Baghdad rather than New York, and at the worst, the Amendment Conference would be lost in the babble of war.

The Parliamentarians' Tour

In addition, PGA's initial attempt to attract press attention to the Amendment Conference was a dismal failure. In November, Tovish organized the three-country caravan that he'd had to postpone from the spring. Two U.S. Senators (Jeffords and Harkin), two members of the House (Green and Downey), and two British M.P.s flew to Moscow, where they met up with Suleimenov and Evgeny Velikov, the Vice President of the Soviet Academy of Sciences and Gorbachev's unofficial scientific advisor. From New York, Tovish brought copies of the open letter to Presidents Bush and Gorbachev, and to Prime Minister Margaret Thatcher, with 2057 signatures of members of the parliaments of countries that had no nuclear weapons.[38] The eight legislators had asked for personal meetings with all three heads of state, to present the letter and to discuss the Amendment Conference and the test ban issue. Only Gorbachev agreed to meet with them personally. The British government, in the midst of its crisis of succession from Margaret Thatcher to John Major, fobbed them off on Deputy Foreign Minister Douglas Hogg; in the United States, they were given an audience with National Security Advisor Brent Scowcroft.

In all three meetings, they argued that the world's concern about Iraq as a future nuclear weapon state[39] should lead the three major nuclear weapon states to press for a quick CTB, to reduce the "prestige" value of nuclear weaponry; to make it possible to sanction Iraq, if it tested a weapon, for violating a global norm; and perhaps even to preclude Iraq from being able to demonstrate membership in the nuclear club by conducting a nuclear test. Oddly, the PTBT's amendment clause, which Iraq

Olafur Ragnar Grimsson (center), president of Parliamentarians for Global Action, introduces Olzhas Suleimenov (left), founder of Nevada-Semipalatinsk, to Indonesian Foreign Minister Ali Alatas, who became president of the Amendment Conference (photograph by Nina Tovish).

had accepted along with the rest of the Treaty, provided that an amendment "shall enter into force for all Parties upon the deposit of instruments of ratification by a majority of all the Parties [including the depositaries],"[40] so by using the amendment route, rather than negotiating a new CTB, the countries of the world could impose on Iraq a legal restraint against all testing. In addition, since Gorbachev had long advocated a CTB, they urged him to support the tactic of adjourning rather than ending the Amendment Conference in January in order to keep the issue on the world's agenda.

In three days, the delegation moved from Moscow to London, Washington, and New York. Gorbachev said that he understood both points and would think about them, but he told the legislators that "you don't have my voucher [yet]." The British official restated his government's official position that testing would be needed for as long as deterrence was necessary. Scowcroft agreed with the legislators on the importance of nonproliferation policy but said that he could not agree with them about the desirability of a CTB.[41]

The three-country tour was intended as much to attract public notice to the Amendment Conference in the United States as to educate the three heads of state. Suleimenov, among others, spoke at a rally across the street from the White House after the meeting with Scowcroft, PGA issued press releases and held press conferences in each city, and the legislators met with the editorial boards of the Washington Post and the New York Times. However, only about sixty people, nearly half of them Kazakhs on a peace mission, attended the rally, and the only press reports of the trip were an item on the Tass news wire, a story in Iowa about Senator Harkin's participation, and a Gannett News Service account of Senator Jeffords' planned visit to Moscow.[42]

Three weeks later, on the eve of the Conference, the Washington Post editorially noted that "sentiment to extend the [PTBT] to underground tests is growing, notably in the Soviet Union but also in this country." The Post's view of this development, however, was anything but positive: "As long as the United States retains bombs, it must have the safest and most efficient ones, it must be confident that they work and it must make sure deterrence remains credible. These are the purposes served by testing. Americans need not apologize for it."[43] To the extent that the conveners of the Amendment Conference intended to use it to stimulate and change American public opinion,[44] they had a steep hill still to climb.

Notes

1. Final Declaration of the Third Non-Proliferation Treaty Review Conference, NPT/CONF.III/64/I, Annex I, p. 14, September 25, 1985.

2. Tom A. Zamora, *Arms Control Debate Blocks Consensus at Fourth NPT Review Conference* Oct. 29, 1990 (Federation of American Scientists report), p. 4.

3. Charles Van Doren and George Bunn, "Progress and Peril at the Fourth NPT Review Conference," *Arms Control Today* October, 1990, p. 8.

4. NPT/CONF.IV/L.1, Aug. 24, 1990.

5. Statement to the IV RC NPT by the Non-Aligned and Other States Parties to the NPT not taking part in the East European or Western Groups (undated, distributed August 24, 1990).

6. NPT/CONF.IV/L.4, Sept. 5, 1990.

7. NPT/CONF.IV/L.3, Sept. 3, 1990.

8. Memorandum to LAWS Board of Directors and National Advisory Board from George Bunn, LAWS Observer to the NPT Review Conference, Sept. 20, 1990.

9. Zamora, p. 3.

10. Bunn, p. 4.

11. NPT Fourth Review Conference, Drafting Committee: Revised proposals regarding Article VI and preambular paragraphs 8 to 12, pp. 10–12 (Sept. 13, 1990).

12. *Ibid.,* pp. 6–8.

13. Van Doren and Bunn, p. 9.

14. Draft consensus text for Paragraph 7 offered by the Swedish ambassador, Sept. 14, 1990.

15. Zamora, p. 4.

16. Zamora, p. 4.

17. Interview with Aaron Tovish, who also observed the Review Conference, in Washington, D.C., Sept. 21, 1990.

18. Zamora, p. 4.

19. The United States had allowed the summer, 1990, session of the Conference on Disarmament to discuss, but not to begin negotiating, a comprehensive test ban. But when that session ended, the U.S. had refused to agree that those discussions could resume at the following winter's session. Some observers speculated that the purpose of the American refusal was to reserve something that it could concede in the Final Document of the Review Conference. Interview with Aaron Tovish, who also observed the Review Conference, in Washington, D.C., Sept. 21, 1990.

20. Zamora, p. 4. Although Mexico prevented consensus on this occasion, and the President's proposal probably could have obtained a majority vote, the principle of requiring unanimity is one that, in the long run, probably favors the Western states. Since the United States would lose subsequent votes, "the best alternative for the US was no vote and no final document." Warren Donnelly of the Congressional Research Service, quoted in *Arms Control Reporter,* Non-proliferation Treaty, Sec. 602.B.181 (Oct., 1990).

21. At the Fourth NPT Review Conference "neither [Mexico nor the United States] had strict instructions to return home with a final document, nor did they consider the lack of one to be a major catastrophe." Zamora, p. 1.

22. Van Doren and Bunn, p. 12.

23. Bunn, p. 3.

24. Reuters, "Deadlock Threatens Future of Nuclear Treaty," *New York Times* Sept. 16, 1990, p. 5, col. 1.

25. The Treaty was transmitted to the Senate on June 28. The Foreign Relations Committee held hearings in July and reported them to the Senate on September 14. *Threshold Test Ban and Peaceful Nuclear Explosions Treaties,* Exec. Rept. 101–31, 101st Cong., 2d Sess. (Sept. 14, 1990), pp. 1–8.

26. Rick Atkinson, "Gulf Crisis Poses Dilemma for U.S. Military Facing Cutbacks," *Washington Post* Dec. 23, 1990, p. A1, col. 2.

27. U.S. Comprehensive Test Ban Coalition, *Comprehensive Test Ban News* June 27, 1990.

28. *Congressional Record* 101st Cong., 2d Sess., Sept. 18, 1990, p. H 7795.

29. Women's International League for Peace and Freedom, "How to Promote 'Egg Shell' Letter-Writing Campaign," (flyer and coupons). Other small-scale projects by Coalition members in this period included creating amendment conference Christmas cards to send to members of Congress, advertisements in local papers, and ringing of church bells in Cleveland, Portland, and Cambridge (MA) on the occasion of each nuclear test. "News from the Grassroots" in U.S. Comprehensive Test Ban Coalition, *Comprehensive Test Ban News* June 27, 1990.

30. Congressional Record, p. H 7795.

31. *Ibid.,* p. H 7796 (remarks of Mr. Kyl).

32. *Congressional Record* pp. H 7812–13.

33. See *Exec. M, Nuclear Test Ban Treaty, Hearings before the Committee on Foreign Relations* 88th Cong., 1st Sess (August, 1963), p. 274 (testimony of Gen. Maxwell D. Taylor).

34. *Threshold Test Ban and Peaceful Nuclear Explosions Treaties,* Exec. Rept. 101–31, 101st Cong., 2d Sess. (Sept. 14, 1990), pp. 173–74.

35. National Defense Authorization Act for Fiscal Year 1991, Public Law No. 101–510, 104 Stat. 1485, November 15, 1990.

36. Minutes, U.S. Comprehensive Test Ban Coalition, Sept. 7, 1990.

37. See U.S. Comprehensive Test Ban Coalition, Press Packet of Nuclear Test Ban Events in Conjunction with The Test Ban Treaty Conference.

38. "Tripartite Delegation Meets Gorbachev," *Global Action* December, 1990, p. 1.

39. At the time of their meetings, senior U.S. national security officials were arguing that a war against Iraq might be necessary in part because Iraq seemed bent on acquiring a nuclear weapons capability.

40. Treaty Banning Nuclear Weapon Tests in the Atmosphere, in Outer Space and Under Water, Art. II, Sec. 2.

41. Interviews with Aaron Tovish in Washington, D.C., Nov. 27 and 28, 1990. It was not clear whether Scowcroft was stating his own view or merely repeating the official position of the Bush administration. In 1986, while out of the government, Scowcroft had co-authored, with 22 other national security experts, a Council of Foreign Relations Report on "new approaches to non-proliferation." The report concluded that "a comprehensive test ban treaty could make a significant contribution to containing proliferation. . . . [A]bstinence from testing would mean that they [proliferators] could not demonstrate the achievement of a nuclear explosive capability or have full confidence that they had achieved it; and [it] would effectively preclude the development of . . . advanced types of explosives [and] help preserve the viability of the Non-proliferation Treaty by providing the most widely demanded response to [the non-nuclear weapon states'] complaint[s]." Containing Nuclear Proliferation: A New Assessment, Summary Report of the U.S. Panel on New Approaches to Non-Proliferation, in Council on Foreign Relations, *Blocking the Spread of Nuclear Weapons* (New York: Council on Foreign Relations, 1986), p. 12.

42. Telephone interview with Aaron Tovish, Dec. 5, 1990.

43. "Ban Underground Tests?" *Washington Post* Dec. 17, 1990, p. A10, col. 1 (editorial). Much of the editorial echoes views expressed the same day in a *Post* op-ed by Kathleen Bailey, who as a government official a year earlier had announced the United States' plan to veto the proposed PTBT amendment. Kathleen Bailey, "This is Not Arms Control," *Washington Post* Dec. 17, 1990, p. A11, col. 1. For a rejoinder, see Paul Warnke, "Disarming Logic," *Washington Post* Dec. 22, 1990, p. A13.

44. Asked why the Conference should go ahead in view of the announced U.S. and U.K. vetoes, Marin-Bosch told a reporter, "Because [most] countries . . . have no leverage as far as pressuring [the U.S. and U.K.] to come to an agreement, so this is a way of having some public opinion focused on this issue. This is an issue that has virtually disappeared from public consciousness, especially in the United States, and I think it is important to revive it." "CTB is Part of NPT," *Disarmament Times* May, 1990, p. 3, col. 3 (interview with Miguel Marin-Bosch).

6

The Conference

No one associated with the PTBT Amendment Conference—no diplomat, no PGA staff member, no peace activist—ever believed that the Conference would amend the Treaty. At some points early in the process of bringing about the Conference, some CTB advocates hoped that to avoid the embarrassment of voting against the rest of the world, the United States and Britain might agree to resume trilateral CTB negotiations, permit the CD to begin multilateral negotiations, or announce a limit on the number of tests they would conduct each year; others predicted that the United States and Britain would be willing to vote alone against an amendment, or to boycott future meetings of the Amendment Conference, rather than make even the slightest concession toward further constraints in its test program. In any event, by the time the Conference opened on January 7, the only unresolved issue was whether, in some form, it would survive the two week session to become an enduring institution for putting pressure on Britain and the United States to negotiate a CTB, either in a large forum such as the Amendment Conference or a smaller one such as a committee of the CD or, most likely, bilateral or trilateral talks. With respect to the endgame, a limited range of possibilities occupied everyone's mind.

First, the conference could recess for a year or two, and it might establish one or more working groups to study or discuss relevant issues during the interim. This outcome was the best that the Mexican government, its allies, and Parliamentarians for Global Action could hope for, and it seemed plausible, given the numerical superiority of the non-aligned bloc, the rules of the Convention that procedural issues could be decided by majority vote and that the Chair could decide what issues were "procedural," and the fact that during the fall, Foreign Minister Alatas had agreed to be the non-aligned candidate for Chair, and the Western countries had decided not to oppose him.[1] The non-aligned countries could move to recess the Conference to keep the process going; if Britain or the United States claimed that the issue was "substantive," Alatas could rule it procedural, requiring only a majority vote. Britain and the United States would then face the difficult choice of boycotting or participating in the second session, and meanwhile they and their allies would lose a highly politicized roll call vote in a Conference that might achieve more visibility than one ballot among many in a session of the General Assembly. Given the prospect of losing a vote, the United States might even agree to the recess and to participate at a later date, some thought, in exchange for other concessions such as a two-year lapse with no interim working groups.

At the other end of the spectrum, the Conference could simply dissolve after two weeks, as Britain and the United States desired. If enough European states were willing to vote against a recess, and enough non-aligned states could be persuaded either to abstain or not to be present for the vote, the United States might actually be able to prevail in its view that the Conference should be a one-time event rather than an ongoing institution.

Between these extremes lay several middle options. For example, the Conference could decide to recess without setting a specific date for another meeting, leaving that question to the discretion of Alatas. Although Indonesia was one of the countries that had called for the Conference, the United States might accept this concept because it would not guarantee a second session, and perhaps because it would then retain the power, through diplomatic and economic pressure on Indonesia, to try to prevent a resumption of the event. Alatas himself was reported to have told the six originating countries that he favored this resolution of the recess issue.[2] Another conceivable type of compromise would involve ending the Conference by consensus on the basis of minor concessions, symbolic or genuine, by some or all of the depositaries. For example, the United States had not agreed, at the end of the summer session of the Conference on Disarmament, to continue in existence the committee of that body charged with discussing test ban issues. This committee could be re-authorized with its prior mandate, or it could be strengthened by giving it the power to begin to negotiate a CTB, with the understanding that nothing could be achieved in the negotiations without U.S. and British concurrence. Along the same lines, the United States might agree, as part of a compromise, to reopen the "step-by-step" talks with the Soviet Union; the administration was coming under strong pressure from Congress and from the Soviet government to do so in any event.

On all sides, governments and non-governmental advocates focused their moves to achieve the result they desired with respect to the end of the two-week Conference. On the surface the delegations were occupied with test ban policy. The entire first week of the Conference was devoted to delegations' lengthy, formal readings of their general policy statements, many of which repeated the substance of statements made at the June

Meeting or the views of other delegations. But behind the scenes the only real issue was the question of the future of the Amendment Conference itself, and a great deal of activity was devoted to the inevitable confrontation over this question.

The General Assembly Resolution

Mexico made the first move, several weeks before the Conference began. In the General Assembly, where it was sure to have the votes it needed, it introduced still another resolution on the question of the Amendment Conference. The first draft of Marin's resolution was weak; indeed, it was silent on the key issue of continuing the Conference after its initial session. Marin didn't think that a strong resolution could be adopted; in addition, he may have been under tight control from Mexico City following criticism in the Western press of his single-minded focus on the CTB issue in the NPT Review Conference. But Tovish and William Epstein spoke with disarmament experts on many United Nations delegations and succeeded in obtaining from several of them authorization to tell Marin that at meetings of the requesting countries, they would speak up to strengthen the Mexican resolution.[3] In its final form, the resolution not only called on states to contribute to the success of the Conference but recommended that "intensive efforts continue, under the auspices of the Amendment Conference, until a comprehensive nuclear-test-ban treaty is achieved." While this language did not specify that the Conference would have more than one session, it implied it, because efforts could hardly continue under the "auspices" of a non-existent body. To make the point that the Conference would have work to do between sessions, the resolution recommended that the Conference establish a working group to study various aspects of a test ban treaty and report its conclusions to the Conference. Finally, to take account of the certain Western objection that the Conference on Disarmament was the proper body to deal with the test ban issue, the resolution stressed "the importance of ensuring adequate co-ordination among the various negotiating forums" concerned with the issue.[4] This resolution would not bind any country, but it would demonstrate world-wide support for the Conference to continue and therefore provide political support to those within each non-aligned foreign ministry who would be inclined, in January, to argue in favor of a vote to recess the Conference.

The Mexican resolution was easily approved by the General Assembly, and as in previous years, only Britain and the United States opposed it. But this time, there were only 116 votes in favor (as opposed to 127 in 1989), and 27 abstentions (compared with 22).[5] The difference was accounted for principally by the revolutions that had occurred in Eastern Europe in the fall of 1989. The former members of the Warsaw Pact, including Bulgaria, Czechoslovakia, Hungary, Poland and Romania, which had once followed the Soviet Union in voting with the non-aligned on the Amendment Conference, were now eager to join the European Economic Community and were therefore following the lead of the NATO countries;[6] by the end of the Conference, many delegates referred to them jokingly as the "neo-NATO countries" because they appeared to want to be economically as successful as their West European counterparts and saw political conformity to Western European positions as a necessary but not sufficient condition for such an outcome.[7] Their abstentions in the United Nations left them free to abstain, or even to vote no, if they had to vote on recessing the Conference.

Visibility

A second tactic of those who wanted the Conference to continue was to try to bring it greater visibility so that elected governments voting to abort the process would have to pay a higher price in terms of jeopardizing political support from their domestic constituencies. The first effort in this direction—the trip of the legislators to Moscow, London and Washington—had been a media failure, but PGA, the U.S. Coalition, International Physicians for the Prevention of Nuclear War and others renewed their efforts, as January approached, to attract media attention. They made three kinds of efforts to get attention. Only one of them worked, but its success was spectacular.

Their first approach was to take advantage of the fact that the United States Conference of Mayors had endorsed the CTB and had scheduled a special workshop for American and Soviet mayors on the day before the Conference was to open. The Conference of Mayors had been able to get a room in the United Nations for the session; it had been able to line up Paul Warnke, the former chief U.S. arms control negotiator, and Carl Sagan, the famous astronomer, as speakers; it had located seven mayors of Soviet cities (including Murmansk, near the Novaya Zemlya test site) who would attend; and New York's Mayor David Dinkins had agreed to attend and to make the opening address.[8] Nevertheless, only seven American mayors attended the meeting, and it received virtually no publicity.

Second, the test ban movement organized two public demonstrations. The first took place at the Nevada Test Site two days before the Conference was to open. It attracted three thousand participants, including Olzhas Suleimenov whose mass demonstrations in Kazakhstan had closed down the Soviet test site there and propelled him into the Supreme Soviet. The Nevada demonstration also resulted in the arrest of seven hundred people who committed civil disobedience by crossing the Site's boundary. But unlike a similar action several years earlier, the demonstration and arrests did not receive press attention outside of Nevada.[9] The second demonstration was to take place outside of the United Nations building half way through the Conference, for which 2000 people were expected.[10] But a severe snowstorm forced the organizers to move the rally into a church, only 400 activists turned out, and, more ominously, by this time the CTB issue was rapidly being displaced, even on the agendas of its ardent followers, by the imminence of the deadline the U.N. Security Council had given Iraq for the removal of its forces from Kuwait. Even as the rally was being held, Congress was voting to authorize war,[11] and several of the rally's speakers departed from their planned texts to plead for peace in the Persian Gulf. Peter, Paul and Mary's Peter Yarrow interrupted his rendition of "Where Have All the Flowers Gone?" to say a word, not about nuclear testing, but about the lives about to be wasted in conventional warfare. As a press event, the rally was a near-bust. The *New York Times* ignored it, and although two New York television stations sent camera crews, a Cable News Network crew left without filming because, although it had planned to take some footage of Dr. Bernard Lown's address, it was unwilling to wait while Corbin Harney, a leader of the Western Shoshone nation in Nevada (which claims the Test Site as its land), chanted a seven-minute opening prayer in his native tongue.[12]

Finally, test ban advocates made a concerted effort to persuade reporters, columnists and opinion leaders to write about the Amendment Conference in the days before and during its opening days. They bombarded established columnists with material about the Conference, and they called on as many scientific and political experts as they could, requesting them to submit opinion pieces. To their relief, this type of effort was finally rewarded. Shortly before the Conference assembled, several columns urging its success appeared in newspapers often read by diplomats and American policy-makers. These pieces included opinion essays by Jerome Wiesner in the *New York Times,* Paul Warnke in the *Washington Post,* Walter Clemens in the *Christian Science Monitor,* Tom Wicker in the *New York Times,* Mary McGrory in the *Washington Post,* and George Bunn in the *Christian Science Monitor.*[13] The *Boston Globe* editorially urged President Bush to reverse his position, and *USA Today* editorialized that "The USA took the lead [in 1963] in steering the world away from [a] menacing future. We must take the lead again. We must put an end to nuclear testing."[14] In addition, as the Conference opened, the *New York Times* gave it a significant story, with a picture, in its News of the Week in Review section; the *New Yorker Magazine* devoted the lead article in its "Talk of the Town" section to the contrast between the President's use of multilateral consultations to "marshall . . . a global consensus against Saddam Hussein" and his "willingness to defy an equally united world community on an equally grave issue;" and Anthony Lewis, writing in the *New York*

Sri Lankan Ambassador Edmond Jayasinghe (second from right), congratulates Indonesian Foreign Minister Ali Alatas on his election as president of the Amendment Conference. U.N. Secretary-General Javier Perez de Cuellar (left) and Conference Secretary-General Sohrab Kehradi look on (U.N. Photo 177194 by Milton Grant).

Times, charged that the real reason for the President's stance on testing was to throw "what may seem to him a relatively small bone" to conservatives.[15] In case any delegates missed any of these articles and columns, the non-governmental organizations at the Conference distributed reprints widely. In addition, both Greenpeace and PGA held press conferences during the first week of the Conference, and they asked their overseas chapters and members to fax copies of any stories in foreign newspapers to their New York offices so that the delegates would know that they knew that their foreign ministries had also seen the publicity.

The non-aligned countries made more subtle efforts, as well, to project the importance of the Conference to national governments. They had already persuaded United Nations Secretary General Perez de Cuellar to address the Conference on its opening day (knowing that most delegates would report his participation in cables to their capitals); now they persuaded him to make the General Assembly Hall, rather than a smaller conference room, available for the opening session.

The Western Strategy

The Western response was equal and opposite. Just as the non-aligned countries had taken a strong position in the United Nations resolution in favor of continuation of the Conference, the Western countries tried their best, before the Conference opened, to disable it, and in the opening days, they did what they could to convince the non-aligned that they expected to shut down the effort completely.

The United States' most significant effort to derail the Conference was an attempt to incapacitate one of its most effective leaders, Marin-Bosch. Marin's performance at the NPT Review Conference had infuriated the national security community in the United States, whose members believed that he had set back the cause of non-proliferation by preventing agreement on elements in the proposed final statement that would have strengthened the NPT. The distress was great enough to reach the White House, and when George Bush visited Mexican President Carlos Salinas de Gortari in Mexico City in November, 1990, to discuss a free trade agreement between the two countries, he asked Salinas to reverse Mexico's policy with respect to the Amendment Conference. Salinas replied that each of the two governments had its own test ban policy.[16] Nevertheless, it was not clear that the Mexican government would continue to back Marin, since it very much wanted the free trade agreement. At some point during the following month, Marin proposed a set of instructions for the delegation to the Amendment Conference, including a proposed direction to lead an effort to keep the Conference going after January. His request was denied by the Foreign Ministry, and only his threat to resign produced a reversal in his favor, and to a direction from Salinas to continue on the course he had been taking.[17] The Mexican Foreign Ministry sent Deputy Foreign Minister Andres Rozental to New York at the outset of the Conference, possibly to supersede Marin, but he ended up delivering, as Mexico's address to the Conference, a speech very similar to what Marin himself would have said. It included a suggestion that the Conference examine a system of imposing sanctions on any country that violated the Treaty as amended.[18] Since sanctions was a new idea for the international community (though it had first been floated during the tripartite legislative tour of capitals), its examination would obviously require more than the two week opening session. In addition, although Rozental's speech did not explicitly address continuation of the Conference, Marin advocated it within the non-aligned caucus, and he revealed in a public meeting that he had done so.[19] Marin's hand may have been strengthened further by the very favorable reaction of the Mexican press to Rozental's speech.[20]

The second prong of the Western strategy was to lobby for votes to end the Conference after the initial two week period. The United States announced in public that it "urge[d] other parties to join in bringing this process to a close" and stated that it would not participate in or provide any financial support to a continued Conference.[21] Behind this rhetoric lay American military alliances and American economic power. Its NATO allies, all of which (except Britain) had abstained on Marin's General Assembly resolution, intimated that they had instructions not to support continuation of the Conference, and at a meeting with Greenpeace members on January 9, Canada's ambassador, Peggy Mason, said that Canada had instructions not merely to abstain, but to vote against a second session.[22] (Of course such revelations were two-edged; Canadian members of PGA and Greenpeace immediately notified Canadian newspapers, in order to suggest to the Canadian public that its government was not willing to continue the process of disarmament negotiations).[23] American economic power did not have to be asserted as explicitly. In the opening days of the Conference, several non-aligned countries seemed unwilling to follow the lead of Mexico, Mauritius, the Philippines, and others who urged them to be ready to vote against the United States and its allies. "The lowering of political punch by the non-aligned is due to the international economic situation," Marin lamented. "The focus of [many governments, including my own] is not on CTB, but on something else. So whenever the person behind the 'U.S.' nameplate screams, they begin to re-evaluate their position."[24]

The Numbers Game

Despite the non-aligned group's numerical superiority in the Conference and the British and American power to veto an amendment, numbers mattered to both sides. PGA worried that unless its forces could see that they would win a vote on continuing the Conference by a substantial margin, individual non-aligned states would begin to peel away from the non-aligned group and to accept whatever terms the West offered, rather than bring the matter to a vote in which the non-aligned group would be divided. Under the rules of the Conference, abstentions would not be considered in the vote count,[25] which explained why Canada and perhaps other Western countries might vote negatively, though they had abstained on Marin's General Assembly resolution. The Western group, together with the formerly socialist countries of Eastern Europe, could cast as many as 30 votes against continuation of the Conference; PGA and its allies wanted to be sure of at least 40 votes in favor of a recess, and it hoped for 55. But Tovish noted, during the first days of the Conference, that only about 40 non-aligned countries had sent representatives to participate, and some of them were already wavering on the question of a recess and might abstain. Tovish decided on a strategy of changing the numerical balance by packing the Conference. The U.S. Comprehensive Test Ban Coalition made a list of thirty non-aligned treaty parties that had not fielded delegations. It designated as "lobby day" the morning before the scheduled "parade of tests" demonstration, and it assigned about 50 members of its constituent organizations, who had come to New York to observe the Conference and to protest U.S. policy, to visit the United Nations Missions of these countries and to urge their participation in the Conference. These volunteers, many of them doctors associated with Physicians for Social Responsibility and International Physicians for the Prevention of Nuclear War, fanned out through a snow storm to explain to the missing countries the international significance of the vote that would occur at the end of the following week.

Their work turned out to be both rewarding and successful. Ambassadors from many of the small non-aligned countries graciously received the citizen-lobbyists; they were as surprised by the house calls from American doctors as the Indonesian Foreign Minister had been by the visit of a member of the Icelandic parliament. Several of them spent more than an hour with the Americans; some offered to speak in their home towns; and fourteen additional countries promised to attend the Conference if a vote became imminent.[26]

The numbers game was not lost on the West, either. At Conference sessions, a member of the American delegation could be seen moving from chair to chair at the rear of the chamber, checking off attendance on her list of parties. It seemed unlikely that the United States would actually discourage any country from attending (most of the absences were due to the inability of small delegations to field representatives to attend the Conference), but its count would enable it to assess its likelihood of being able to win a vote decisively.

While some Coalition volunteers sought participation by the missing non-aligned nations, others visited delegates from Eastern and Western block countries to try to persuade some of them to support a continued Conference or at least to abstain.[27] Because delegates from these larger countries were usually present on the floor of the Conference chamber, the volunteers (who, as accredited representatives of non-governmental organizations, had seats at the back of the room) often buttonholed them when they entered or left the room. The diplomats were accustomed to working in the hermetically sealed atmosphere of the United Nations headquarters building, to which only they and the U.N. staff were generally admitted, and while they seemed bemused by all the lobbying, they also seemed pleased by the unprecedented attention that they were receiving.

At the same time, and probably with somewhat more effect, PGA urged its parliamentary members in Western capitals to press their governments not to vote to terminate the process. Tovish calculated that if even one or two European countries could be persuaded to abstain and to express its willingness to attend future sessions, the Western group would experience a massive fracture, because any government would have a hard time explaining to its constituents why it took a harder line than its Continental neighbor.[28] Furthermore, any division within the Western contingent could cause wavering non-aligned countries to firm up their commitment to vote to keep the forum alive.

More Markers

As in the June meeting, a key element of both sides' strategy was to accumulate markers on the record; that is, formal statements, during the "general debate," that would purport to commit a government to a position on the key procedural issue of adjournment. In most of the general debate scheduled for the first five days of the Conference, delegations spoke of the desire of their countries to achieve (or in the case of Britain and the United States, to defer) a CTB, and several delegations confined their remarks to this substantive issue, making essentially the same points about the dangers of the arms race, the importance to non-proliferation of a CTB, and the verifiability of such a Treaty, that had been stated during the "general exchange of views" at the June meeting.[29] But a larger number of delegations inserted into their formal statements either explicit statements or broad hints about their views on the future of the Conference itself, forecasting for other delegations how they would vote if a consensus compromise were not reached.

Few Western or formerly socialist countries would follow the United States in stating that they would refuse to participate in future meetings, but many of them disparaged the utility of the Conference as a negotiating body, implying that after two weeks it would have served its purpose, which they defined as giving "impetus" to the work of the Conference on Disarmament, even though the United States would continue to use its procedural veto to prevent that body from beginning to negotiate a CTB. Thus Denmark believed that "the objective of this conference should be to give impetus to [the CD] which is the proper . . . forum,"[30] Norway asserted that "instead of follow-up actions within the framework of the Amendment Conference, we should increase our efforts to find ways and means to succeed in Geneva,"[31] Japan hoped that the Conference would "serve as an important catalyst" to the CD,[32] Germany considered the CD to be "the appropriate international forum" for dealing with a test ban, [33] and Poland considered the "real value" of the Conference to be "in stimulating" U.S.-Soviet negotiations.[34]

The non-aligned states laid down their markers as well. The most important of them was the statement of Alatas, speaking on the opening day as President of the Conference. Most delegates expected that in his Presidential address, he would feel constrained from taking a firm position on the issues before the Conference. But Alatas surprised both PGA and the delegates with a fiery speech indicating that he would not moderate his views to accommodate the United States. "Questions of verification . . . have now . . . been practically resolved," he declared. "Confidence in the reliability and safety of nuclear weapons can be obtained by methods and advanced technical means without having to resort to actual weapons tests. . . . [g]overnments should no more seek refuge in arguments long since shown to be untenable or irrelevant."[35]

Other countries were in a position to signal their intentions regarding the Conference as an institution. For Sri Lanka, Jayasinghe said that he wanted "to place on record that it was never the intention of the co-sponsors of the Amendment Conference that it should be terminated with one session."[36] Brazil, whose president had recently reached a bilateral agreement with Argentina to forswear underground nuclear testing, said that "the time allocated to this exercise is clearly insufficient."[37] Egypt, which a year earlier had helped to broker agreement between the U.S. and the non-aligned countries, noted its willingness "to work . . . under the auspices of the Amendment Conference now and to continue to do so until [a CTB has been achieved]."[38] Mauritius said that if the Conference did not set up a permanent working group it should "be postponed to meet again next year. It could then decide, in the light of the proceedings of the [CD], whether the 'working group' should then be set up or whether this Amendment Conference should then take any other decision."[39] Venezuela, speaking through the Deputy Foreign Minister sent to New York for the occasion, also advocated a recess of a year or two, during which a smaller group could continue discussions and report to the General Assembly.[40] The Philippine government suggested that a working group be designated to study "control, institutional mechanisms and legal aspects" of a Treaty and that the Conference should resume "at the latest by June, 1992."[41]

The First Non-Aligned Caucus

A further element of the non-aligned countries' strategy was to use a formal caucus to develop a position behind which most, if not all member countries could unite. The Western countries did not have a formal caucus (one whose meetings were announced by the Secretary-General of the Conference), but the non-aligned group of countries was so large that its members could meet together only by scheduling time for such an event in a United Nations conference room and making it a formal event.

Because it had hosted the most recent summit of non-aligned heads of state, Yugoslavia chaired the caucus. But Yugoslavia was torn by ethnic divisions and many predicted its imminent collapse as a national state; in addition, its economy, like that of most countries in 1991, was fragile. Accordingly, it was not in a position to take as strong a leadership role among the non-aligned group as it had in the years leading up to the

Conference. Aware of these difficulties, Marin prepared to guide Darko Silovic, the new Yugoslavian ambassador to the United Nations, through the steps that he would have to follow to generate a position for the non-aligned group. Silovic was in an unusually delicate position. As a member of the group of six countries that had initiated the Conference call, Yugoslavia would be expected to play a leading role on behalf of the non-aligned, and its chairmanship of the non-aligned group enhanced its status even further. But the shift in voting patterns of the formerly socialist countries left Yugoslavia as perhaps the only non-Communist country in Europe that was not conforming its positions on procedural issues to those favored by most NATO countries.[42]

When the non-aligned caucus met the day after the opening session, Marin distributed a list of four principles on which he hoped the non-aligned delegates could agree. The first of them was that the issues were sufficiently complicated as to require further discussion. Second, the Conference should be reconvened in 1992 or 1993 to ensure "adequate follow-up," and an "intersessional working group" should meanwhile discuss the issues. Third, the CD should be given a negotiating mandate, to complement the work of the Conference. Finally, "as far as possible," voting should be avoided.[43]

The response in the caucus to the Mexican proposals was cool. It was clear that the United States would not agree to them, so despite Marin's language about avoiding votes if possible, the only way that his ideas could be put into force would be to outvote the Western bloc. A few delegations stated their willingness to vote if need be, but the "mood" of the caucus was to work something out with the West rather than to vote on a recess.[44] Marin had foreseen this division and had advised Silovic to say, at the end of the caucus, that if there were no objection, he took the sense of the meeting to be that the chair of the caucus was authorized to consult with individual caucus members and to firm up a proposed caucus position. But whether through oversight or a deliberate decision, Silovic failed to make the statement, and the meeting ended with no clear outcome.[45] Faced with this default, Marin began to fill the void, working the halls to consult with non-aligned participants. And as the Western delegates spread around the floor of the Conference urging delegates to vote to end it, several delegations reacted by becoming more committed to confrontation, if confrontation were required to make something come out of the Conference process. Nevertheless, Marin found it "hard to find something that will satisfy the six [originators] and also not cause many of the non-aligned to abstain."[46]

Meanwhile, Grimsson activated PGA's parliamentary network to light a fire under the Yugoslavian delegation. One of PGA's officers was Miran Mejak, a member of the Yugoslav parliament. In December, he had posed a parliamentary question to his government, inquiring what stance it would take in the Conference. The answer had followed the line taken by many Western European countries: "our delegation will advocate . . . establishment of an ad hoc committee at the [CD] with an adequate mandate."[47] Grimsson concluded that Silovic's failure to catalyze the non-aligned might have resulted from weak instructions from Belgrade. At his suggestion, Mejak immediately went to see senior officials in his capital. After some discussion, they promised to send Silovic a cable that same day, instructing him "to endeavor that the amendment process not be allowed to come to an end on January 18, and that this date be postponed or that a second session be held in the near future."[48]

The American Hard Line

Ironically, Marin and his supporters were given a major boost when the American delegate made her country's speech on the Conference's fourth day. Even before this event, the United States had signalled that it would be uncompromising on procedural issues. The Conference was managed, as was traditional, by a "General Committee" consisting of the President, the Chair of the Credentials Committee, and the ten vice-presidents, two from each of five traditional voting blocs. The commonality of views on test ban issues among the countries of Asia, Africa, and Latin America, coupled with Alatas' chairmanship of the General Committee, guaranteed their control of the General Committee.[49] Nevertheless, at the General Committee's first meeting, the Netherlands and New Zealand, who were presumed to be acting at the behest of Britain and the United States, raised two issues about the "informal meeting" that had been scheduled at which non-governmental organizations would address the Conference. Neither of these issues had been addressed by the Meeting in June. First, the Western countries wanted to establish that the United Nations would not issue a press release summarizing their testimony, as it did with respect to delegates' plenary statements. Second, they wanted the notice of the informal meeting to be printed on the back page of the United Nations' daily Journal, under "Announcements," rather than on the front page, under "Other Meetings." A substantial argument ensued, which Alatas finally ended by giving the informal meeting top billing but ruling out a press release. Nevertheless, this wrangle delayed a session of the Conference by 45 minutes and showed all of the delegates that no procedural issue was so trivial as to make the Western countries work with the others in an easy-going way.

The American delegate's speech, though not unexpected, was a much more significant blow to the idea that compromise was possible. Ms. Hoinkes probably had no choice, given the policy statements that Washington had issued for a decade, but to reiterate the American hard line. Strung together succinctly, however, the various elements of the United States' test ban refrain seemed like a blast of icy water directed at many delegates' hopes for some sort of consensus.

Ms. Hoinkes began by reminding the delegates that the United States "does not support negotiation of a comprehensive test ban at the present time," and that "so long as nuclear weapons continue to play a critical role in our national security, we must have a sensible testing program." Even if the United States did favor a CTB, it would not want to amend the PTBT because that would "seriously jeopardize the continued viability of the existing treaty regime." Therefore "the United States will not participate in, or provide any financial support to, any continuation of this conference in any manner beyond the scheduled—and agreed—two week session [and urges other parties to not to support continuation]." As for the other negotiating fora, the United States would be willing to re-establish a committee of the Conference on Disarmament "on the same non-negotiating basis" as last year and, after "a period of time," to "propose to the Soviet Union negotiations on possible further steps in the area of nuclear testing." In saying that the United States remains committed to the step-by-step approach, however, "I do not want to create any misunderstanding. We have not identified any further limitations on nuclear weapon tests, beyond those now contained in the [150-kt Threshold Treaty] that would be in our national security interest." Finally, as to the Conference itself, amending the PTBT was a poor idea because consideration of test ban issues "is a serious undertaking that should be undertaken in a serious manner. It should not become the subject of political gamesmanship. . . ."[50]

Tovish was delighted with the speech, and particularly with Hoinkes' implication that the work for which nearly a hundred ambassadors had assembled was not "serious;" he believed that her words would radicalize the fence-sitters among the non-aligned, giving them no basis on which to hope for any compromise with the United States.[51] Nevertheless, the first whiff of compromise was already in the air. Just before Hoinkes had spoken, the Ambassador from New Zealand had hosted a lunch with Jayasinghe, the ambassadors from Britain, Canada and Nigeria, and, though she had no diplomatic status, Frances Wilde, a member of the New Zealand parliament who was an officer of PGA. At the lunch, he'd floated the idea of a consensus decision to authorize Alatas, after consultation among parties, to reconvene the Conference in his discretion.[52]

While Tovish was pleased that the West had felt sufficient pressure to initiate discussion about compromise, he was ambivalent about New Zealand's specific proposal. Leaving everything to Alatas' discretion guaranteed nothing, and Indonesia could come under pressure from the United States to abstain from renewing the Conference. On the other hand, Alatas would probably feel accountable to all of the parties, and particularly to his co-initiators among the group of six. The leaders of the activist organizations, particularly Eric Fersht of Greenpeace and William Monning of the International Physicians, believed that a consensus to reconvene the Conference, but without any specific time frame, would be disastrous; it would make all of the diplomats happy, but it would leave the peace organizations without any target date around which to organize their public relations and lobbying activities, and they would be unable to get governments to focus on an event that had no definite schedule.[53] Maxime Faille, who had left the United Nations secretariat during the fall to rejoin to PGA staff, believed that the New Zealand proposal could be the basis for an agreement, if Alatas' discretion were confined. Within PGA, he advanced the idea of having the Conference's General Committee meet by a fixed date to decide whether to recommend to Alatas that the Conference be reconvened. Since the non-aligned had a majority on the General Committee, this procedure would make it very likely that the Conference would meet again before the NPT came up for renewal in 1995.[54]

Delegate and Critics

Late on the Friday afternoon of the first week—at the mid-point of the Conference—critics of American test ban policy had the opportunity to confront Ms. Hoinkes. Many of them had come from distant states to observe the Conference, and they wanted to have the opportunity to speak directly to a government official. At first, Ms. Hoinkes insisted on meeting with a small representative group, but when Carolyn Cottom, the CTB Coalition's director, insisted that she see everyone, she agreed, although, not aware of how many people were involved, she insisted that the meeting take place in the Delegates' Lounge at the United Nations, rather than in a conference room.

The Delegates' Lounge is a large room, thickly carpeted and nicely furnished; the diplomatic conversations there are usually conducted in hushed tones. What happened that afternoon must have been unprecedented in United Nations history. As Ms. Hoinkes seated herself on a sofa, seventy people of all ages, races, accents and modes of dress arrayed themselves in chairs and on the floor around her. For an hour, she listened patiently to dozens of her critics' short statements, many deeply emotional, many focused on issues that were rarely if ever addressed in the federal inter-agency debates. Some of the speakers pleaded, some shouted, some wept; few of them had ever had the opportunity to address the United States government about a cause on which they had worked for decades.

A Western Shoshone leader spoke first. "You made a Treaty with my people," he told her. "But now you continue to take my land and to poison

my water." Tears streamed down the face of the woman who followed him:
"I lost a brother to radiation from the atmospheric tests of the 1950's and
my father is dying of cancer now," she cried. "My grandchildren are now
being exposed because underground tests still vent some radioactivity. I
need to know when we can expect relief. Will my great grandchildren be
safe? My great-great grandchildren?"

"What struck me about your speech [to the delegates] was its complete
absence of hope," another activist complained. "You couldn't even identify
any limitations on testing that would be acceptable to the government." A
woman shouted, "You squander my money while 10,000 people in my city
live on the street. I'm ashamed of how you spoke at the United Nations
representing me," and another asked, "I wonder why you're smiling as you
hear this. We're serious and we're crying. Don't you take us seriously?"

Hoinkes responded in a professional manner, too cool in temperament
for the emotionally charged crowd, but making the best case she could, to
this audience, to justify her government's policies. "Perhaps one of the
reasons why I'm smiling is that I have a lot in common with what you are
working for. [We are all trying to prevent nuclear proliferation but] the
question is whether this particular measure [a CTB] is at the top of our list
of priorities . . . and there we have some differences. . . . We don't think
that the link to testing is as keen as it seemed when we entered into the
NPT."

Her response did not and could not have satisfied her critics. "You've
presented your case well," one told her. "But it insults our intelligence to
say that we have to proceed bilaterally with the Soviets when we all know
that the Soviets are willing to stop testing if we do so." The last person to
speak told her, "The rest of the world sees these issues [CTB and prolifer-
ation] as connected. It's you who are living in isolation."

Politics at the Mid-Point

While Ms. Hoinkes was meeting the activists, the General Committee
was meeting to try to develop some structure for the second week of the
Conference, including the all-important question of how the Conference
would deal with the question of its own continued existence. Earlier in the
day, the Japanese delegate had held a lunch to which he had invited the
delegates from Egypt, Venezuela, and the Philippines. Japan was solidly in
the Western camp, Venezuela and the Philippines had emerged as leaders
of the group who wanted the Conference continued, and the Egyptian
delegation had helped to broker the deal, a year earlier, through which the
West and the non-aligned had agreed on a date and place for the Conference.
Over lunch, the Venezuelan Deputy Foreign Minister had suggested a new
compromise: Alatas would meet with a working group of delegates during

the United Nations session in the fall (thereby avoiding the expense of a special meeting), and this group would report to the full Conference, which would be reconvened during 1992. "Or at the latest in 1993," the Egyptian delegate added.[55]

But whatever the substance of a compromise, there remained the problem of either obtaining Western consent or forcing a vote. On this procedural question, progress could be measured in millimeters at best. The most outspoken non-aligned delegates had begun to prepare for a vote, which, after Hoinkes' speech, seemed more and more likely. They had prepared two resolutions. Under the first, the Conference would decide to hold a second session "no later than June, 1992." Under the second, an intersessional working group of 15 states would be established, which would "meet in New York . . . adopt its own procedures . . . and report . . . to the next session of the Conference." Financing would be shared according to the same formula that was applied to the Conference, and the United Nations secretariat would be requested to provide facilities for both the working group and the reconvened Conference.[56]

Some of the non-aligned delegates had a draft of this resolution in their pockets during the meeting of the General Committee, but circulating it proved premature. In the meeting, the Dutch delegate argued for giving maximum flexibility to Alatas with respect to resolving how the meeting would end. Consistent with his role as President of the Conference, Alatas himself advocated finding a consensus and avoiding a vote. But the delegate from Tanzania noted that consensus might not be possible. "We all desire consensus," he said, "but the Treaty provides for voting if necessary. Voting is an open option." The delegate from the Philippines added, "We agree. When a country passes national legislation, we vote on it rather than seek a hopeless consensus."

Despite the militancy of the most determined non-aligned countries, Tovish concluded that even a fairly weak consensus compromise that would keep the Western countries involved in the process would be better than an outcome in which, outvoted, they might unilaterally abandon the process, leaving the non-aligned with an empty shell. Furthermore, he doubted that most of the non-aligned would press for a vote if any plausible compromise were possible. At a Sunday morning strategy meeting before the second week of the session, the PGA staff concluded that they could, if necessary, recommend to non-aligned delegates that they agree to a consensus decision to allow Alatas to reconvene the Conference at his discretion, provided that the General Committee would work on test ban issues in the interim and report periodically to the parties. If the stalemate in the CD continued and Alatas did not reconvene the Conference after several years, they reasoned, they could rekindle the issue by instigating resolutions in the United Nations and in parliaments across the globe, urging that the Conference hold another session.

But Tovish and his PGA colleagues also believed that even this weak a compromise was unlikely, because they calculated that Hoinkes had inflexible instructions to refuse to allow the Conference any further life. Furthermore, with a Gulf war imminent, it was doubtful that she could get her instructions changed on short notice by an interagency committee in Washington, even if she requested it. On the other hand, they fretted that if President Bush actually launched a war against Iraq during the next few days, the United States would have a free hand to close down the Conference permanently. They reasoned that virtually no countries would vote against the U.S. while its soldiers were dying in the Middle East to enforce the United Nations' demand that Iraq withdraw from Kuwait.[57] Nevertheless, some of the non-aligned delegates drew the opposite conclusion: that few governments would be pleased that the United States had moved so quickly toward a military attack on Iraq, and they might show their displeasure in many small ways, such as by continuing the Amendment Conference over U.S. objections.[58]

Tovish began the second week of the conference working on two alternative tracks, both of which assumed that no war would begin before the week ended. He kept abreast, as best he could, of all compromises that had been floated, and who supported them. At the same time, on the assumption that a vote on continuation would eventually occur, he worked to line up as large a bloc as possible to outvote the West. He arranged for follow-up calls to the countries that had not yet appeared at the Conference, wrote to the Yugoslavian delegation to tell it that PGA knew that the delegation had instructions to try for a second session, and, with the concurrence of the Mexican delegation, encouraged the Venezuelan deputy foreign minister to call a meeting of the 41 Conference requestors if Silovic did not bring the entire group of non-aligned countries together in the near future.[59]

The Paradox of Time

On the first morning of the second week, the Conference ran out of steam. It had scheduled a day and a half of meetings of the "Committee of the Whole," a format in which essentially the same group of people would continue to read prepared statements and would continue to avoid any public colloquy or other dialogue, but in which they would at least not have to distribute scores of copies to each other. In principle, the agenda for the Committee of the Whole was to discuss the proposed amendment and the verification protocol that the six originators had also circulated.[60] In fact, after only six delegations had spoken (for a total of a little more than an hour) in the Committee of the Whole, Alatas noted that no other delegations were prepared to speak, and the Committee agreed to cancel its proceedings for the rest of the day. The irony was patent: the non-aligned countries claimed that the Conference had to be continued in existence because it did not have enough time, in a two-week session, in which to do its work, but the calendar for the two week period was far from full, and the Conference had not established even one small working group for interactive conversations about the CTB amendment, the verification arrangements, or any other topic. In reality, of course, the irony was more apparent than real, because without United States cooperation, working groups could not have done meaningful work, and the non-aligned needed more Conference time not for immediate negotiations, but to keep the pressure up.

Meanwhile, out of sight, the delegates continued to slog through their real work of deciding on the future of the institution. At a caucus of Western countries, European delegations pressed the United States delegation to ascertain whether it would accept any compromise that kept the Conference alive. Ms. Hoinkes eventually conceded that the United States wanted the Conference to end with a statement by Alatas to which everyone could agree, rather than with a vote, and that the United States might be willing to have him say that the work begun by the Conference would continue, allowing each delegation to interpret such a phrase as it wished. Thus, the question of whether the Amendment Conference could be reconvened would be left completely ambiguous, with some countries believing that Alatas could call it together again and others concluding that it had ended, with its "work" to be transferred to the CD. But the United States delegation asked that the Western group not reveal even that slight hint of flexibility with as much as four days remaining in the life of the Conference, lest the non-aligned group pocket it and demand more.[61]

Even as the Western group met, the Yugoslavian log-jam broke, and a caucus of the non-aligned countries was scheduled for the following afternoon.[62] By this time, the deadline for Iraqi withdrawal from Kuwait was little more than 24 hours away, and the final effort for a negotiated settlement—the visit by the United Nations Secretary-General to Iraq's President Saddam Hussein—had failed.[63] Tovish was frantically working to develop a strategy for salvaging the Conference in the event of war. Finally, he hit upon one, and after testing it out on a few key non-aligned delegations, he approached an Indonesian delegate—a close associate of President Alatas—at the end of the meeting of the Committee of the Whole. He suggested that if war were to occur, Alatas could announce to the delegates that useful work being impossible under the circumstances, the Conference should be suspended and reconvened at the "earliest practicable time." This resolution, he reasoned, would recognize the real inability of delegates to focus on the CTB question during the opening days of a major war, keep the Conference alive as a juridical entity, make it relatively more likely (compared to several other scenarios) that the Conference would eventually reconvene (because there would have been no finely tuned compromise regarding the end of the session), and might even be welcomed by the United States delegation because it would "put it out of its misery."[64] Alatas could not himself suspend the Conference, but he could propose suspension to the delegates. His proposal might easily carry without a call for a record vote. Tovish was aware of a potentially serious flaw in his plan—that if the Conference recessed until the call of its President, without establishing a specific date—its continuation might depend not only on Indonesia's willingness to call a second meeting, but also on Alatas' personal status. For example, if he left the foreign ministry or the Indonesian government, he would almost certainly lack the power to call a meeting, but at the same time, his successor might also lack the power because it had been vested in him personally. Nevertheless, this plan was the best one that Tovish could devise for a war setting.[65]

On-Stage and Off-Stage

The following day, delegates acted out an increasingly strange drama. The imminence of war preoccupied the delegates privately; a few yards from where they met, the United Nations Security Council was making a final attempt to persuade Iraq to withdraw its troops, and outside the building, thousands of demonstrators were chanting to protest the American drive to war. But no hint of the crisis infiltrated the Conference proceedings; on the floor, delegates continued to read formal statements about the work that still needed to be done to develop an effective verification system, or the role that the CD should play.[66]

To the extent that concern about war left the delegates with residual energy for their work, their real focus remained the question of the Conference's own future, and a few views on this question were expressed (as additional markers) in the floor statements, though they consumed only a small fraction of the approximately two hours of Conference time. The Philippine delegation reiterated its proposal for a reconvened Conference in 1992 or 1993, and it responded to Western claims that the non-aligned were being too "confrontational" by characterizing as confrontational the continued testing of nuclear weapons, despite the pleas of numerous General Assembly resolutions.[67] Nigeria pointed out that "there is absolutely nothing, and I repeat nothing, that this Conference can do to make the CD adopt a negotiating mandate for its work," and proposed "that this Conference agrees to suspend further action between now and the end of 1993 . . . to give the CD enough opportunity to conclude the elaboration of a

CTB [Treaty, but reconvene then, if necessary, for] full consideration of the amendment proposal."[68] The Peruvian delegate also urged that the Conference have a second session.[69] With the non-aligned caucus just hours away, one of the purpose of these statements was to impress Silovic with the breadth and depth of non-aligned support for continuing the Conference.[70]

Meanwhile, the six originating countries, consulting with other non-aligned countries one by one, had obtained from many of them an agreement that if a reasonable compromise with the West could not be achieved, the non-aligned would vote for the resolutions that their leading delegations had circulated.[71] They hoped that in its afternoon caucus, the non-aligned group would ratify this strategy, although some non-aligned delegates were less inclined than the six originators to maintain a working group between sessions. For their part, PGA and Greenpeace staff members spent the morning talking to as many non-aligned delegates as possible, and they urged them to speak up at the non-aligned caucus in favor of outvoting the West rather than accepting a compromise that did not clearly keep the Conference in being.[72]

The United States also worked the halls, asking its potential supporters for its support. It let them know that it would accept any final statement by Alatas (as opposed to the Conference), provided that it fairly characterized the various views of groups of delegations. The U.S. could also accept, if necessary, a statement by Alatas that he planned to continue to consult with delegates, but it could not accept a statement in which he said that he planned to reconvene the Conference. In the view of the United States, he lacked the power to do so.[73]

In fact, the delegation of the United States held the even stronger view, though neither it nor any other delegation surfaced the issue, that not even the Conference could decide to continue itself, except by unanimous consent which the U.S., among others, would deny. For this view of the limited power of the majority, the United States delegation relied (in its internal analysis) on precisely the rule of procedure that it had fought for, and that the Mexican delegation had so worried about, at the Meeting in June: that "decisions adopted by consensus may not be reconsidered unless the Conference reaches a consensus on such reconsideration."[74] Perhaps aware that it was on weak ground as a result of the uncontested Mexican statement to the effect that the rule applied only to decisions "adopted during [the] Conference,"[75] the United States delegation also relied on the fact that the Conference had decided, on its opening day (and therefore "during" the Conference), to adopt an agenda that included, as one item, "Closure of the Conference."[76] But the United States delegation gave no indication that it intended to assert or rely upon its reading of these rules (as opposed to its threat to boycott further proceedings) in order to derail a vote to continue the meeting.[77]

The Second Non-Aligned Caucus

The second non-aligned caucus followed the track that the six originating parties had hoped it would. Perhaps because he'd received the cable from Belgrade that Tovish had stimulated through Mejak, Silovic himself laid out the position of the six originators.[78] Prompted by Silovic's initiative, behind the scenes encouragement from a few delegates, and suggestions from PGA and Greenpeace, countries other than the other five originators did the rest of the talking. The Pakistani delegate said that while every delegation hoped for compromise, the Conference would not fulfill any useful purpose if it did not either amend the PTBT or remain in existence to try again in better times. Nothing less than a definite date for continuation of the Conference would be acceptable. The Nigerian representative reminded the non-aligned nations that the origin of the non-aligned movement had been integrally connected with the test ban issue and said that they had to stand up for their core principle of ending nuclear tests. Bangladesh, the Philippines, and Tanzania were equally firm, Tanzania reminding delegates once again that it might be necessary to vote because the West might refuse to consent to continuation.

Silovic continued to play his part. At the end of the meeting, he said that in the absence of objection, it was his understanding that with a small delegation including Pakistan and Mexico, he would tell Alatas that the non-aligned group favored the two resolutions that the six originators had been circulating and would urge Alatas to try to obtain the consent of the Western countries to their substance.[79]

Barring the intervention of war, Tovish expected that Alatas would then present the non-aligned proposals to the Western group, which would reject them. Alatas would next spend about a day trying to ascertain whether the Western countries had any flexibility to agree to a continued conference, an unlikely possibility because the privately whispered United States position had moved only very slightly, from unwillingness to allow Alatas to reconvene the Conference to a willingness to let him do so but only with the consent, at that time, of all parties. Tovish would have been happy to encourage the non-aligned to jettison their second resolution (for a continuing working group) in order to get Western consent to a 1993 meeting, but he doubted that the West would so agree. He believed that the attempt to negotiate a compromise would continue inconclusively until the last possible minute (the beginning of the final scheduled meeting of the Conference, on Friday, January 18, at 3 PM), and that the real moment of truth would arrive only if and when Alatas notified delegates of a change of room, from Conference Room 4, in which they usually met, to one of the rooms equipped with electronic voting machinery. Only then would the Western countries go as far as they could to reach agreement. If their offer was still not sufficient, the Conference would vote.[80]

The President's Draft
and the Non-Aligned Response

The next day, PGA scored an important breakthrough. Five years earlier, at the urging of Ole Esperson, a PGA parliamentarian, the Danish parliament had passed a resolution supporting the idea of an amendment conference.[81] Now, at Tovish's urging, Esperson reminded the Danish Foreign Minister, on the floor of the parliament, of Denmark's support for the Conference and asked whether Denmark would vote for its continuation even if the United States opposed it. Esperson did not relent until the Foreign Minister pledged that Denmark would do so. PGA quickly spread word of this commitment to delegations from all over the world, making it very difficult for the Danish delegation to the Amendment Conference to try, even if it were inclined to do so, to have this new policy reversed.[82] Denmark's determination to vote with the non-aligned against its NATO ally put instant pressure on its neighbors Sweden and Norway.

That afternoon, Alatas held separate meetings with the six originators, the Western group, and the larger bloc of non-aligned countries. In each meeting, he distributed a "non-paper" that he had written, reflecting his own ideas for ending the Conference. He suggested that by consensus, the Conference adopt a declaration stating that because "further work needed to be undertaken," Alatas should "conduct consultations with a view to achieving progress [on verification and possible sanctions] and resuming the work of the Conference at an appropriate time." Under the President's draft, no date would be specified, and no interim working groups would be established.[83]

On hearing that the Western countries objected even to what it regarded as Alatas' weak proposal, the delegation of the Philippines asked Mexico to introduce the non-aligned position as a formal resolution. The Philippine ambassador was keenly aware that the Rules of the Conference provided that unless otherwise agreed, the Conference could not vote on a proposal unless it had been circulated in six languages 24 hours before the vote.[84] Only two days remained, at this point, before the Conference was scheduled to hold its final meeting.[85] Marin consulted Alatas about introducing the draft, but Alatas put him off, noting that the non-aligned draft was, in effect, a substitute for a paragraph in his own draft, which was still a "non-paper," not yet ripe for introduction.[86]

Later in the afternoon, Alatas convened a meeting of about 25 delegations representing all major groups at the Conference, to discuss his proposal. None of the groups of delegates was delighted with the President's formulation, but the non-aligned were more disappointed than the West. Ms. Hoinkes said that the United States could live with parts of his draft if it were expressed as a Presidential declaration, but could not accept it as a statement of the Conference to which the United States would have to agree, because it could not consent to resumption of the Conference even without a specified date. The non-aligned group countered with an alternate section for a declaration by the Conference, one that was only slightly watered down from the resolutions that they had earlier circulated. Under their proposal, the delegates would agree "to reconvene the Conference no later than September, 1993 and to establish an intersessional working group, composed of fifteen to twenty countries, in order to continue the consideration of verification of compliance of a CTBT. The working group will submit a report to the Conference at its reconvened session."[87] The Mexican delegation tried on the role of broker; it circulated a paragraph on behalf of the originators (but for the moment, without Yugoslavia, which had again gotten cold feet) and the Philippines. This draft used some of Alatas' language but added to it all of the key phrases from the non-aligned draft.[88]

Once again, the Conference was at an impasse on the only real issue to be negotiated. Now there were three proposals, and although the President was somewhere between the other two, neither of the major blocs seemed ready to accept his proffered compromise. At 6:30 in the evening, immediately after the meeting with Alatas ended, the non-aligned bloc met again to consider strategy. They got only as far as reporting, to the non-aligned delegates who had not attended the meeting with the President, what Alatas had proposed. Half an hour into the meeting, a delegate entered and whispered something to Silovic, who immediately reported that the armed forces of the United States had begun to drop bombs on Iraq. The meeting ended at once; the delegates, like everyone else, were eager to watch television reports from the war front. As Tovish had anticipated, the advent of combat quickly changed the dynamics of the Conference. Within an hour, Alatas had notified key delegations by telephone that in view of the impossibility of continuing to work under the circumstances, he was considering proposing that the Conference suspend its work immediately and reconvene in September, during the annual meeting of the General Assembly.[89]

War

The next morning, as the United States Defense Department provided its initial reports on its first attacks on Iraq, Alatas convened the General Committee. He let it be known that as the Foreign Minister of a Moslem country, he wanted to return home as soon as possible. Following up his telephone calls, he proposed suspending the Conference and holding "consultations" at the General Assembly to decide (as one delegate recalled his words) "what would happen next." Before the non-aligned could object to this vague formulation, two of the Western representatives—Finland and the Netherlands—objected, saying that work should continue for the one remaining day of the Conference. Their view was consistent with that of the United States; Ms. Hoinkes was at that very moment telling American observers of the Conference that, "our minds are to some degree somewhere else but the most effective way of dealing with this subject [the Conference] is to let it run its course. [Acceptance of a Presidential proposal to suspend the Conference until a later date] would be quite unwise."[90] But members of the six originators didn't like the President's formulation, either; they were willing to interrupt their work, but they wanted a real commitment that the process wouldn't fade out and be put to rest in September. The Conference was, in the opinion of a member of the Philippine delegation who credited Imelda Marcos with the phrase, in a state of "suspended animosity."

At PGA, Tovish believed that Alatas' concept of leaving it to himself to reconvene the Conference after appropriate consultations wasn't so bad, and that although Marin should be the one to make the judgment call, the non-aligned should probably accept it.[91] One of his allies explained that the non-aligned would be in a stronger position to bargain at the General Assembly than at the Conference. Several non-aligned countries would send much higher-level diplomats to the General Assembly, who would be more willing to decide to vote against the United States. In addition, CTB advocates would have two more of the CD's fruitless semi-annual sessions on the record. In addition, a non-aligned delegate observed that by September, the United States might have an army of occupation in Iraq, an eventuality that might increase the solidarity of third world countries.

The clock now approached the point at which only a little more than 24 hours remained before the final meeting of the Conference. If the six originators didn't file a formal proposal for continuation of the Conference, the Western countries might later complain that they hadn't been given adequate notice as required by the Rules. Still hoping for a negotiated compromise, but believing that they had little choice but to protect the vote that might become necessary, the six, now joined by the Philippines, filed a "draft decision," using the language that they had drafted the previous day.[92]

Two hours later, the President convened the Conference in secret session. The non-aligned proposal was distributed as the delegates assembled, but four other texts were also being passed around within political groupings on the floor.[93] Of the other documents, the most important was a "non-paper" distributed by Australia and New Zealand, consisting of a proposed consensus draft. This draft, however, merely reiterated the Western position that the Conference should be terminated. The most committed delegates within the non-aligned group were pleased by the proliferation of drafts; it signified the collapse of consensus and the greater likelihood of a vote. Furthermore, the non-aligned group was the only one that had filed with the Secretariat, so theirs was the only one distributed officially, on letterhead, with an official document number. This gave it both a psychological and a legal legitimacy: if the Conference did not reach a consensus compromise, this would be the text on which a vote would be taken.[94]

In what turned out to be only a brief public session, the President reviewed his attempts to reach a compromise through consultation. He then promised to continue, through further meetings during the evening and the next morning, to press for agreement. But, he cautioned—and this was the first time he'd said it in a meeting open to all delegates—if agreement could not be reached, it might be necessary to vote the next afternoon.

Although some delegates may have seen the meeting as a rather perfunctory Presidential report, a member of the non-aligned leadership thought it extremely significant, because in the final days of the session, the key battle had become a struggle for the loyalty of Alatas. He'd been very active in his attempts to secure consensus, but beyond that, he'd kept his views to himself since his opening speech on the desirability of a test ban. Despite being Foreign Minister of one of the co-sponsors of the non-aligned resolution, he'd never spoken a word to other delegates in support of the non-aligned goal of continuing the Conference, even in private.[95] His aides had been equally reticent. Where did he stand on this question? Some non-aligned delegates read his silence as neutrality. Others thought that he was secretly on their side but could not reveal that fact for fear of being accused by the West of being biased. Still others thought that he actually preferred any consensus arrangement to a divided vote for continuation, because he would get more credit, and seem more the statesman, if he reconciled the seemingly unreconcilable parties.

The non-aligned group continued, in the absence of a sign of approval from Alatas for a strategy of voting, to be divided. Even within the leadership group, some worried that winning a vote over a solid bloc of Western "nays" would be pyrrhic because Western countries would then be committed against the process and might even join a U.S.-led boycott. Indeed, over a lunch attended that day by Ms. Hoinkes, several other Western delegates, and several non-aligned delegates, a Western member had asked rhetorically, "What do you really want? You can get a piece of paper but you'll drive us all away from the Conference and spoil the atmosphere at the CD. Or you can agree to a more moderate formulation that we can all live with and we'll argue about all this some other day."[96]

Other non-aligned delegations thought that despite this private bravado, a Western boycott was unlikely, but these delegations simply did not want to take a stand on the record against the United States, particularly on the first or second day of a war. As a result, the Mexican delegation feared that although they would win a vote if they pressed for one, some non-aligned countries would resent them for making them go on the record against the United States, and this consideration gave it pause against pressing for confrontation, particularly after it had taken its lumps in the Western press following the NPT Review Conference.[97]

Alatas' performance in the short closed meeting therefore rallied some members in the non-aligned leadership group. Not only had Alatas mentioned the possibility of voting, but "he went through a song and dance about how hard he'd tried to forge a compromise [which I read as the beginning of the process of saying aloud that voting was legitimate]."[98] Not only that, but minutes after the meeting ended, Tovish learned from the UN Secretariat that Alatas had scheduled the following afternoon's final meeting for the General Assembly Hall, a room fully equipped for electronic voting.[99]

Immediately after the session, the delegates from Yugoslavia and Sri Lanka accepted an invitation from the Indonesian delegate (an offer probably extended at Alatas' initiative) to meet with the Western group to discuss which elements from among the various drafts "would be acceptable to a wide spectrum" of countries.[100] The delegates from these three countries did not tell their colleagues among the non-aligned co-sponsors before they attended the meeting, but for more than an hour, they worked over three of the texts that had been circulating. Although they were not fully satisfied with their product, they agreed to allow members of the Western group to draw up a composite draft which they would present the following day for consideration by the rest of the six.[101]

Right after that meeting, the three non-aligned ambassadors met with Marin and others from among the six, and it became clear that although everyone was willing to examine the composite draft in the morning, it was unlikely to be acceptable to Mexico, the Philippines, and others who had supported the non-aligned draft. At the same time, the British delegate checked with London, which also rejected the composite.[102]

The meeting between the non-aligned members who'd met with the West and the non-aligned delegates who expressed skepticism about their work had just ended when Iraq attacked Tel Aviv and Haifa with Scud missiles.

On the morning of the final day, the compromise surfaced. In their concentration on its text, the delegates blocked out, to the extent possible, the escalating crisis outside their walls. The draft consisted of two parts. First, the delegates would adopt a consensus document through which the parties would agree that "further work needed to be undertaken," and urged the Conference on Disarmament to "resume and increase" its substantive work. The proposed consensus resolution would be coupled with a Presidential statement in which he would declare that "it is understood that I will undertake consultations . . . with an objective of reviewing the progress . . . and of seeking the views of the States Parties, concerning further actions to be undertaken by them."[103] It was not lost on the more determined non-aligned delegates that neither part of the document stated or implied that the Conference would ever meet again; some of them even began to wonder whether by working at length to produce the composite draft the previous evening, the Yugoslavians and others had been trying to signal their increasing distance from the non-aligned group.

The delegates were supposed to meet in a previously scheduled open session, but this formal meeting was delayed for two hours while behind closed doors, Alatas presided over a large informal meeting with leading delegates from all factions. By this time the composite had been criticized by Washington as well as London, and with the non-aligned leadership also opposed, it was clear that it could not be the basis for consensus. The delegate representing Indonesia suggested that the parties make one last effort to compromise, this time not on the basis of the defunct composite, but rather by accepting the draft that Alatas had written two days before. The Western group and the non-aligned leadership agreed that early in the afternoon, each of them would hold one more caucus to see whether they could accept the President's wording.[104]

The Endgame

Nearly two hours after the open meeting was to have begun, a third of the delegates, including virtually all of the key players, were absent; they were still ensconced in the private meeting with Alatas. The rest milled around the floor of the Conference chamber, grumbling about the delay. Greenpeace and PGA officers wandered around, checking attendance so that they could telephone delegations that might be needed for an afternoon vote. All groups were fully focussed on the Conference; the Gulf War, a day and a half old, seemed already to have receded into the background; the United Nations headquarters building, only days earlier the site of emergency meetings, television lights and mass demonstrations, was, except for the knot of activity around the Amendment Conference, nearly silent and deserted.

As delegates entered the Conference room, word spread quickly that Alatas' meeting had not gone well, and that the odds for consensus were rapidly falling; Greenpeace staff members handed delegates copies of the non-aligned resolution, on which the organization had overprinted "VOTE YES." With it, they gave delegates a copy of a press release stating that "it looks likely that a vote will occur today" with only the U.S. and U.K. expected to vote against continuation.[105] The implicit message was that the world was watching what the delegates did, and that their governments would be held to account by their constituents if they scuttled the process.

One of the non-aligned negotiators, taking his seat on the floor, said that he was not merely astonished, but "shocked" by what seemed to be a breakdown of the consultation process.[106] Australia circulated an unsigned "draft final declaration" incorporating the composite that had just been trashed; many delegates joked aloud about the anonymous nature of this document (which implied, by being unsigned, that its authors didn't really know who was willing to support it publicly), and some non-aligned delegates expressed anger that ever since the previous evening, Western delegates had been spreading "false rumors" that the non-aligned group had agreed to it.[107]

Convening what turned out to be a brief session, Alatas said that intensive negotiations were "continuing," but it was apparent to everyone that a vote on the non-aligned resolution was increasingly likely. Greenpeace members rushed to the phones, and PGA staff members to their fax machines; within an hour, the two organizations had alerted the U.N. Missions of thirty absent countries that their votes would be needed in the afternoon.[108]

At 2:30, in the General Assembly hall, U.N. technicians were testing the electronic voting system. For perhaps the first time in history, the names of 117 countries were flashed on the voting screens without the inclusion of France and China, countries that were members of the United Nations but had never signed the PTBT. Spotting Tovish in the corridors, Silovic revealed his astonishment: "You people really have an amazing amount of influence. Twenty-five countries are here because the peace groups called them. When we call them on behalf of the Non-aligned Movement, we can't get them to come to a meeting."[109]

But the meeting hall remained empty for a long time; delegates milled in the hallway while for the insiders in both camps, the last set of secret caucuses began, the Western countries in one room, the sponsors of the non-aligned draft in another. The Western group emerged first, its members looking very somber. They could be overheard asking each other how they would vote on various formulations that might be put before them when the final non-aligned caucus broke. Clearly there was no unanimity.

The caucus of the non-aligned leadership went on much longer, delaying the final plenary by nearly two hours. Within the non-aligned group, the fractures that had been developing throughout the Conference now became more pronounced. Indonesia again suggested accepting Alatas' draft, which, rather than specifying a deadline for resuming the Conference, empowered Alatas to "conduct consultations with a view to achieving progress on [verification and possible sanctions] and resuming the work of the Conference at an appropriate time."[110.] Yugoslavia and Peru were the first to agree to this suggestion, arguing that by so doing, the non-aligned were much more likely to attract Western European votes.[111] Sri Lanka soon followed in arguing for the President's formulation;[112] Jayasinghe was persuaded by his Yugoslavian and Peruvian colleagues, and he also wanted to avoid a threatened statement on the record by the British government to the effect that, like the United States, it was committed to boycotting any future session.[113] The Deputy Foreign Minister from Venezuela didn't speak at all. Marin wanted to hold out for a specific date by which the Conference would resume, but as chair of the group, he felt that he could not insist on having his way over what he regarded as a "veto" by at least two members of his group.[114] Three other factors may also have influenced Marin to agree to the President's language. According to another delegate who was in the room, after some press accounts had singled him out as the spoiler at Geneva, neither he nor any other delegate wanted to be the martyr who pressed for a deadline without the support even of the six originators. Second, with the non-aligned countries divided on strategy, Sweden, Norway, and others close to the Western group would feel considerably less pressure to follow Denmark's lead in voting for continuation. In addition, Marin's instructions from Mexico City had insisted that he show some flexibility, and perhaps to enforce that command, Andres Rozental, the Mexican Deputy Foreign Minister who had made the main plenary statement for Mexico, had told the United States delegate that Marin would be flexible, and she had cleverly let other delegates knew that she'd heard from Rozental about Marin's instructions.[115]

In the end, only the Philippines and Nigeria, which had also co-sponsored the non-aligned resolution, firmly advocated insisting on a deadline for Conference resumption. They argued that since the hard line taken by the U.S. and Britain necessitated a vote in any event, the non-aligned might as well press for a vote on what they really wanted.[116] But deserted by their allies, they finally agreed to go along with the others in a strategic retreat.[117]

The debate between the Yugoslavian and Peruvian delegates, on the one hand, and the Philippine and Nigerian delegates, on the other, did not reflect differing assessments of the likelihood for gaining a last-minute consensus. When they agreed to Alatas' formulation, none of the non-aligned leadership expected that it would bring about consensus, for they all suspected that the United States and perhaps Britain had instructions to refuse to agree to any draft that even implied continuation of the

Conference as an institution. But Yugoslavia and Peru, followed by Indonesia and Sri Lanka, argued that, at the very least, a few Western nations might support them, and others would abstain. Even a handful of Western votes would give new legitimacy to the Conference and make it more likely that it would one day be reconstituted.[118]

Alatas' formulation must have split the difference as finely as possible, for its acceptance by the non-aligned leadership instantly divided its nongovernmental supporters, as the idea of leaving the future of the Conference in Alatas' hands had done when the delegate from New Zealand had first floated it.[119] Tovish welcomed the compromise because he believed that it represented acceptance of the Conference as a continuing international body.[120] Eric Fersht of Greenpeace, with whom Tovish had been working closely for two weeks, thought that the effort had failed. In addition to worrying that the lack of a target date would make political organizing in Europe more difficult, he reasoned that PGA would be hard pressed to get the non-aligned countries even to think about reconvening the Conference before 1993, or to press for a new meeting before the NPT extension conference in the spring of 1995. The phrasing, he believed, would enable the United States and its Western allies to drag out the "consultations" past the critical point in 1995 during which the non-aligned would have the greatest leverage over the depositaries.[121] For an hour as delegates assembled in the General Assembly hall, Tovish and Fersht sat together in the gallery, arguing about whether the new text—now beyond their ability to change—would renew the Conference or bury it.[122]

Alatas brought the Conference to order for the final time. Marin proposed the new non-aligned text as a modification of the non-aligned draft circulated the previous day, and he requested a recorded vote.

Following U.N. custom, Alatas allowed delegates to make statements before voting. Most chose not to do so, but the British ambassador announced his regret that the conference had failed to come to a consensus conclusion, and that "some" had forced the delegates to underline this failure by requiring them to vote. More significantly, the Swedish delegate signalled other moderate Western countries before the vote by saying that although the final text was not in complete congruence with its view, Sweden would support it. Two minutes later, Hungary expressed the view of European countries more sympathetic with the views expressed by the United States. Saying that questions having to do with international security could be decided only with the full consent of the parties involved, Hungary planned to abstain.

The speakers finished; the scoreboard of countries lit up; it was time to vote. Delegates pushed buttons on their desks, lighting markers like traffic lights on the big board: green for yes, amber for abstentions, red for no. The machinery flashed the count. Ninety-five countries had voted, and the

The electronic voting board in the General Assembly hall flashes the result of the vote on the proposal regarding continuation of the conference (U.N. Photo 177212 by Milton Grant).

non-aligned proposal had passed, 74 to 2, with 19 abstentions. Seven members of the Western group had supported it; all but two of the other Western countries had abstained. True to their principle of not intimating any support for the amendment process, Britain and the United States had voted against even this weak statement of support for continuation of the Conference.[123]

After the vote, Alatas permitted the delegates a second opportunity to explain their votes for the record. Three of the statements were noteworthy. The Canadian ambassador explained her abstention by asserting that the non-aligned text inaccurately stated that the parties "agreed" to give Alatas certain continuing instructions whereas, in fact, "there is no such agreement; holding a vote can't create an agreement where there is none."[124]

The Philippine ambassador made a brave attempt to resurrect, under the banner of the decision that had been approved, the arrangements that the non-aligned had given up at the eleventh hour. He told the delegates, on the record, that "we voted 'yes' on the understanding that the consultations that you would conduct would include a working group on verification. Ideally this should take place during the next General Assembly session. Further, my delegation believes that an 'appropriate time' for resuming the work of the Conference, at the very latest should be in September, 1993, two years ahead of the final review of the NPT."[125]

The American delegate, however, laid down an ominous marker pointing in the opposite direction. She said that despite the view of the American government that the Conference was not well conceived, "as depositaries we carried out our responsibilities [to call an Amendment Conference], as we always will, when 1/3 of the parties call for it. That exercise will conclude today, and should the requisite number call again, we'll carry out our duties."[126] The implication, which she did not need to state, was that the United States believed that the Conference lacked the power to perpetuate itself, so that even if Alatas interpreted the decision to permit him to reconvene the Conference and tried to do so, the U.S. would not recognize the validity of his act. It would insist that if any countries wanted a new Amendment Conference, they would again have to assemble 39 or 40 countries in support of a petition to the depositaries, a much more arduous process and one that the United States might more easily prevent. By making this statement on the record, the United States protected its position of principle better than it could have done by objecting to the non-aligned proposal as a non-consensual "reconsideration" in alleged violation of the rules of the Conference. If it had interposed a procedural objection before the vote, Alatas would probably have overruled it formally. By avoiding such a ruling, the U.S. escaped having its legal opinion about the longevity of the Conference undercut by a negative Presidential ruling or a vote of the Conference upholding the President's view.

The endgame had been played out; the final moments had arrived. Keenly aware of the ambiguity of what had been agreed, Alatas closed the meeting by saying that the Conference had highlighted the urgent need for the conclusion of a CTB, and that since the Conference had taken a decision "entrusting certain responsibilities to me" he would "try to fulfill them as best I can." He made no attempt to describe what those responsibilities were, and no one expected that he would.

Notes

1. See Chapter 4, text following note 71.

2. Interview with Kennedy Graham, Secretary-General of Parliamentarians for Global Action, in New York City, Jan. 7, 1990. It might seem unlikely that a government official would want to put his country in a position in which the United States would have an incentive to exert pressure against it, but it should be kept in mind that the United States uses carrots such as foreign aid more often than sticks to achieve its foreign policy objectives. A simpler theory is that Alatas intended to press for a successful conclusion of the amendment process as swiftly

as possible, and he trusted himself to reconvene the Conference if given the power to do so.

3. Telephone interview with Aaron Tovish, Sept. 5, 1991.

4. A/RES/45/50, Dec. 13, 1990.

5. A/45/PV.54, p. 16, Dec. 18, 1990.

6. As the ambassador from Czechoslovakia put it, "We [have now] placed at the forefront of our endeavors considerations that we felt were closer to reality, rather than some desires that had remained unfulfilled for many years." A/45/PV.54, p. 14 (statement of Mr. Nejedly).

7. The pun was usually attributed to Marin-Bosch.

8. "U.S., Soviet Mayors to Meet on Nuclear Test Ban Treaty," News from the United States Conference of Mayors, Jan. 6, 1990 (press release).

9. The public relations expert who dealt with the press on behalf of PGA and other groups opposed to nuclear testing believes that the difference in press coverage between the two events can be explained by the fact that in the first one, celebrities had participated and several of them, including Teri Garr and Martin Sheen, had been arrested. Interview with Trudy Mason in New York City, Jan. 8, 1991.

10. U.S. Comprehensive Test Ban Coalition, January Calendar of New York Events (undated); interview with Trudy Mason in New York City, Jan. 8, 1991.

11. Adam Clymer, "Congress Acts to Authorize War in Gulf," *New York Times* Jan. 13, 1991, p. 1.

12. Interview with Trudy Mason, handling press for PGA, in New York City, Jan. 12, 1991.

13. Jerome Wiesner, "Why Don't We Stop Testing the Bomb," *New York Times* Dec. 23, 1990, p. 11; Paul Warnke, "The Nuclear Siren Song," *Washington Post* Dec. 9, 1990, p. K7; Walter C. Clemens, Jr., "Can a Poet Stop Nuclear Testing?" *Christian Science Monitor,* Dec. 26, 1990; Tom Wicker, "How to Help Hussein," *New York Times* Dec. 26, 1990, p. A31; Mary McGrory, "Bush Shuns Nuclear Test Ban," *Washington Post* Jan. 1, 1991, p. A2; George Bunn, "U.S. Should Agree to Ban Underground Nuclear Testing," *Christian Science Monitor* Dec. 31, 1991, p. 19.

14. "Ending nuclear-weapons creep," *Boston Globe* Dec. 5, 1990 (editorial); "USA should press for test ban treaty," *USA Today* Jan. 7, 1991, p. 10A (editorial).

15. Michael Gordon, "Bomb Tests Not Gone or Forgotten," *New York Times* Jan. 6, 1991, Sec. 4, p. 4; Notes and Comment, *The New Yorker* Jan. 14, 1991, p. 21; Anthony Lewis, "The Nuclear Priority," *New York Times* Jan. 7, 1991, p. A18.

16. Interview with Amb. Miguel Marin-Bosch, in New York City, Jan. 6, 1990.

17. Interviews with a non-governmental activist with knowledge of these events, in New York City, Jan. 10, 1991. Marin may also have been aided by the Mexican Foreign Ministry's awareness that the United States government wanted the free trade agreement at least as much as it did, and by the fact that with a Gulf war and destruction of Middle East oil fields impending, the United States might soon need Mexico's oil. Interview with a United Nations official in New York City, Jan. 7, 1991.

18. Address of Deputy Foreign Minister Andres Rozental, Jan. 8, 1991.

19. Miguel Marin-Bosch, briefing for non-governmental organizations at United Nations headquarters, Jan. 9, 1990.

20. See "No a Ensayos Nucleares," *Excelsior,* Jan. 9, 1991 (editorial); "Pide Mexico en la ONU cese total de ensayos nucleares," *El Universal,* Jan. 9, 1991, p. 1.

21. Statement of Mary Elizabeth Hoinkes, head of the U.S. delegation, Jan. 10, 1991.

22. Interview with Eric Fersht, Greenpeace, Jan. 10, 1991.

23. See, e.g., Margaret Terel, "Waterloo MP can't understand opposition to nuclear test ban," *Kitchener-Waterloo Record* Jan. 10, 1991, p. A3.

24. Miguel Marin-Bosch, briefing for non-governmental organizations at United Nations headquarters, Jan. 9, 1990.

25. PTBT/CONF/3, Rule 31.

26. Lobby Day debriefing session, Jan. 11, 1991.

27. See U.S. Comprehensive Test Ban Coalition, Lobbying Day Target Lists (Jan. 11, 1991).

28. Telephone interview with Aaron Tovish, Jan. 7, 1991.

29. See, e.g., Amb. Maj Britt Theorin of Sweden, Jan. 8, 1991; Amb. Ahmad Kamal of Pakistan, Jan. 9, 1991; Amb. Kamal Kharrazi of Iran, Jan. 9, 1991.

30. Amb. K.-A. Eiliasen of Denmark, Jan. 8, 1991.

31. Amb. Svein Saether of Norway, Jan. 8, 1991.

32. Amb. Mitsuro Donowaki of Japan, Jan. 8, 1991.

33. Amb. Hans Joachim Vergau of Germany, Jan. 8, 1991.

34. Amb. Stanislaw Pawlak of Poland, Jan. 9, 1991.

35. Pres. Ali Alatas, Jan. 7, 1991.

36. Amb. Edmond Jayasinghe, for Sri Lanka, Jan. 8, 1991.

37. Amb. Ronaldo Mota Sardenberg of Brazil, Jan. 8, 1991.

38. Mr. Amre M. Moussa of Egypt, Jan. 8, 1991.

39. Mr. Paul Raymond Beringer of Mauritius, Jan. 10, 1991.

40. Amb. Adolfo R. Taylhardat of Venezuela, Jan. 10, 1991.

41. Amb. Sedfrey A. Ordonez of the Philippines, Jan. 8, 1991.

42. The views of Ireland and Switzerland on procedural issues were not discernable in the early stages of the Conference.

43. Non-paper presented by Mexico to the non-aligned caucus on Jan. 8, 1991 (undated).

44. Interview with Edmond Jayasinghe in New York City, Jan. 8, 1991.

45. Interview with a member of a non-aligned delegation, in New York City, Jan. 10, 1991.

46. Miguel Marin-Bosch, briefing for non-governmental organizations, Jan. 9, 1991.

47. Letter to Aaron Tovish from Miran Mejak, Jan. 8, 1991.

48. Letter to Aaron Tovish from Miran Mejak, Jan. 11, 1991.

49. The General Committee included, in addition to Alatas, Finland as Chair of the Credentials Committee; the Netherlands and New Zealand as the Western members; Bulgaria and Byelorussia and the Eastern members; Tanzania and Senegal from Africa; Sri Lanka and the Philippines from Asia; and Venezuela and Mexico from Latin America—a 7 to 5 split in favor of the non-aligned even if Byelorussia voted with the West.

50. Ms. Mary Elizabeth Hoinkes, Head of U.S. Delegation, for the United States, Jan. 10, 1991.

51. Interview with Aaron Tovish in New York City, Jan. 10, 1991; telephone interview with Aaron Tovish, Sept. 5, 1991.

52. Telephone interview with Aaron Tovish, Jan. 10, 1991.

53. Eric Fersht and William Monning, in strategy meeting of non-governmental organizations, Jan. 10, 1991.

54. Interview with Maxime Faille, in New York City, Jan. 10, 1991.

55. Interview with a member of a non-aligned delegation, Jan. 11, 1991.

56. "Draft language for resolutions at PTBT Amendment Conference," undated but in existence by Jan. 11, 1991.

57. Interview with Aaron Tovish in New York City, Jan. 13, 1991.

58. Interview with a non-aligned delegate, Jan. 15, 1991.

59. Interviews with Aaron Tovish in New York City, Jan. 13–14, 1991.

60. The proposed verification system embodied in the originating countries' draft had been compiled at PGA's request by the Verification Technology Information Centre (VERTIC) of London, an private arms control organization with scientific advisors from several European countries, the United States, and New Zealand. See Verification Technology Information Centre, "The Verification of a Global Comprehensive Test Ban Treaty" (1991). VERTIC's plan, including a global network of seismic stations, satellite imagery, the use of airborne sensors, data exchanges, and challenge on-site inspections, had been translated into proposed treaty text by Professor David A. Koplow of Georgetown University Law Center and then distributed by the originating countries with a letter stating their "hope that it will be the object of careful consideration at the Conference." PTBT/CONF/6, Dec. 12, 1990.

61. Interview with a member of a Western delegation, Jan. 14, 1991.

62. Announcement of the Secretary-General of the Conference in the Committee of the Whole, Jan. 14, 1991.

63. Patrick Tyler, "U.N. Chief's Talks with Iraqis Bring No Sign of Change," *New York Times* Jan. 14, 1991, p. A1.

64. Interview with Aaron Tovish, Jan. 14, 1991.

65. Telephone interview with Aaron Tovish, Jan. 15, 1991.

66. One observer wrote that "One of the curious political phenomena . . . was the relative absence of reference to the Gulf Crisis. . . . This is not the first time that political events in the real world have been blocked out at UN headquarters through a denial process by most delegates. Psychiatrists call this malady 'group dissociative disorder.'" Homer Jack, "Gulf Crisis has Little Impact," *Disarmament Times* Jan. 14, 1991, p. 2. Jack's description of the lack of reference to impending war was accurate, but the cause was political, not psychological. Delegates seemed very aware of the approaching conflict, but speeches for the record in international meetings are official statements approved by officers committees in their governments and rarely encompass the speaker's subjective reactions to events.

67. Amb. Nicasio G. Valderrama, Jan. 15, 1991.

68. Amb. Bariyu A. Adeyemi, Jan. 15, 1991.

69. Amb. Jose Antonio Bellina, Jan. 15, 1991.

70. Interview with a non-aligned delegate, Jan. 15, 1991.

71. See text at note 56. Most of the negotiation among non-aligned delegations was undertaken by their younger members; that is, by officials under 40 years of age. Interview with a younger member of a non-aligned delegation in New York City, Jan. 15, 1991. This practice spared most Ambassadors from much time-consuming and sometimes unproductive work, but there was more to this age breakdown than that. In several cases, the younger members of the delegations were more committed to and idealistic about a CTB than their seniors (for whom this Conference was just another diplomatic event) and therefore had more energy for the task.

72. Interviews with Maxime Faille of PGA and Eric Fersht of Greenpeace, Jan. 15, 1991.

73. Conversation between Ms. Hoinkes and a delegate from Czechoslovakia in the author's presence.

74. PTBT/CONF/3, Rule 29.

75. PTBT/CONF/M/SR.13, p. 6; see Chapter 4, text at note 88.

76. PTBT/CONF/1, p. 18; interview with Ms. Mary Elizabeth Hoinkes in New York City, Jan. 15, 1991. This argument also had a weakness. Although the agenda did include this phrase, prior agenda items included consideration of the proposed amendment and "other matters." By recessing during consideration of either of those agenda items, the delegates would never reach the item denominated as "Closure." Therefore they could argue that a lengthy recess was not a reconsideration of their commitment that the Conference would eventually end.

77. The author did not hear from any delegate any hint of such a strategy; in order not to affect the very event he was reporting on, he did not ask Ms. Hoinkes whether she planned to assert her understanding of the rules.

78. The relevance of Tovish's communication with his Yugoslav parliamentarian can be inferred from the fact that earlier in the day, before the meeting, Silovic himself referred to Mejak, telling Tovish that Mejak had misunderstood the view of the Yugoslavian government when he'd sent Tovish his first letter, note 47. Telephone interview with Aaron Tovish, Jan. 15, 1991. (To stimulate a more active role by Silovic, Tovish had earlier sent copies of both letters from Mejak to the Yugoslavian mission, inquiring as to the real Yugoslavian position. See letter to "Slobodan" from Aaron Tovish, Jan. 13, 1991).

79. Interview with a delegate from a non-aligned country, Jan. 15, 1991; telephone interview with Aaron Tovish, Jan. 15, 1991, after Tovish had been briefed by a different non-aligned delegate.

80. Telephone interview with Aaron Tovish, Jan. 15, 1991.

81. Resolution of 24 April, 1986, reprinted in Parliamentarians for Global Action, A New Road to a Comprehensive Test Ban (New York: Parliamentarians for Global Action, Second Edition, June, 1988), p. 61.

82. Telephone interview with Aaron Tovish, Sept. 5, 1991.

83. "Draft Declaration," a "non-paper" circulated by Alatas, Jan. 16, 1991.

84. PTBT/CONF/3, Rule 24.

85. Interview with Virgilio Reyes of the delegation of the Philippines, Jan. 17, 1991.

86. *Ibid.*

87. Undated, unsigned draft circulated by a group of non-aligned countries, Jan. 16, 1991.

88. Unsigned, undated "draft decision" circulated by six delegations, Jan. 16, 1991.

89. Telephone interview with Aaron Tovish, Jan. 16, 1991. Tovish had heard about Alatas' call from a member of a non-aligned delegation.

90. U.S. Delegate Mary Elizabeth Hoinkes, speaking to representatives of non-governmental organizations at the Conference, Jan. 17, 1991.

91. Interview with Aaron Tovish, Jan. 17, 1991.

92. PTBT/CONF/L.1 (provisional), Jan. 17, 1991. See Appendix D for the pertinent text. Even though they filed more than 24 hours before the final meeting, the sponsors worried that the West would still make procedural objections to their proposal, on the ground that although the proposal was to be circulated at a meeting that afternoon, not all delegations might be present, and some of them would therefore not receive a copy until the next morning. Interview with a non-aligned delegate, Jan. 17, 1991.

93. As the delegates assembled, PGA staff members were also passing out a document of their own, a compilation of recent letters to President Bush from members of Congress, including some Democratic Congressional leaders, and Congressional resolutions, all urging support of a CTB amendment and some urging "at the very least . . . a continuation of the Conference." See, e.g., H. Con. Res. 16, 102d Cong., 1st Sess. (Jan. 8, 1991); Letter to President George Bush from Reps. Wayne Owens, Dante Fascell, Richard Gephardt, *et al.* Jan. 14, 1991; S. Con Res. 1 (Jan. 16, 1991). The purpose of this activity was, of course, to impress upon delegates that notwithstanding the attitude of the executive branch of the U.S. government, members of Congress were not only aware of their work but supported a CTB.

94. Interview with a Western (but not American) delegate, Jan. 17, 1991.

95. Interview with a non-aligned delegate, Jan. 17, 1991.

96. Interview with a non-aligned delegate, Jan. 17, 1991.

97. Interview with a member of the Mexican delegation, Jan. 17, 1991.

98. Interview with a non-aligned delegate, Jan. 17, 1991.

99. Interview with Aaron Tovish, Jan. 17, 1991.

100. Telephone interview with Amb. Edmond Jayasinghe of Sri Lanka, Jan. 21, 1991.

101. Telephone interview with Amb. Edmond Jayasinghe of Sri Lanka, Jan. 21, 1991.

102. The following morning, the British ambassador told the Sri Lankan ambassador of London's rejection. Telephone interview with Amb. Edmond Jayasinghe of Sri Lanka, Jan. 21, 1991.

103. "Draft Final Declaration," unsigned but dated Jan. 17, 1991 and circulated by Australia on Jan. 18, 1991.

104. Telephone interview with Amb. Edmond Jayasinghe of Sri Lanka, Jan. 21, 1991.

105. Greenpeace USA, press release, Jan. 18, 1991.

106. Comment by the ambassador from a non-aligned country active in the negotiations, overheard on the floor, Jan. 18, 1991.

107. Interview with a non-aligned delegate, Jan. 18, 1991.

108. Interview with Eric Fersht, Greenpeace, Jan. 18, 1991.

109. Interview with Aaron Tovish, Jan. 18, 1991. Alatas, too, expressed his amazement during the final moments of the Conference when, after expressing his gratitude to the U.N. staff he also thanked "the representatives of the non-governmental organizations who have been with us all the time—I might also say all over us all the time (laughter)—inspiring us [and] urging us to move forward."

110. Draft decision, unsigned, dated Jan. 18, 1991 and distributed by the non-aligned leadership at 4:02 P.M.

111. Interviews with two non-aligned delegates, Jan. 18, 1991, and telephone interview with Amb. Edmond Jayasinghe of Sri Lanka, Jan. 21, 1991.

112. Interview with a non-aligned delegate, Jan. 18, 1991.

113. The British had said that if given a date, they wouldn't attend, and Jayasinghe suspected, based on statements from Western European countries to the effect that they "couldn't work outside of the NATO framework," that the United States' other major NATO allies also would have boycotted the session. Telephone with Amb. Edmond Jayasinghe, Jan. 21, 1991.

114. Interview with Amb. Miguel Marin-Bosch, Jan. 18, 1991.

115. Telephone interview with Amb. Edmond Jayasinghe of Sri Lanka, Jan. 21, 1991.

116. Telephone interview with Amb. Edmond Jayasinghe, Jan. 21, 1991.

117. Interviews with two non-aligned delegates, Jan. 18, 1991.

118. As Ambassador Jayasinghe put it, "The middle ground people have a big role to play. The nuclear powers will be more susceptible when they talk. When [the time comes to] continue the dialogue, they are in a better position to talk to the U.S., and to explain their own difficulties. . . . [They can say] 'we don't like to embarrass you publicly, so you need to listen to us behind the scenes.'" Telephone interview with Amb. Edmond Jayasinghe of Sri Lanka, Jan. 21, 1991.

119. See text at note 52.

120. Interview with Aaron Tovish, Jan. 18, 1991.

121. Interview with Eric Fersht, Jan. 18, 1991.

122. See Chapter 7, text before and after note 5.

123. Amendment Conference, Ninth Plenary Meeting, Recorded Vote Ser. No. 113, Jan. 18, 1991. The roll call vote is reported in Appendix E. The delegate from the Cape Verde Islands arrived too late to vote but announced that he would have voted in favor of the decision. The Western states supporting the non-aligned initiative were Australia, Denmark, Iceland, Ireland, New Zealand, Norway and Sweden, prompting a non-aligned delegate interviewed right after the vote to observe, "We traded a date for seven Nordic and Pacific votes." He may have understated the terms of the trade, however, because removing the 1993 date from the draft may also have moved several states from voting no to abstaining. The fact that Britain voted against even this draft, rather than abstaining, may warrant taking with a grain of salt the British complaint that "some" delegates forced a vote rather than permitting consensus. It seems likely that the non-aligned would

have had to have gone considerably further to avoid British opposition, raising questions about which delegates were the ones who really blocked consensus and required the Conference to vote.

124. Amb. Peggy Mason, Jan. 18, 1991.
125. Amb. Sedfrey Ordonez, Jan. 18, 1991.
126. Mary Elizabeth Hoinkes, for the United States, Jan. 18, 1991.

7

Perspectives

Procedure and Substance

By dint of their training in the mastery of courtroom and legislative processes, lawyers are accustomed to thinking that procedure is everything; in a famous opinion, Justice Felix Frankfurter once wrote that "the history of American freedom is, in no small measure, the history of procedure."[1] A close look at the origin and course of the Partial Test Ban Treaty Amendment Conference suggests that for activists and diplomats, no less than for attorneys, the real struggle takes place at the level of procedure.

To begin with, the whole effort was made possible because the PTBT included a clause specifying what in 1963 was an unusually open procedure for considering an amendment to a Treaty. A more restrictive procedure, such as one permitting amendments only at the initiative of the depositary governments, could in principle have provided a focus for PGA's effort; countries could have petitioned the depositaries to act. But the fact that the Treaty specified a relatively democratic method for initiating consideration of an amendment made it much more likely that a group of governments would take PGA's proposal seriously. Resolutions that passed overwhelmingly because of the one-country, one-vote procedures of the United Nations General Assembly also helped to legitimate the conference call and to give political support to nations inclined to join it.

As soon as the requisite number of countries had petitioned for a conference, diplomats became consumed with procedure. The issues of where the conference would occur, when it would begin, and how long it would last became paramount, and representatives of the nations of the world fought over these questions for nearly a year. Although issues of meeting arrangements may seem trivial at first blush, real political influence may be affected by their resolution. For example, countries were probably more ready to accept Marin-Bosch's emphasis on the CTB issue at the NPT Review Conference because the issue had recently been highlighted in two weeks of speeches at the organizing Meeting of the Amendment Conference. The vote at the Conference was as large as it was because the

Conference was in New York, where virtually every country has a permanent Mission, rather than Geneva, where many fewer countries are represented, and the New York venue also made it possible for American peace activists to visit Missions of several absent countries to persuade them to participate.

At the preparatory Meeting, delegates made speeches about their countries' views on nuclear testing, but procedural questions dominated the real agenda. Leading delegations on both sides embedded procedural "markers" in their statements of test ban policy, signalling their commitment to particular outcomes on the ultimate issue of the duration of the Conference and such subsidiary issues as whether it would work through continuing committees, whether non-governmental organizations would be allowed to participate, and under what conditions a majority could rule. Behind the scenes, in the closed committees of the Meeting, all the significant struggles involved procedural issues, from the central question of the method by which the Conference could decide to perpetuate itself to the largely symbolic question of whether the United Nations' Secretary-General would be allowed to open the Conference. The wrangling over these issues was so intense that an Australian diplomat remarked, "Looking at the documents, one gets no idea of the protracted disputes which preceded them. However, the discussions and then negotiations were some of the most difficult I have experienced."[2]

The Conference itself was devoted to virtually nothing but procedure. To be sure, many hours were devoted to the reading of policy statements about nuclear testing, but many of them made the same points that had been asserted in the speeches at the Meeting, and in previous speeches at the Conference; delegates engaged in no dialogue to probe each others' views; and in corridor conversation, the substance of the nuclear test ban issue was virtually ignored. The six non-aligned initiators had circulated a lengthy and very detailed verification plan,[3] but fewer than five delegates commented on it, and the Conference did not use any of its time for interactive discussion either of the merits of a comprehensive test ban or of the verification mechanisms that had been proposed. By contrast, virtually the entire two week session was devoted to resolving a procedural question that to many lay observers of world affairs is the quintessential caricature of diplomacy: whether to hold another meeting. This issue was the subject of formal statements in plenary and committee meetings, strategy sessions, caucuses, corridor lobbying, telephone calls, lunches, dinners and receptions. The intensity of delegates' attention to this question appeared even to displace their focus on the outbreak of war. The issue was also the subject of the Conference's only vote.

Moreover, the actual effect of the delegates' vote was to decide nothing, and, as if to say that they could never get their fill of arguing over whether to meet again, to leave that question to be resolved through subsequent procedural maneuvering. The resolution that they so reluctantly resolved by a vote rather than by consensus mandated "the President of the Conference to conduct consultations with a view to achieving progress on [verification and possible sanctions] and resuming the work of the Conference at an appropriate time."[4] This text raises five critical questions of interpretation.

First, as Aaron Tovish recognized when he first heard the proposal that eventually became the outcome, even the term "President of the Conference" is ambiguous. Obviously the delegates meant Alatas, but what did they intend to happen if Alatas resigned as President, or, more realistically, ceased to be Foreign Minister of Indonesia, either because he took a different post in his government or retired to private life? Did they intend that he should conduct these consultations as, for example, a Minister of the Interior who had no other foreign policy duties, or as a private citizen? If not, or if Alatas became disabled while Foreign Minister, who would undertake the consultations and have whatever powers Alatas might possess to reconvene the Conference? The Conference had ten Vice-Presidents, but the resolution voted by the delegates did not refer to them, and even if an explicit reference were not necessary, none would be the clear inheritor of Alatas' delegated power because none was senior to any other. Would his power pass, not to one of the Vice-Presidents, but to the next Foreign Minister of Indonesia? Or would the power to hold consultations and perhaps reconvene the Conference cease to exist if Alatas were no longer willing or able to exercise it?

Second, whom was Alatas supposed to consult, and how? The issues of verification and sanctions involve complex technical and financial issues, which none of the nuclear powers, except perhaps the Soviet Union, was willing to negotiate about; certainly none had expressed any willingness to consult with Alatas about them. Furthermore, real progress on these subjects would require meetings of experts and much staff work, resources that were not at Alatas' disposal. Of course the references to these issues were probably conceived of to rationalize, in the absence of a real intersessional working group, a pause followed by the possibility of a resumed Conference. Still, the inclusion of such references as guideposts could eventually give opponents of a resumed Conference a basis for saying that the Conference had established certain preconditions for such a meeting, and that they had not been met.

Third, did the resolution in fact establish preconditions, and if so, what were they? Alatas was clearly authorized to conduct consultations. The consulting parties were clearly supposed to have a "view" to achieving progress on certain issues and to "resuming the work" of the Conference. But the resolution was less clear on whether Alatas could himself call the

Conference into session again. It left ambiguous whether the achievement of any progress was required before the Conference could resume and, more important operationally, who would decide either this question or the ultimate question of whether and when to hold a new session. If the consultations were somehow pertinent to the reconvention decision, what decision mechanism was implied? Did there have to be consensus among the consulted parties that the work of the Conference should be resumed, or would it be sufficient if a substantial number of them (or Alatas alone after such consultations) thought that resumption was desirable? The wording of the resolution even left open the possibility implied by the United States' delegate: that following consultations, even if everyone thought the work of the Conference should be resumed, that event would legally require new petitions to the depositaries by a third of the parties, and new negotiations on the necessary financial arrangements.

Fourth, what was the difference between resuming "the work of" the Conference and resuming the Conference itself? The resolution seemed to use these three extra words to avoid saying that the Conference itself could be resumed. Although no delegation stated such an interpretation during the Conference, countries that did not want a highly visible meeting at United Nations headquarters could later argue, based on this language, that even if the consultations warranted further discussion of a CTB or its subsidiary issues, any further work should take place in the CD.[5]

Finally, if the Conference itself could be reconvened without new petitions, when would "an appropriate time" occur? Was the appropriateness of time to be measured merely by the passage of some years (warranting a fresh look at the amendment issue) or the achievement of some progress, however measured, on the verification and sanctions issues? Or could Western countries (particularly those that had voted in favor of the resolution) legitimately assert that it would be "appropriate" to resume the Conference only when there was some hope of progress; e.g., when the American and British governments changed their policies and favored a CTB, or perhaps when they not only favored a CTB but believed that amending the PTBT was the best way to achieve one?

The ambiguity of these phrases virtually ensured that the same kinds of procedural arguments and devices that had attended the creation of the Conference would characterize all approaches to its continuance. Non-aligned diplomats would be on familiar ground as they approached their next task, of using General Assembly resolutions and other vehicles to persuade first the Western countries that had supported them, then the Western nations that had abstained, and finally the recalcitrant nuclear weapon states, to participate in another round of meetings.[6]

Despite the diplomatic focus on procedure before, during and after the Conference, it is also possible, from a different vantage point, to conclude that procedure is almost irrelevant to the real international politics of the comprehensive test ban question. Consider, for example, the perspective of a policy planner in the United States Department of Defense or National Security Council. Whether out of genuine concern about the future of American deterrence, or as a result of pressure from the weapons laboratories, or because continued testing had become a tenet of faith for conservatives, opposition to amending the PTBT was, for the Reagan and Bush administrations, "a given."[7]

The Amendment Conference was never taken very seriously, except as a public relations problem. Even after it became clear that a third of the parties had called for the Conference and the United States would have to help to convene it, the event was "not even a thorn in our side, but just a gnat buzzing around our eyeglasses," a matter not of national security policy but of "conference management."[8] It therefore didn't really matter whether Conference decisions were made by consensus, a two-thirds vote, or a majority, or whether the Conference was held in New York or Geneva, or whether non-governmental organizations participated. The inevitable result would be no change in American policy.

Reconciliation of these two perspectives involves the distinction between long-term and short-term outlooks. For the activists and diplomats who gave birth and nurture to the Conference, the five-year campaign was one more episode in an effort that has now been underway for nearly 40 years. At some points during the process of obtaining requests to hold the Conference, some of its sponsors defined success as making the American or British administrations reconsider their policies, or requiring them to pay a political price, domestically or internationally, for their reluctance to halt testing. But their real achievement, sometimes invisible as an objective even to themselves, involved agenda setting for global arms control over a term much longer than the life of the Conference, perhaps extending to or even beyond the end of the century.

In the 1960s, a preponderance of the world's nations committed themselves to the idea that a halt in the qualitative nuclear arms race, for which a test ban was a necessary if not sufficient condition, was very important. In the 1980s, the Reagan, Bush, and Thatcher administrations not only rejected that idea for themselves but sought to persuade their publics and other governments that the highest priority in future nuclear arms control efforts should be given to percentage reductions in arsenals, through the process of bilateral negotiations for strategic arms reductions. For those who believed that obtaining a CTB would remain an important objective, it became important to keep the test ban issue high on the list of the unfinished arms control tasks of the world community, so that governments, including at least several Western nations, would not permanently accept the Anglo-American outlook.

The procedural devices available to Conference supporters lent themselves to this agenda-setting task. By raising the issue in governments and parliaments, by forcing every foreign ministry to confront a decision as to whether it would join the Conference call, by making governments take sides on a score of other contentious questions, by providing a "news hook" for columns and editorials, and by making the issue the pivot point for the Fourth NPT Review Conference and the 1995 NPT extension conference, test ban proponents effectively used the machinery established under the PTBT to sustain the test ban issue through several long years in which, Gorbachev's unilateral moratorium of 1985 having failed, there were few other opportunities for public activity or media attention. At the same time, the British and American governments measured success in terms of a short-term objective, preventing further testing limitations on their watch. Both sides got what they thought they needed.

The distinction between procedure and substance can be overdrawn. In this instance the procedural efforts of PGA and others achieved a considerable degree of long-run agenda setting and had little immediate effect on nuclear testing. Nevertheless, similar activities could potentially have a greater influence on policy to the extent that they pose either of two immediate threats to governments that defend continued nuclear testing.

First, because the press loves nothing more than conflict, the opportunities framed by procedural battles could have attracted media attention to the Amendment Conference and therefore cost Western governments some public support from their moderate swing voters.[9] Here, the U.S. and Britain probably benefitted serendipitously from the fact that the U.N. Security Council set the deadline for Iraqi withdrawal from Kuwait three days before the end of the Amendment Conference; when the U.S. initiated combat a day after the deadline had passed, the chance that even a hotly contested vote at the final session would be widely reported dropped substantially, and Western governments almost escaped without any negative press.[10] "We did not get one item in the press," Ms. Hoinkes asserted, somewhat prematurely. "The . . . lack of attention this whole exercise drew to itself will encourage people, including the NGO's [non-governmental organizations], to reassess whether they've got their priorities straight."[11]

The fact that the United States received any negative commentary for its stand in the Amendment Conference was due, in large measure, to still more dogged labor by Tovish and by Eric Fersht of Greenpeace. They had taken Suleimenov to meet with the editorial board of the *New York Times* and had then instigated additional visits and calls from activists in order to persuade the *Times* to editorialize about the Amendment Conference.[12] Shortly after the Conference ended, the *Times* blasted the Bush administration with a scathing Sunday editorial. It accused the U.S. government of "alienating other nations with its intransigence" at the Conference, and said that Mrs. Hoinkes had "gratuitously offended" other countries by "patronizingly" saying that test ban negotiations "should be conducted in a serious manner," thereby implying that the Amendment Conference was trivial or a matter of amusement. "For the U.S. to insist on testing undermines nuclear arms control and sends the wrong message to potential nuclear powers," the *Times* added.[13]

Second, while the availability of procedure may be sufficient to keep a public issue alive, the particular procedures that are applicable can have an influence on the outcome. At the PTBT Amendment Conference, the U.S. and Britain had complete control over blocking a CTB because the Treaty's amendment clause prevented amendments from being adopted without their concurrence. But at the NPT Review Conference, the requirement for consensus was two-edged; both Mexico and the United States could stand each other off because either could block a final report, and since the positive accomplishments of the Review Conference were likely to be embodied, eventually, in other agreements, Mexico may have been in the stronger position to bargain. At the Amendment Conference, secondary issues were subject to voting, and at the NPT extension conference, the future of an important treaty will also be subject to a vote. Procedural arrangements may facilitate or impair majority rule, and the United States will not always enjoy rules as favorable as those that the nuclear powers had written into the 1963 Treaty which, unlike subsequent multilateral arms control agreements, they simply drafted and signed and then opened for signature by other governments.[14]

The End of Nuclear Testing

Despite the Bush administration's dogged resistance to significant constraints on nuclear testing, American participation in the negotiation of a CTB is, in all likelihood, likely to begin within months or years; the striking changes in the world just since the inauguration of President Bush make it exceedingly unlikely that the United States can resist further restrictions on testing for as long as another decade, or even that its government will want to do so. Several events, in particular, have made continued nuclear weapons testing by the United States seem an anachronistic vestige of a cold war already receding rapidly in memory.

First, the Soviet Union disintegrated, and although it fragmented into successor states having *de facto* possession of nuclear weapons, the way in which the transfer of power took place reduced significantly the likelihood that a superpower arms race would resume. In particular, the divisions within the Soviet military revealed during the coup attempt of August, 1991, and the collapse of the Communist party in the aftermath of the coup's failure, made it much less likely that hardliners would be able to seize power and renew cold war military threats to American and European security. Furthermore, the former Soviet republics having strategic nuclear weapons were quick to state their desire either to divest themselves of them or to place them under controls,[15] and the two republics with nuclear test sites ordered testing halted.[16]

Second, although it was possible to imagine future governments of the Soviet republics considerably more nationalistic than those that emerged in 1991, the republics' need to focus on their economic crises, brought on in part by decades of excessive investment in armed forces, made it unlikely that even such governments would desire or be able to renew cold war competition and military threats to American and European security.

Third, the beginning of a process of reciprocated unilateral arms control initiatives by Presidents Bush and Gorbachev in the fall of 1991 began to transform what had been decades of superpower competition from an arms race to a peace race; as part of the new dynamic, President Gorbachev immediately began to press his American counterpart on testing restraints and Russia's President Boris Yeltsin echoed his call early in 1992.[17] Fourth, the discovery of Iraq's secret programs to acquire nuclear weapons,[18] new concerns about the nuclear weapon ambitions of Iran, Algeria, and North Korea,[19] the realization that dissolution of the Soviet Union could instantly create a dozen nuclear-armed nations,[20] and the fear that former Soviet bomb designers would emigrate to third world countries desiring their services have heightened all countries' awareness that nuclear proliferation is a serious threat to international security.[21] Compared to the risks of further proliferation, the possibility seems relatively remote that republics of the former Soviet Union would agree to adhere to a CTB with rigorous verification provisions and then try to evade it; that if they did try, their violations would be unidentified by the monitoring systems and unreported by their own people; and that even then they would obtain any genuine military advantage from a few clandestine subkiloton tests.

Testing will probably wind down in three phases. The first phase has already arrived; testing is already being conducted at a rate lower than at any time since the Eisenhower-Khrushchev moratorium. This slowdown occurred not because of public or international pressure for a CTB, but as a result of the collapse of the Warsaw Pact and the Soviet Union, the budgetary crises in the United States, and the emergence of powerful environmental and nationalist movements in the Soviet republics (and particularly in Kazakhstan). In the second phase, the United States and Russia may ratify the *de facto* slowdown through mutual moratoria on testing or by negotiating a new threshold test ban treaty. The real question is when and how the *coup de grace* will be administered to nuclear testing, through a negotiated multilateral comprehensive test ban treaty.

Why Testing Has Slowed Down

Testing has slowed in recent years primarily because the development and testing of new types of nuclear bombs and warheads is an increasingly expensive undertaking, and in the United States, the justification for increasing annual outlays ended in 1989. In 1989 and 1990, the Warsaw Pact began to collapse, and the Berlin Wall was dismantled; the Soviet Union abandoned its hegemony over Eastern Europe while it struggled for its own economic and political survival. At the same time, most of the nuclear weapons programs championed by the Reagan administration were nearing completion, and others were canceled.[22]

During the Cold War, the United States Congress was willing to appropriate spending approximately $ 450 to 650 million per year for testing (in addition to about twice that amount for nuclear weapon research and development) because the military competition between the super-powers, including continued testing by the other side, appeared to warrant it.[23] But the Soviet Union began to become unable to compete. In addition, because of pressure from its citizens, led by Suleimenov, it virtually halted its test program.[24] These developments occurred just as the United States government started to realize the need for fiscal austerity, including defense spending cutbacks, after a decade of record budget deficits. From 1988 to 1990, Congress showed only a slight interest in pressing the President to negotiate further limits on testing,[25] and equally little interest in reducing the testing budget.[26] But because of budgetary pressure, Congress was also unwilling to allow the funds allocated for tests to rise as their cost increased, and the number of U.S. tests each year therefore had to drop as a result of ordinary inflation.[27] From 1988 to 1990, the number of Soviet tests fell from 17 to seven to one, and the number of American tests dropped from 14 to 11 to 8.[28] Congressional experts expected that the new level of about eight to ten U.S. tests per year, rather than about 17 tests per year, would continue until further reduced by further budget crises or new arms control agreements.[29]

The U.S. government might use the *de facto* reduction in its testing program to stave off pressure for a CTB and show its domestic critics that it is on the road, if barely so, to a comprehensive test ban. Notwithstanding its frequent claim that "we have not identified any further limitations . . . that would be in our national security interest,"[30] the United States was under real pressure in the early 1990s to show some movement. President Reagan had pledged the United States to talks on a series of steps leading to a CTB, and President Bush was criticized domestically and internationally for breaking that promise. In a hearing, Senator Sam Nunn, the Chair of the Senate Armed Services Committee, had with some difficulty extracted from the Director of the Arms Control and Disarmament Agency an assurance that the negotiating "pause" after entry into force of the Threshold Test Ban Treaty would be a period of "months" rather than "years."[31] Academic and political support for a "phased" approach to a CTB had grown,[32] and in 1991 the Soviet Union put more public pressure on the United States by announcing a new moratorium on tests as part of its reciprocation of President Bush's unilateral arms control measures.[33] There seemed little reason for the U.S. government not to bow to the inevitable and obligate itself, if not to a moratorium on testing, then at least to the testing limits imposed by its budget; without any significant national security consequences, it could also accept (either unilaterally or in an agreement with the successor states of the Soviet Union) yield limits much lower than the 150 kiloton level set by the Threshold agreement.[34] Furthermore, a low-kiloton threshold limit seems a likely next step if only because it would give hardliners a new opportunity to waste years, as they did before the Threshold Test Ban was ratified, investigating "how precisely the . . . threshold can be measured."[35]

The Final Phase

Unilateral retrenchments imposed by budget constraints and local protests will not bring a permanent halt to nuclear testing even by the United States and Russia, much less Britain, France, China, and the countries that have not signed the NPT. Only a CTB with rigorous verification provisions to assure signatories that others are also in compliance will really produce an end to nuclear explosions. Meanwhile, although an interim bilateral agreement could have some political significance, it will not materially affect either the nuclear arms race or nuclear proliferation. Under a 10 kiloton threshold, new low-yield tactical nuclear weapons could be developed and fully tested, and "with the possible exception of some x-ray laser experiments, much research on third-generation directed-energy nuclear devices could be carried out."[36] In addition, "a quota is apt to do very little to change the expected status of nuclear testing worldwide from what would occur at any rate."[37]

What can be done to achieve the CTB after all the decades of missed opportunity? It is plain, as virtually all of the delegates to the Amendment Conference recognized, that the policy of the United States government must be changed. Under Gorbachev, the Soviet Union was eager to negotiate an end to testing, and this attitude seemed to be shared by Russian President Boris Yeltsin. The British test only in Nevada, so an end to testing in the United States would terminate British explosions even in the unlikely event that a policy change in Washington did not produce a similar change of heart in London. Even France has said that it would stop testing if the United States, Britain, and the Soviet Union did so.[38] The overwhelming majority of NATO and non-aligned countries either already support a CTB or would eagerly support a superpower-initiated CTB agreement. China remains recalcitrant, but it is doubtful that China could remain for long as the only country in the world conducting nuclear weapon tests without experiencing severe political pressure from all of the countries with which it deals. Only the United States' government's eagerness to continue to test blocks the road to a CTB.

It would be tempting to draw the simple conclusion that substituting a Democratic for a Republican President is both a necessary and sufficient condition for obtaining a comprehensive test ban. The support that both President Jimmy Carter and candidate Michael Dukakis gave to a CTB is indeed relevant; it seems easier for Democrats to accept or even embrace an end to testing than for moderate Republicans to do so, perhaps because, as Anthony Lewis put it in describing President Bush's hostility to a CTB, that the real reason for it "appears to be a mind-set among certain conservatives, a belief that continued nuclear testing is a symbol of American status and power in the world [and] refusing even to talk about a test ban may seem . . . a relatively small bone to toss to the right."[39]

On the other hand, Carter's failure to come even close to delivering a CTB, while partly attributable to Soviet foot-dragging on verification in the Brezhnev era, suggests that even a Democratic administration might not make a permanent and complete ban on testing a high priority or avoid deep internal division if it did so. Any administration, of whatever political party, will have to contend with pressure and obstruction from the national laboratories and their allies in the Departments of Defense and Energy, and any administration will have other arms control objectives that also seem important. If the internal resistance to cutting the numbers of strategic weapons is fairly small compared to the internal resistance to a CTB, even a Democratic administration may be tempted to relegate the test ban issue to rhetoric, a token effort, or a second term in office. Furthermore, a moderate Republican administration might reckon the risks of internal opposition somewhat differently. The most significant card that the laboratories and their allies can play is to produce 34 Senators to support them in blocking Senate consent to ratification of a CTB, the nightmare scenario that has plagued Presidents ever since the Senate refused to permit the United States to become part of the League of Nations. A Republican President who negotiated a CTB might be able to produce support from loyal Republican Senators that a Democratic administration could not rely upon.

The strategy of test ban proponents must therefore be long-term and non-partisan. In addition, because many different opportunities exist for exerting pressure, a strategy must focus on several of them simultaneously.

Theory. To begin with, what CTB proponents ask for must take account of reality. Virtually all of the arguments for continued American testing have collapsed, but a little bit of life remains in the reliability and safety arguments, and CTB advocates should be willing to tolerate a short delay in the effective date of a CTB to accommodate reliability and safety concerns that may be legitimate and can be satisfied by a relatively short period of explosive testing.[40]

With respect to reliability, some additional testing may be needed because the primary triggers used in several U.S. warheads were not designed to be "robust;" that is, because of Defense Department and weapons laboratory practices, they are more sensitive than they need be to relatively slight changes in the composition of their non-nuclear components, such as the surrounding conventional explosives.[41] A few tests of redesigned primaries, before a CTB is negotiated, while it is being negotiated, or before a negotiated CTB becomes effective may help to reassure Defense Department officials of the long-term reliability of existing warhead designs.[42]

Safety presents similar short-term problems. Many people think that present designs, or those already under development, present a sufficiently low risk of accidental detonation, and that additional tests to redesign current systems for additional safety features are not necessary.[43] On the other hand, after concerns were raised in 1990 about the safety of certain weapons systems,[44] a panel of the House Committee on Armed Services asked Professor Sidney D. Drell of Stanford University and two colleagues to perform a study and report to the Committee. In its report, the Drell committee recommended that all nuclear bombs loaded onto aircraft should be built with insensitive high explosive and fire-resistent pits and that a further review should be undertaken of the "acceptability" of retaining missile systems (including the Trident II missile) without redesigning them for insensitive high explosive, non-detonable propellant, and fire-resistent pits.[45] Although the Committee did not explicitly deal with testing in their evaluation, Dr. Drell believed that "we can and should make important progress toward enhanced safety . . . in a number of ways that do not require underground test explosions. . . . However to go further and design new warheads with safety-optimized designs, or just simply safer configurations, it will be necessary to perform underground nuclear tests. . . . [T]he number of tests would be limited."[46] The tests needed for this purpose could be conducted within "yield limits in the range of 10 kilotons or thereabouts."[47] Testing of a redesigned Trident II missile may have become unnecessary in January, 1992, when the Department of Energy decided to cancel production of the Trident warhead and to substitute an older type of warhead. On the other hand, the replacement warhead chosen by the U.S. government was also one that did not use insensitive high explosive, rather than the MX Missile warhead, which does incorporate it.[48]

In order to resolve questions about both reliability and safety, therefore, CTB advocates should be willing to tolerate a short period of low-yield testing as a prelude to the entry into force of a CTB. To prevent the interim regime from becoming the permanent arrangement, however, it would be better to begin negotiating a CTB at the earliest possible date, and to provide for the transition period in the agreement itself, with a complete ban on tests taking effect after a few years in which existing nuclear weapon states could conduct a strictly limited number of tests with yields lower than 10 kilotons.[49]

The President. What the President should do to achieve a CTB is obvious. He should reverse the policy established by President Reagan of regarding a ban on testing as, at best, only a distant and theoretical objective. To say that testing will be needed for as long as the United States relies on nuclear deterrence is to say that no person now alive will ever know a world without nuclear testing. This policy cannot be justified by any of the rationales usually offered for the need to test, such as improving the reliability or safety of stockpiled weapons. It can only be based on more tenuous rationales such as not upsetting the laboratory scientists or their Congressional allies, not being willing to insist that Congress provide the perhaps larger amounts of funding necessary to maintain stockpile reliability without testing, or belief that somehow, some day, tests will produce a new superweapon (such as a perfect missile defense) that will enable the United States to achieve a degree of national security it has not known since the dawn of the atomic age. Similarly, the president should reject his secretary of energy's most recent justification for testing, the facile claim that as the number of nuclear weapons in the superpowers' arsenals decline, testing is even more necessary to preserve confidence in those that remain.[50] Under this logic, if genuine nuclear disarmament became feasible, the U.S. would need a greatly expanded testing program.

The President should therefore seek, as quickly as possible, to negotiate a CTB, though perhaps a CTB that would enter into force after a few years during which the United States would be able to conduct a limited number of tests of warheads redesigned to maximize safety features and to remain reliable without further explosive testing.[51] The initial negotiations should include Russia and Kazakhstan; to the extent that Britain, France, or China are genuinely interested in achieving a CTB in the near future, they should be permitted to participate, but problems that they raise (e.g., French or Chinese objections to intrusive verification) should not prevent early agreement by the United States and former Soviet republics to halt their testing.

A successful CTB will have to be multilateral, so the Conference on Disarmament should have a role in drafting the agreement once the broad outlines of the pact have been defined by the superpowers. The United States and the former Soviet republics need not fear that other countries will water down the verification regime that they impose on themselves; the multilateral treaty can provide, as the draft developed during the Carter years did, that any parties can negotiate among themselves a separate verification agreement that is more stringent than the verification provisions of the multilateral accord.[52]

If the President of the United States is willing to negotiate a CTB agreement in good faith and to involve other nations through the Conference on Disarmament, it is unlikely that anyone will press for the PTBT Amendment Conference to reconvene. It will sufficiently have fulfilled its mission.[53]

The United States Congress. If the President does not initiate these steps, Congress should continue to press him. For three years during the Reagan administration, the House (but not the Senate) passed amendments to the annual Defense Authorization bills that would have limited tests to 1 kiloton if the Soviets had followed suit and permitted strict verification.[54] More recently, Congress expressed in law its judgment that the United States should continue its bilateral talks with the Soviet Union to achieve further testing limitations, including a CTB,[55] and it has insisted that the Department of Energy report to it on which warheads could be reliably remanufactured without further testing or with minimal testing.[56] If it can find the political will to do so, Congress should again attempt to limit U.S. testing, as the House would have done during the Reagan years. It should refuse to authorize funds for testing except for a small number of low-yield tests necessary to improve the safety and reliability of types of bombs and warheads already in the stockpile. To enforce its policy of limiting tests to those that are essential, it should require the Department of Energy to justify each proposed test in a classified report to the House and Senate Armed Services Committees, and it should change its procedures so that instead of merely authorizing funds for testing, it would by annual legislation approve or modify the program of tests that the Department proposes to conduct.

In addition, Congress should immediately provide by law that no nuclear testing may be conducted by or in the United States after January 1, 1995, unless after that date a successor state of the Soviet Union conducts a nuclear test or refuses to cooperate in the establishment of a reciprocal monitoring system.[57] Congress cannot effectively micro-manage the negotiation of a multilateral CTB, but by cutting off funds for unnecessary testing, even in a way that it could itself later revoke, it can alter the incentives so that the executive branch will see the wisdom of negotiating world-wide restraints rather than tolerating unilateral ones.

Finally, Congress should take steps to prevent Livermore and Los Alamos National Laboratories from exercising inordinate influence to keep U.S. testing going. Three types of actions are necessary.

First, members of Congress should educate themselves with respect to how the laboratories influence policy. They should understand the degree to which the Defense Department, the Department of Energy, the State Department, the Arms Control and Disarmament Agency, the National Security Council, the President, and the Congress itself are dependent on assessments (on such issues as stockpile safety and reliability) by the two laboratories that design new types of weapons.[58] They should know how many times, over thirty years, the laboratories have intervened, often with erroneous or misleading information, to prevent Presidents from negotiating a CTB.[59] They should be aware of how unlikely it is that the laboratory directors or other senior management, all of whom rise from careers within the laboratories rather than being selected from outside,[60] will ever provide new perspectives on the need for testing. Members of Congress are familiar with lobbyists pleading for special causes in the name of the public interest; they should hear the laboratories' arguments for continued funding of nuclear explosive research with at least as skeptical an attitude as they exhibit when others request public funds. In particular, they should be consider the possibility that the nuclear weapons designers, whose views are represented by their laboratory directors, are threatened by a test ban with a sudden and dramatic loss of personal power and prestige.[61] Representatives and senators should also realize that when they hear stockpile reliability or safety arguments from the Joint Chiefs of Staff or other federal agencies, they are almost certainly receiving warmed-over advice from the laboratories rather than separate judgments.

Second, to help assess the laboratories' claims, Congress should create an independent commission to report periodically to itself and to the President on the need for continued nuclear tests and on what tests, if any, should be authorized by law. To prevent laboratory domination of the commission, no full-time government official or past or present laboratory employee or consultant should be a member. Instead, its composition should be selected from among prominent American scientists, particularly those based at universities. Just as the appointment of an independent President's Science Advisory Committee was the critical step in liberating President Eisenhower from dependence on self-serving technical advice from his weapons laboratories, the creation of such a commission could help now to provide balanced counsel to the United States government.

Third, to help the laboratories understand that an end to testing need not mean the end of their institutional lives or a devaluation of the work of the scientists who work for them, Congress should encourage the laboratories to diversify their research more than they have already done.[62]

The Department of Energy and the laboratories themselves appear to welcome such diversification as a hedge against the end of nuclear weapons competition with Russia or other countries. At a Congressional hearing in 1990, the Secretary of Energy pointed to laboratory support for several non-defense projects such as mathematics education and superconductivity. He said that "we are already on the very steep slope of transitioning these laboratories to even more non-nuclear weapons programs and activities," and that "I feel that we are underway with a whole new and exciting role for all of our national laboratories, in particular those that have been labeled as the bomb laboratories in the past, which is simply fast becoming a misnomer."[63] The director of Los Alamos National Laboratory testified that "our role will change to reflect the new world order" and cited current laboratory work in environmental degradation, oil exploration, health care, and computer modeling for law enforcement.[64] Despite this verbiage, in recent years the percentage of laboratory funds invested in nuclear weapons activities has been going up rather than down, from about 50% in the early 1980s[65] to about 64% in Fiscal Year 1991.[66]

Congress should recognize that although the weapons laboratories may have less nuclear weapons development work to do in the future, they are important national assets. The laboratory directors have given thought to the role that their institutions could play in the development of high-technology civilian projects, such as superconducting materials and high-definition television, but funds for projects such as these have remained only a small fraction of the laboratories budgets. Rather than continuing to operate the laboratories as nuclear weapon centers and lobbyists,[67] or cutting their budgets, Congress should provide funds so that they can help to keep the United States on the cutting edge of technology.[68] This may not satisfy some of the weapons laboratory scientists, who fear becoming "just another Argonne or Brookhaven,"[69] but other scientists would likely welcome the opportunity to spend more time on high-technology work serving national priorities in the civilian sector. Specific projects could be recommended and evaluated by the same high-level scientific advisory commission that evaluated the need for any future nuclear weapons tests. At the same time, Congress should provide that no more than 25% of the work of any national laboratory should be devoted to nuclear weapons research or development.

U.S. Allies and Non-Aligned Countries. As the non-aligned countries recognized throughout the period leading up to the Amendment Conference, countries that are not testing nuclear weapons have only limited influence on the test ban process, and they can exercise what influence they have primarily by helping to set the international arms control agenda. They played this role with some success before and during the Amendment Conference, in that the test ban issue was given considerable prominence, at a time when it might otherwise have been dormant, through the events at the Fourth NPT Review Conference and through the press stories and columns generated by the onset of the Amendment Conference.

It is hard to see how a second session of the Amendment Conference in 1993 could have even that much effect if the United States government is still adamantly opposed to a test ban at that time. On the other hand, if the United States and the former Soviet republics are still engaged at that time in a process of reciprocating each other's unilateral arms control initiatives, a resumption of the Conference at that time could provide an occasion for national security officials to review U.S. test ban policy. These officials might believe that the Amendment Conference was too large a forum for the initial work of drafting a CTB Treaty, but a reconvened Conference could nevertheless then provide real impetus to bilateral or trilateral negotiations. Similarly, if the Labor Party wins the 1992 British election and its leaders continue to desire negotiation of a CTB, an impending second session of the Amendment Conference would provide an early focus for a prompt review of test ban policy in both London and Washington.

A resumed Conference early in 1995, on the eve of the NPT extension conference, is a different matter. At that time, the non-aligned countries will have their greatest degree of leverage over the superpowers' test ban policies because of their ability to undermine the Non-Proliferation Treaty by extending its life for only a short time.

Unfortunately for them, this threat is as useless and as dangerous as a nuclear weapon, and for the same reasons. As the United States has recognized, the NPT serves most countries' interests; starting a process that could lead to its demise is a very risky game, because while the success of this strategy (resulting in a permanent NPT *and* a CTB) would be of great value, its failure (resulting in a decaying NPT and no ban on testing) would hurt nearly everyone. Unless the United States changes its view of a CTB, reconvening the Amendment Conference in 1995 could produce a months-long game of chicken. The consequences would be unpredictable, but a plausible scenario would be that the NPT would be extended only for five years, with the non-aligned states hinting that in the absence of a CTB they would allow no further extensions. Five years later, they might feel a need to make good on that implicit threat, propelling them in the direction of destroying a valuable treaty.

Unless there is a significant change in the attitudes or personnel of the American or British governments in 1992, therefore, the strategy of trying to amend the Partial Test Ban Treaty may have served its purpose and may have reached the end of its useful life. To keep the CTB issue prominent in world affairs in the face of continued U.S. and U.K. resistance, the non-aligned countries should make a somewhat different move. Instead of proposing a CTB to the superpowers, as they did in the Amendment Conference, they should draft and sign such a treaty and open it to signature by all countries.[70] They could write this new Treaty either in a new forum that they would create on their own initiative, or in a second (or third) session of the Amendment Conference. Of course writing an entirely new Treaty in the Amendment Conference would go beyond the terms of reference of that body, but there is a strikingly successful precedent for such a move. In 1787, the delegates who went to Philadelphia to amend the Articles of Confederation changed course and wrote an entirely new instrument: the Constitution of the United States. An equally dramatic change of direction might be easier for the non-aligned countries to undertake if the United States follows through on its threat to boycott a second session of the Conference.

To put pressure on the nuclear weapon states, the new CTB Treaty should take effect when 75 countries sign it and have an effective life of four years, but it should also specify that it will become a permanent obligation if before that four-year period expires, the United States, Britain, France, China, Russia and Kazakhstan become parties. Thus the nuclear weapon states (and the country with the former Soviet Union's main test area) will have it in their power by their own adherence to bind all other signatories to a permanent ban on tests. Furthermore, every time a country decides to join the treaty, there will be occasion for press attention, and more pressure for all of the nuclear weapon states to join the bandwagon. Press attention would be particularly focused as the deadline for nuclear weapon state signatures approached. India and Pakistan could increase the pressure still further by announcing that if the nuclear weapon states signed the CTB, they would at long last join the Non-Proliferation Treaty.

The developed countries that are U.S. allies also have an important role to play in the process of moving the world toward a CTB. At least in public, they claim to believe that a CTB is a priority; almost none of their governments accept the statement of the Reagan and Bush administrations that a CTB must be regarded only as a distant goal.[71] If these democratically elected governments do not really believe what they are saying, they should level with their constituents and accept political responsibility for what may be a less popular position. If, on the other hand, their private views are consistent with their public rhetoric, they should make their opinions known in serious, private communications with their American and British allies. The heads of government of these countries, including particularly the leaders of the economic superpowers Germany and Japan, should advocate a CTB directly to the American President and the British Prime Minister; in the increasingly multi-polar world, they can lead, rather than merely follow, on the issue of nuclear testing.

In the final analysis, of course, the responsibility for ending testing lies with the leadership of the countries that continue to engage in it, and particularly with the President of the United States, who should realize that as it has in past decades, a window of opportunity in which to end nuclear testing may soon close. The Soviet Union strongly favored a CTB in 1958, but the United States was ambivalent. President Kennedy dearly wanted a comprehensive ban in 1963, but by then the Soviets were ambivalent at best. Both countries' leaders wanted a ban for about six months in late 1977 and early 1978, but the period in which agreement was possible was too short, given mutual suspicions and the welter of other arms control negotiations that the two countries had undertaken. The Soviets strongly supported a CTB after 1985, but by then the United States was no longer interested. If at any time during the long history of this issue, a Gorbachev had faced a Kennedy or a Carter, it seems likely that a comprehensive test ban would have been concluded in short order. For the moment, the Russian leadership appears to favor a negotiated end to testing; the U.S. should not wait to change its policy until the day when a resurgent Russian military-industrial complex changes its government's attitude toward such a ban.[72]

For 35 years, the opportunities to end nuclear weapons testing have been squandered. Now the issue is again becoming prominent as a result of continued concern about proliferation and the herculean efforts of a few determined individuals, such as Aaron Tovish, Olafur Grimsson, Alphonso Garcia-Robles, and Miguel Marin-Bosch; a small number of peace organizations; and the quiet, steady commitment of most of the world's governments. Through the 1980s, they kept the nuclear testing question on the diplomatic agenda. It remains to be seen whether their work and their beliefs, applied over the next five or ten years, can change the policies of the most powerful nations of the world.

Notes

1. Malinski v. New York, 324 U.S. 401, 414 (1945) (Frankfurter, J., concurring).

2. Quoted in Limited Test Ban Treaty, Chronology 1990, *The Arms Control Reporter* p. 601.B.25, June, 1990.

3. See Chapter 6, note 60.

4. PTBT/CONF/13, Paragraph 26, Feb. 11, 1991. For the full text, see Appendix D.

5. The subtlety of this distinction may have escaped some observers. While an official Soviet foreign ministry spokesperson was careful to say that Alatas would consult "on the question of when and how the Conference's work could be resumed," the Tass reporter paraphrasing his remarks in English said that the

objective of the consultations would include "deciding where and when the conference could resume its work." Compare Official Kremlin Int'l News Broadcast, Briefing by Vitaly Churkin, Head of the Information Directory of the U.S.S.R. Foreign Ministry, Federal Information Systems Corp., Jan. 28, 1991, with Tass in English, "Foreign Ministry Briefing on 25th January," British Broadcasting Corp., Summary of World Broadcasts, p. SU/0981/A1/1, Jan. 28, 1991. Similarly, William Epstein reported that "seven Western nations that were expected to abstain voted instead to reconvene the Conference." William Epstein, "January meeting keeps hope alive," *Bulletin of the Atomic Scientists* April, 1991, p. 10. Since Epstein is a consultant to PGA, his paraphrase of the text might be attributable to putting the best face on the outcome rather than any oversight of the precise words of the compromise.

6. As of the summer of 1991, Parliamentarians for Global Action's strategy was to persuade Alatas to conduct his consultations during the 1991 General Assembly, with a view to convening a second session of the Amendment Conference in the fall of 1992. Interview with Aaron Tovish in Stockholm, Sweden, July 1, 1991.

7. Interview with Mary Elizabeth Hoinkes, Chair of the U.S. interagency working group on the PTBT Amendment Conference, in Washington, D.C., March 21, 1990.

8. Telephone interview with a member of the Policy Planning Staff, U.S. Department of State, Jan. 16, 1990.

9. An example of this kind of media criticism is the editorial that appeared in the *Toronto Star*: "Canada couldn't even bring itself to vote in favor of a future conference, let alone argue vociferously for a complete ban on tests of nuclear arms." "Nuclear tests go on," *Toronto Star*, Jan. 28, 1991, p. A16 (editorial).

10. Aside from the *New York Times* editorial reported below, no United States newspaper or wire service appears to have reported any news about the Conference, including the vote on its final day. NEXIS search, Jan. 30, 1991, and telephone interview with Aaron Tovish, Jan. 30, 1991.

11. "Hoinkes: 'It is Over,'" *Disarmament Times* January 24, 1991, p. 3 (interview).

12. During the closing days of the Conference, for example, the *Times'* editorial offices were visited by Eric Fersht of Greenpeace and Sheldon Cohen of PGA. Telephone interview with Aaron Tovish, Jan. 29, 1991.

13. "Self-Defeating on Nuclear Tests," *New York Times* Jan. 27, 1991, Sec. 4, p. 16, col. 1 (editorial). This editorial marked a major turnaround for the editorial board of the *Times*. Five years earlier, when Tovish and Grimsson were in the early stages of organizing the effort that led to the Conference, the *Times* had said that a CTB "would appear to do a great deal more for the Soviet Union than it has yet admitted" and that while a test ban would freeze warhead designs, "not all changes have been bad." "The Test Ban Shibboleth," *New York Times* March 31, 1986, p. A18 (editorial).

14. By contrast, the United States and the Soviet Union presented identical texts of a draft non-proliferation treaty to the Eighteen Nation Disarmament Committee in 1967, but their drafts had to be revised in response to the concerns of non-aligned states. United States Arms Control and Disarmament Agency, *Arms*

Control and Disarmament Agreements: Texts and Histories of the Negotiations (Washington, D.C.: U.S. Arms Control and Disarmament Agency 1990), p. 92. Similarly, the United States and the Soviet Union presented to the forerunner of the Conference on Disarmament two identical draft texts of a Convention to restrict environmental modification during wartime, but other nations' objections led to modifications of the text and to the adoption of several "understandings." *Ibid.*, p. 212.

15. In his inaugural address, Ukrainian President Leonid M. Kravchuk said that Ukraine would seek to eliminate all nuclear weapons on its territory through negotiations with the United States; his foreign minister expressed interest in taking up an American offer of funds to assist the Soviet republics in dismantling their nuclear weapons. "Ukraine's Chief Says Atom Arms Will be Scrapped," *New York Times* Dec. 6, 1991, p. A 10; Eric Schmitt, "U.S. Confident on Soviet A-Weapons," *New York Times* Dec. 6, 1991, p. A 10. Days later, Russia, Ukraine and Byelorussia formed the Commonwealth of Independent States; in their chartering agreement, declaring that the Soviet Union had ceased to exist, they stated that they would "respect each other's desire to achieve the status of nuclear-free zone and neutral state" and that they had "decided to preserve . . . united control over nuclear weapons." "Text of Agreement by Slav Republics Creating a Common-wealth," Reuters, Dec. 8, 1991.

16. Vanora Bennett, "Yeltsin Braces Russians for Hardship, Bans Nuclear Tests," Reuters, Oct. 28, 1991 (one year moratorium); "Kazakhstan President Bans Nuclear Arms Tests at Semipalatinsk," Reuters, Aug. 29, 1991.

17. In September, 1991, President Bush announced a series of unilateral arms control initiatives, including destruction of all U.S. ground-launched, short-range nuclear missiles and the removal of tactical nuclear weapons from ships. He also proposed new arms control negotiations with the Soviet Union, including talks on enhancing the physical security of nuclear weapons and on preventing accidental or unauthorized launches. Remarks by President Bush on Reducing U.S. and Soviet Nuclear Weapons, *New York Times* September 28, 1991, p. 4. President Gorbachev's immediate response was positive, but it included a complaint that "President Bush told me that indeed the issue of nuclear tests hadn't been raised in these proposals. However, the President himself and his Cabinet had in mind that this issue naturally would have to be looked upon in the new context arising from the proposals. Myself, I think that we now have an opportunity to make an unprecedented step and to start mutually discontinuing our nuclear tests." Excerpts From Gorbachev's Remarks on Cuts, *New York Times* September 29, 1991, p. 12. A week later, while matching and in some cases going beyond the American arms control initiatives, Gorbachev announced a one-year moratorium on Soviet nuclear tests and called for the other nuclear powers to follow its example "and in this way a road will be opened for earliest and complete cessation of all nuclear tests." Gorbachev's Remarks on Nuclear Arms Cuts, *New York Times* October 6, 1991, p. 12. On January 29, 1992, President Yeltsin called for a CTB, a phased reduction, or at least a resumption of bilateral talks on test limitations. Official Kremlin Int'l News Broadcast, Federal News Service, Jan. 29, 1992.

18. See, e.g., R. Jeffrey Smith, "Arms-Grade Uranium Believed Found in Iraq; Concern Arises About Progress on A-bomb," *Washington Post* Nov. 26, 1991, p. A 15.

19. Richard Boucher, State Department Briefing, Nov. 15, 1991 (U.S. has raised with India concern about Indian plans to sell a research reactor to Iran); "Reactor plea," *The Times* Nov. 16, 1991 (Washington believes that Tehran "is determined to develop nuclear weapons"); Elaine Sciolino with Eric Schmitt, "Algerian Reactor: A Chinese Export," *New York Times* Nov. 15, 1991, p. A1; Thomas L. Friedman, "China Stalls Anti-Atom Effort on Korea," *New York Times* Nov. 15, 1991, p. A 12.

20. In December, 1991, tactical nuclear weapons were stationed, albeit under guard by "elite Russian-dominated military forces," in all twelve Soviet republics. Eric Schmitt, "U.S. Confident on Soviet A-Weapons," *New York Times* Dec. 6, 1991, p. A 10.

21. Shortly before President Bush announced his arms control initiatives, the President of Kazakhstan told ABC-TV that he opposed the removal of nuclear weapons from his republic. Fred Hiatt, "Some Soviet Republics Seeking Separate Armies", *Washington Post* September 17, 1991, p. 1. The President reportedly acted because of "escalating concern in Washington that Soviet authorities might not be able to maintain control over their nuclear weapon stockpile." Michael Gordon, "The Nuclear Specter," *New York Times* September 28, 1991, p. 1. In the speech announcing his initiatives, the President added that "some 15 nations have [ballistic missiles] now, and in less than a decade, that number could grow to 20. The recent conflict in the Persian Gulf demonstrates in no uncertain terms that the time has come for strong action on this growing threat to world peace." Remarks by President Bush on Reducing U.S. and Soviet Nuclear Weapons, *New York Times* September 28, 1991, p. 4. Only a month after the President acted, Arzamas 16, one of the Soviet Union's nuclear weapons design centers established Chetek, a "private enterprise" established to sell underground nuclear explosions (to dispose of toxic wastes and decommissioned nuclear reactors) and other nuclear technology for hard currency. William C. Potter, "Russia's Nuclear Enterpreneurs," *New York Times* November 7, 1991, p. A29; William J. Broad, "A Soviet Company Offers Nuclear Blasts for Sale to Anyone With the Cash," *New York Times* November 7, 1991, p. A18.

22. Most of the Reagan programs had completed or were about to complete the testing stage. The sea-launched and ground-launched cruise missile warheads had become operational in 1983; the MX missile warhead in 1986; and the Trident II (D5) missile in 1988. The advanced cruise missile warhead was scheduled to become operational in 1991. International Foundation, "Toward a Comprehensive Nuclear-warhead Test Ban," (The International Foundation: Moscow, U.S.S.R. and Washington, D.C. 1991), pp. 41–45. Three other warheads (for the "follow-on-to-Lance" short range missile, the Sea-lance antisubmarine weapon, and the 155 mm. artillery shell) were canceled in 1990. *Ibid.,* p. 44.

23. The figure for the entire research, development and testing budget is from International Foundation, p 39. The figure for the testing component is from a telephone interview with Christopher Paine, assistant to Senator Edward M. Kennedy, Jan 30, 1991.

24. The Soviet Union conducted only one test in 1990, and none in 1991. In the spring of 1991, President Gorbachev visited Kazakhstan and promised that there would be only a "few more tests" at the Semipalatinsk test site. A report circulated in the Soviet Union to the effect that the Soviet military had already lowered four nuclear devices into the ground at the site and that they could no longer be removed—they had to be detonated. The Ministry of Defense reportedly offered Kazakhstan six billion rubles for the right to conduct a last series of explosions at the site. Y. Grubin, "Broken Illusions," Soviet Press Digest (SovData Dialine), June 30, 1991. Nevertheless, a few days after the failed coup attempt, Kazakhstan President Nursultan Nazarbayev banned all tests at the site. "Soviet Communist party suspended," The (London) Daily Telegraph, August 30, 1991, p. 1. Shortly thereafter, Soviet President Mikhail Gorbachev formally announced a new one year unilateral Soviet moratorium on testing. Gorbachev's Remarks on Nuclear Arms Cuts, *New York Times* October 6, 1991, p. 12.

25. See the discussion of the Bosco amendment in Chapter 5, text at notes 28–35.

26. See the discussion of the DeFazio amendment in Chapter 5, text at note 27. In 1990, however, Congress did eliminate a separate budget line for research, development and testing of nuclear directed energy weapons, the nuclear component of the "Star Wars" Strategic Defense Initiative (SDI). Telephone interview with Christopher Paine, assistant to Senator Edward M. Kennedy, Jan 30, 1991. As a result, these programs had to compete for funding with other nuclear weapons programs, and for Fiscal Year 1991, the budget level for nuclear SDI dropped from $ 170 million to about $ 91 million. Breck Henderson, "X-ray Laser Research Slashed as Congress Cuts SDI Funding," *Aviation Week and Space Technology* Nov. 12, 1990, p. 29. On the other hand, the amount of funding available for nuclear tests was not expected to decline, at least in the short run, because Congress allocated about $ 150 million—the savings from the SDI cut—to research, development and testing to improve the safety and security of nuclear weapons. Paine interview.

27. Paine interview. In January, 1992, Assistant Secretary of Energy Richard Claytor confirmed his department's plan to continue to conduct approximately ten tests per year, even though no nuclear warheads were then on order by the Department of Defense. Jim Wolf, "U.S. to Continue Nuclear Weapons Research Tests," Reuters, Jan. 29, 1992.

28. "Forty-Five Years of Nuclear Testing," *Arms Control Today* November, 1990, pp. 6–7.

29. Paine interview.

30. Mary Elizabeth Hoinkes, for the United States, at the Amendment Conference, Jan. 10, 1991.

31. *Hearing on National Security Implications of Nuclear Testing Agreements before the Senate Committee on Armed Services* 101st Cong., 2d Sess., Sept. 17, 1990, pp. 20–21 (testimony of Amb. Ronald F. Lehman II).

32. Frank von Hippel, Harold A. Feiveson and Christopher E. Paine, "A Low-Threshold Nuclear Test Ban," *International Security* Fall, 1987, pp. 135–51; the Belmont Conference on Nuclear Test Ban Policy (David A. Koplow and Philip G.

Schrag, Rapporteurs), "Phasing Out Nuclear Weapons Tests," *Stanford Journal of International Law* v. 26, p. 205 (1989); David A. Koplow, "The Step-by-Step Approach," *Arms Control Today* November, 1990, p.3; letter to President George Bush from Senator Claiborne Pell, Representative Dante B. Fascell, *et al.*, May 11, 1989.

33. Gorbachev's Remarks on Nuclear Arms Cuts, *New York Times* October 6, 1991, p. 12.

34. The Belmont conferees concluded that even with a yield limit of ten kilotons, the United States could still test the primary "triggers" for thermonuclear explosives, which are the warheads' most critical parts, in some cases boosting the primaries to less than their full design yields. The Belmont Conference on Nuclear Test Ban Policy (David A. Koplow and Philip G. Schrag, Rapporteurs), "Phasing Out Nuclear Weapons Tests," *Stanford Journal of International Law* v. 26, p. 205, 248–49 (1989).

35. Wolfgang K.H. Panofsky, "Straight to a CTB," *Arms Control Today* November, 1990, p. 3, 4.

36. International Foundation, p. 52.

37. Wolfgang K.H. Panofsky, "Straight to a CTB," *Arms Control Today* November, 1990, p. 3, 5.

38. President Mitterand's policy is not, however, without some ambiguity. At a 1989 news conference, he was asked, "Couldn't France make her contribution to the disarmament effort by giving up everything not necessary for her defence and security? For example, by ending nuclear tests in the Pacific, the building of the Hades tactical missile and the weapon it carries, the neutron bomb, or, another example, by giving up her programme for the new generation of strategic submarines?" He replied, "if the United States and the Soviet Union give them up, and Great Britain too, we shall follow suit. I am prepared to stop all nuclear testing immediately, knowing that it is thanks to these tests that we have weapons capable of maintaining us at the necessary credibility threshold. We conduct far fewer tests than the Soviet Union and the United States of America. Asking for the cessation of nuclear tests is tantamount to asking France to give up her nuclear weapons. So let those adopting that line go as far as asking for the elimination of all the nuclear weapons, including the strategic ones of course, of the world's two greatest powers." Embassy of France at London, Speeches and Statements, Sp.St./LON/61/89 (official translation of Press Conference of President M. Francois Mitterand, 18 May 1989). If Mitterand had stopped after the first three sentences of his response, it would be possible to say with assurance that he would reciprocate a halt in testing by the U.S., the U.K. and the U.S.S.R. But his last two sentences equated nuclear testing with possession of a strategic arsenal; in the context of the compound question put to him, he might have been leaving himself room to claim at a later date that superpower nuclear disarmament, rather than only a ban on testing, was a predicate to an end to French tests in the Pacific. Nevertheless, his recitation that the number of French tests was below the number of U.S. or Soviet tests revealed his need for superpower "cover" to justify continued French testing, and beginning in 1989, the number of French tests began to exceed by a substantial amount the number of Soviet explosions.

39. Anthony Lewis, "The Nuclear Priority," *New York Times* January 7, 1991, p. A18, col. 1.

40. The same point is made in Wolfgang K.H. Panofsky, "Straight to a CTB," *Arms Control Today* November, 1990, pp. 3, 5.

41. The fact that current warhead designs are not extremely robust stems from a long-standing Defense Department practice of ordering warheads that use a minimum amount of plutonium. See International Foundation, p. 23. This practice was not controversial, because Department officials did not regard a CTB (for which weapons insensitive to small changes are desirable) as a likely eventuality, and the laboratories were consequently told, at some point after 1971, to design weapons "on the assumption that nuclear weapons testing would continue." Paul Brown, Assistant Associate Director of Lawrence Livermore Laboratory, at a colloquium to the Defense Systems Department of the Laboratory, June 25, 1985, quoted in Hugh E. DeWitt and Gerald E. Marsh, "Weapons design policy impedes test ban," *Bulletin of the Atomic Scientists* November, 1985, p. 10. Given the small probability that a CTB would ever be negotiated (despite the official diplomatic stance of the United States), the Department of Defense probably didn't seek more reliable weapons because such weapons would have weighed more and would therefore have had to have been deployed on more expensive missiles. R. Jeffrey Smith, "Weapons Labs Influence Test Ban Debate," *Science* Sept. 13, 1985, p. 1067, 1069. The problems resulting from minimizing the plutonium appear to have been compensated for by designing the warheads in a way that depended, to produce a specified nuclear yield, on delicate relationships between particular materials and on particular configurations of components. Nevertheless, there remain three options besides claiming that testing will always be necessary because these designs are so sensitive to minor changes. One could simply regard the arsenal as already sufficiently reliable, even if very minor changes are made, as some laboratory scientists do. One could stockpile materials or, if necessary, subsidize the operation of assembly lines to produce them, so that even minor changes will never occur. Or, if there really is a problem, it might be addressed, perhaps at much lower cost, by redesigning the warheads to use a little more plutonium (easily obtainable from warheads being retired as a result of the START agreement and President Bush's unilateral cutbacks of short-range missiles) and conducting a few tests of the redesigned warheads.

42. In the late 1970s, the National Security Council commissioned a panel headed by Dr. Sol Buchsbaum to make suggestions for developing more robust triggers. In 1980, the Panel recommended an Augmented Test Program to develop robust trigger designs that could be used if a CTB were negotiated. Congress added funds to the Department of Energy's budget for this purpose, but after the election of Ronald Reagan, the money was instead reprogrammed to start the X-ray laser program of the Strategic Defense Initiative. Statement of Jeffrey Duncan, legislative assistant to Representative Ed Markey, at Washington Workshop in preparation for Moscow Workshop of the International Foundation, March 20, 1990.

43. International Foundation, p. 26; Ray E. Kidder, "Assessment of the Safety of U.S. Nuclear Weapons and Related Nuclear Test Requirements," Sept. 10, 1990.

44. See Chapter 3, text at notes 82–84.

45. *Report on Nuclear Weapons Safety of the Panel on Nuclear Weapons Safety of the House Committee on Armed Services* 101st Cong., 2d Sess. (December, 1990), pp. 32–33.

46. Memorandum to File regarding CTBT from Dr. Sidney Drell, December 12, 1990, attached to letter to the author from Dr. Drell, Jan. 15, 1991.

47. Letter to the author from Dr. Sidney Drell, Jan. 15, 1991.

48. Asked "to the extent that the Trident II warhead presents a problem, could it be solved without redesign and additional testing by substituting another warhead that already uses IHE?" Dr. Drell replied, "I do not believe that a positive answer to your question on the Trident can be excluded." Letter to Dr. Sidney Drell from the author, Dec. 31, 1990; Letter to the author from Dr. Sidney Drell, Jan. 15, 1991. On the termination of W88 (Trident II) warhead procurement, see R. Jeffrey Smith, "U.S. to Halt H-Bomb Production," *Washington Post,* Jan. 25, 1992, p. A1. Ray Kidder had earlier reported that the "safety concerns could perhaps be resolved in the case of the D5 [Trident II] missile by replacing the W88 warheads with a smaller number of MX W87 warheads" or by a different substitution using W89 SRAM II components, but that the warheads of the older C4/W76 missiles, many of which are still deployed, have no easy substitute. R. E. Kidder, *Report to Congress: Assessment of the Safety of U.S. Nuclear Weapons and Related Nuclear Test Requirements,* UCRL-LR-107454 (Livermore, CA: Lawrence Livermore National Laboratory 1991). Nevertheless, the government reportedly opted for the W76. Smith.

49. In a report to Congress, Ray Kidder has estimated that ten to twenty nuclear tests would be needed to develop warheads with enhanced electrical isolation and insensitive high explosive to replace the existing Minuteman and Trident warheads, and that at least five more tests would probably be needed if the U.S. government followed the Drell Panel recommendation to modify the B61 bomb and the W80-1 air-launched cruise missile to include fire resistant pits. Kidder believes that a better solution to the problem of the potential risk of plutonium dispersal in an accident involving the bombs and air-launched cruise missiles is to prohibit, in peacetime, air transportation of these weapons or their deployment aboard aircraft near operating runways (where a crash might take place). Kidder, 1991, pp. 1–6. President Bush's order to remove strategic bombers from day-to-day alert status has already partially achieved Kidder's recommendation, although as of this writing nuclear bombs continue to be deployed on tactical aircraft.

50. Jim Wolf, "U.S. to Continue Nuclear Weapons Research Tests," *Reuters,* Jan. 29, 1992 (reporting statement of Secretary of Energy James Watkins).

51. The President should direct that while a CTB is being negotiated and during any period of months or years between its negotiation and its entry into force, the laboratory designers should concentrate only on improving safety and reliability, not on developing new types of weapons. This directive would significantly change the design priorities of recent years. For a long time, the Defense Department orders to the laboratories have consigned stockpile endurance and replicability to the lowest category of desired characteristics for new nuclear weapons, a goal "contingent on meeting all the other" specifications, and not a requirement. *Forum on the Involvement of the University of California in Nuclear Testing at Lawrence Livermore and Los Alamos National Laboratories, California*

Senate Committee on Health and Human Services, Feb. 11, 1987, p. 25 (testimony of Paul S. Brown, Assistant Associate Director for Arms Control, Lawrence Livermore National Laboratory).

52. Tripartite [U.S., U.K., U.S.S.R.] Report to the Committee on Disarmament, Paragraphs 20–22, July 30, 1980, reprinted in *Nuclear Weapon Tests: Prohibition or Limitation?* ed. Jozef Goldblat and David Cox (New York: Oxford University Press 1988).

53. As an abstract matter, the CD is a better multilateral forum than the Amendment Conference for negotiation of a CTB. France and China are CD members, but because they are not PTBT parties, they did not participate in the Amendment Conference. On the other hand, the amending the PTBT could have two advantages over negotiating a new CTBT. First, if for domestic reasons, France or China would find it easier to accede to a widely acclaimed CTBT than to help negotiate one, they might prefer to have the multilateral document drawn up in a forum in which they did not have to participate. Second, by dint of the PTBT's amendment clause, an amendment approved by a majority of parties including the depositaries would bind all PTBT parties (e.g., including Iraq) unless they withdrew; by contrast, countries would not be bound by a CTB Treaty unless they made an affirmative decision to do so. It might be easier for some countries (in terms of their domestic politics) to refuse to agree to a test ban than to pull out of a test ban regime.

54. H.R. 4428, Sec. 3036 (99th Cong, 2d Sess.); see Conference Rpt. 99–1001 on S. 2638 (Oct. 14, 1986); H.R. 1748, Sec. 3135 (100th Cong., 1st Sess.); see Conference Rpt. 100–446 on H.R. 1748 (Nov. 17, 1987); H.R. 4264, Sec. 936 (100th Cong., 2d Sess.); see Conference Rpt. 100–989 to H.R. 4481 (Sept. 28, 1988).

55. Pub. Law 101–510, Sec. 3142, 104 Stat. 1485, 1839.

56. Pub. Law. 101–510, Sec. 3131(A), 104 Stat. 1485, 1831.

57. This recommendation differs from the approach taken by 170 members of the House of Representatives in H.R. 3636 (introduced Oct. 24, 1991). That bill would bar tests for one year (a period that would presumably be renewed by Congress annually if conditions did not warrant a change in policy) unless the President certified that the Soviet Union or any successor state of any part of the Soviet Union had tested. The bill therefore provided no phase-out period during which the Department of Energy could make final improvements in the reliability and safety of warhead designs.

58. See, e.g., Chapter 1, text at notes 20, 138–145.

59. See Chapter 1 generally.

60. *Forum on the Involvement of the University of California in Nuclear Testing at Lawrence Livermore and Los Alamos National Laboratories* California Senate Committee on Health and Human Services, Feb. 11, 1987, p. 153 (testimony of Prof. Charles Schwartz). Anthropologist Hugh Gusterson "was often told [by laboratory personnel] that one could not become director of the Laboratory without first being a weapons designer." Hugh Gusterson, "Testing Times: A Nuclear Weapons Laboratory at the End of the Cold War" (provisional title), Ph. D. dissertation, Massachusetts Institute of Technology, 1991 (Second Draft, ch. 4, p. 64).

61. The degree to which the prestige of the employees of the weapon laboratories is directly related to testing is powerfully documented by the anthropologist Hugh Gusterson in a recent Ph. D. dissertation. Gusterson spent a long time at Livermore and learned its power structure and social rituals. He found that Livermore is "a kind of secret society with its own esoteric and powerful knowledge" in which weapons designers are the power elite. "Scientists are the researchers, usually with PhDs, who initiate and help design experiments. Within this group, there is a small cadre of weapons designers, a special elite group who have privileged resources. . . . [One designer] said a designer was anyone who had been through the ritual 'all the way.'" The designers thus rise within the hierarchy by designing and seeing to completion a substantial number of tests. Each part of the design process, which takes years, involves time-honored rituals; for example, "the night before a test the Test Site cafeteria celebrates by serving steak and lobster. Meanwhile the design physicist, like a secluded initiate, customarily sleeps . . . in a special cot covered in government-issued grey blankets in the 'Physics Room' at the control point . . . a special bed which is seen as having ritual, rather than functional, significance. If a test goes well, and it is a designer's first test, their social status is forever changed." Furthermore, one designer "jokingly reported that non-weapons divisions at the Laboratory had 'Third World' status in terms of access to Laboratory resources such as computer time. A disproportionate number of the Laboratory's senior managers were recruited from the weapons design divisions, and I was often told that one could not become director of the Laboratory without first being a weapons designer." Hugh Gusterson, "Testing Times: A Nuclear Weapons Laboratory at the End of the Cold War" (provisional title), Ph. D. dissertation, Massachusetts Institute of Technology, 1991 (Second Draft, ch. 4), pp. 48–65.

62. For a different view, see Jessica Mathews, "Labs in Limbo," *Washington Post* September 27, 1991, p. A29 (the labs are "physically and culturally remote from the marketplace. They excel in engineering but know almost nothing about cost control, high volume production, ease of use or consumer preference . . . . Innovative small businesses don't need help with research and development but with financing and marketing." Mathews proposes that "one weapons design lab . . . may be enough."

63. *Hearing on Department of Energy's National Laboratories before the Senate Subcommittee on Energy Research and Development of the Committee on Energy and Natural Resources* 101st Cong., 2d Sess., July 25, 1990, pp. 8–13 (testimony of Secretary of Energy James D. Watkins).

64. *Id.* at pp. 69–71 (testimony of Siegfried S. Hecker).

65. National Academy of Sciences, *Nuclear Arms Control Background and Issues* (Washington, D.C.: National Academy Press 1985) p. 215.

66. For FY 1991, the operating budget of Los Alamos was $ 942 million. Los Alamos National Laboratory, *Institutional Plan FY 1991–FY 1996* (1990), Table X-1, p. 118. 41% of it was devoted to weapons activities supported by the Department of Energy. *Ibid.,* Table X-2, p. 119. Another 23% of the total budget consisted mostly of SDI work for the Department of Defense. Letter to the author from Dr. Herbert F. York, a former Livermore Laboratory Director, currently Director of the Institute on Global Conflict and Cooperation at the University of

California, San Diego, Jan. 19, 1991. The 64% figure may be understated because it excludes funds devoted to "nuclear safeguards and security."

67. In 1987, lobbying by the weapons laboratories against test limitations generated a Congressional investigation. While the House of Representatives was considering imposing yield restrictions on testing, representatives of the laboratories had held more than 120 meetings with members of Congress, particularly those with "a DOE [Department of Energy] facility in or near their districts" and the Department of Energy had paid $ 550,000 to a private defense contractor to lobby against test restraints. The costs of both sets of activities were borne by the taxpayers. The practices were defended by a Defense Department spokesman as "providing technical information that is really not available anywhere else" rather than lobbying. R. Jeffrey Smith, "DOE Enlists Contractors on Test Ban; Firm, Lab Personnel Aid Lobbying Against Nuclear Restrictions," *Washington Post* May 21, 1987, p. A1; R. Jeffrey Smith, "Hill Panel to Probe Lobbying by DOE and Its Contractors; Effort to Block Nuclear Limits Questioned," *Washington Post* May 22, 1987, p. A7.

68. In 1992, the Bush administration was reported to be preparing to use federal funds to provide "full employment" for 2,000 nuclear scientists from the former Soviet Union, so that they would have job prospects more attractive than designing nuclear weapons for third world countries. Doyle McManus, "U.S to Seek Jobs for 2,000 Soviet Atomic Scientists," *Los Angeles Times* Jan. 24, 1992, Part A, p. 1. See State Department Briefing, Federal News Service, Jan. 24, 1992. If the U.S. government provides retraining and constructive employment for the former Soviet Union's nuclear weapon designers, it should be prepared to do the same thing for their American counterparts.

69. This the attitude of several nuclear weapon scientists interviewed by author Luther Carter in 1990 for a book on the nuclear weapons establishment; they also feared that Livermore and Los Alamos would not continue to enjoy the prosperity they had experienced "through good times and bad" if they did not retain their distinctive mission of developing the nation's nuclear weapons. The reference is to two federal laboratories that do not do nuclear weapons work. Interview with Luther Carter in New York City, Jan. 8, 1991. A Livermore scientist dismissed the possible role of the laboratories in civilian technology, saying that "a non-weapons role for the lab is not a real role. It's an artificial role that might be used for several years until the funding for weapons came back. Our non-weapons projects have never been very impressive." Dan Morain and Robert A. Jones, "Arms Cut Spells 'Turning Point' for Livermore Lab," *Los Angeles Times* Feb. 29, 1988, p. 3, col. 1.

70. Because a multilateral treaty might not satisfy the mutual verification concerns of nuclear weapon states that later joined it, such an agreement should have a clause permitting any parties to negotiate binding side agreements with each other in which they would commit themselves to more stringent verification arrangements. The side agreements would also provide for financing the more stringent systems so that the burdens did not fall on the non-nuclear weapon states.

71. Japan is one of a "number of nations who seek early realization of a comprehensive test ban." Statement of Amb. Mitsuro Donowaki at the Amendment Conference, Jan. 8, 1991. Canada regards conclusion of a CTB as a "priority arms

control objective." Statement of Amb. Peggy Mason, Jan. 10, 1991. For Germany, "the goal of a Comprehensive Test Ban has long been one of the most important issues on the multilateral disarmament agenda." Statement of Amb. Hans Joachim Vergau, Jan 8, 1991. Norway regards a CTB as "essential." Statement of Amb. Svein Saether, Jan. 8, 1991.

72. Efforts to harden Russian policy, invoking the very arguments that American weapons designers have been making for years, are already under way. In February, 1992, Viktor Mikhailov, the Russian deputy minister for nuclear power, expressed his concern that "we might lose the level [of scientific expertise] we now possess" and advocated a resumption of Russian testing after the one-year moratorium declared by President Yeltsin expires. Fred Hiatt, "A-Arms Chief Says Russia Needs Help," *Washington Post* Feb. 5, 1992, p. A22.

Appendix A:
Treaty Banning Nuclear-Weapon Tests in the Atmosphere, in Outer Space, and Under Water

Signed at Moscow, August 5, 1963
Entered into force, October 10, 1963

The Governments of the United States of America, the United Kingdom of Great Britain and Northern Ireland, and the Union of Soviet Socialist Republics, hereinafter referred to as the "Original Parties,"

Proclaiming as their principal aim the speediest possible achievement of an agreement on general and complete disarmament under strict international control in accordance with the objectives of the United Nations which would put an end to the armaments race and eliminate the incentive to the production and testing of all kinds of weapons, including nuclear weapons.

Seeking to achieve the discontinuance of all test explosions of nuclear weapons for all time, determined to continue negotiations to this end, and desiring to put an end to the contamination of man's environment by radioactive substances,

Have agreed as follows:

Article I

1. Each of the Parties to this Treaty undertake to prohibit, to prevent, and not to carry out any nuclear weapon test explosion, or any other nuclear explosion, at any place under its jurisdiction or control:

(a) in the atmosphere; beyond its limits, including outer space; or under water, including territorial waters or high seas; or

(b) in any other environment if such explosion causes radioactive debris to be present outside the territorial limits of the State under whose jurisdiction or control such explosion is conducted. It is understood in this connection that the provisions of this subparagraph are without prejudice to the conclusion of a treaty resulting in the permanent banning of all nuclear test explosions, including all such explosions underground, the conclusion of which, as the Parties have stated in the Preamble to this Treaty, they seek to achieve.

2. Each of the Parties to this Treaty undertakes furthermore to refrain from causing, encouraging, or in any way participating in, the carrying out of any nuclear weapon test explosion, or any other nuclear explosion, anywhere which would take place in any of the environments described, or have the effect referred to, in paragraph 1 of this Article.

Article II

1. Any Party may propose amendments to this Treaty. The text of any proposed amendment shall be submitted to the Depositary Governments which shall circulate it to all Parties to this Treaty. Thereafter, if requested to do so by one-third or more of the Parties, the Depositary Governments shall convene a conference, to which they shall invite all the Parties, to consider such amendment.

2. Any amendment to this Treaty must be approved by a majority of the votes of all the Parties to this Treaty, including the votes of all of the Original Parties. The amendment shall enter into force for all Parties upon the deposit of instruments of ratification by a majority of all the parties, including the instruments of ratification of all of the Original Parties.

Article III

1. This Treaty shall be open to all States for signature. Any State which does not sign this Treaty before its entry into force in accordance with paragraph 3 of this Article may accede to it at any time.

2. This Treaty shall be subject to ratification by signatory States. Instruments of ratification and instruments of accession shall be deposited with the Governments of the Original Parties—the United States of America, the United Kingdom of Great Britain and Northern Ireland, and the Union of Soviet Socialist Republics— which are hereby designated the Depositary Governments.

3. This Treaty shall enter into force after its ratification by all the Original Parties and the deposit of their instruments of ratification.

4. For States whose instruments of ratification or accession are deposited subsequent to the entry into force of this Treaty, it shall enter into force on the date of the deposit of their instruments of ratification or accession.

5. The Depositary Governments shall promptly inform all signatory and acceding States of the date of each signature, the date of deposit of each instrument of ratification and accession to this Treaty, the date of its entry into force, and the date of receipt of any requests for conferences or other notices.

6. This Treaty shall be registered by the Depositary Governments pursuant to Article 102 of the Charter of the United Nations.

Article IV

This Treaty shall be of unlimited duration.

Each Party shall in exercising its national sovereignty have the right to withdraw from the Treaty if it decides that extraordinary events, related to the subject matter of this Treaty, have jeopardized the supreme interests of its country. It shall give notice of such withdrawal to all other Parties to the Treaty three months in advance.

Article V

This Treaty, of which the English and Russian texts are equally authentic, shall be deposited in the archives of the Depositary Governments. Duly certified copies of this Treaty shall be transmitted by the Depositary Governments to the Governments of the signatory and acceding States.

IN WITNESS WHEREOF the undersigned, duly authorized, have signed this Treaty.

DONE in triplicate at the city of Moscow the fifth day of August, one thousand nine hundred and sixty-three.

For the Government of the United States of America	For the Government of the United Kingdom of Great Britain and Northern Ireland	For the Government of the Union of Soviet Socialist Republics
DEAN RUSK	**HOME**	**A. GROMYKO**

Appendix B:
Amendment Proposal

As submitted by Indonesia, Mexico, Peru, Sri Lanka,
Venezuela and Yugoslavia

The Treaty Banning Nuclear Weapon Tests in the Atmosphere, in Outer Space and under Water shall be amended by the addition of the following article and protocols:

Article VI

Protocols annexed to this Treaty constitute an integral part of the Treaty.

Protocol I

States Parties to the Treaty Banning Nuclear Weapon Tests in the Atmosphere, in Outer Space and under Water, in order to achieve the permanent banning of all nuclear explosions, including all such explosions underground, have agreed that in addition to their undertakings in Article I of such Treaty:

1. Each of the Parties of this Protocol undertakes to prohibit, to prevent, and not to carry out any nuclear weapon test explosion, or any other nuclear explosion, at any place under its jurisdiction and control;

(a) underground; or
(b) in any other environment not described in article I, paragraph 1, subparagraph (a) of the Treaty Banning Nuclear Weapon Tests in the Atmosphere, in Outer Space and under Water.

2. Each of the Parties to this Protocol undertakes furthermore to refrain from causing, encouraging, or in any way participating in, the carrying out of any nuclear weapon test explosion, or any other nuclear explosion, anywhere which would take place in any of the environments described in paragraph I of this Protocol.

Protocol II

(The precise provisions of this protocol are not included at this time, but will be submitted later for consideration and agreement at the conference. They will deal with all questions of verification, including in particular, the following:

- international co-operation for seismic and atmospheric data acquisition and analysis,
- installation of special seismic detection networks on the territory of the nuclear weapons States Parties to the Treaty,
- non-interference with national technical means of verification and non-use of concealment measures which impede verification by national technical means,
- on-site inspections, and
- a permanent consultative mechanism to consider questions of compliance and ambiguous situations.)

NOTE: A seventeen page "preliminary draft" of a verification protocol was submitted to the Conference by the same six countries in December, 1990, and given the Document Number PTBT/CONF/6 (Dec. 12, 1990).

Appendix C:
List of States Requesting the Convening
of the Amendment Conference

Bahamas
Bangladesh
Bolivia
Bulgaria
Costa Rica
Cyprus
Democratic Yemen
Dominican Republic
Ecuador
Egypt
German Democratic Republic
Ghana
Guatemala
Honduras
India
Indonesia
Iran
Iraq
Jordan
Liberia
Malaysia

Mexico
Mongolia
Nepal
Nicaragua
Nigeria
Pakistan
Panama
Papua New Guinea
Peru
Philippines
Romania
Sri Lanka
Sudan
Thailand
Togo
United Republic of Tanzania
Venezuela
Yugoslavia
Zaire
Zambia

Appendix D:
Successive Formulations
Regarding the Future
of the Amendment Conference

1. General Assembly Resolution 45/50, Dec. 4, 1990:

The General Assembly . . . recommends that arrangements be made to ensure that intensive efforts continue, under the auspices of the Amendment Conference, until a comprehensive nuclear-test-ban treaty is achieved; recommends also that the Amendment Conference establish a working group, or other means it deems appropriate, to study, *inter alia*, the organization of control, institutional mechanisms and legal aspects of a comprehensive nuclear-test-ban treaty and to report its conclusions to the Conference. . . .

2. Mexican suggestion to the non-aligned caucus, Jan. 8, 1991, distributed to Non-governmental Organizations on Jan. 9, 1991:

Issues are very complicated. . . . Reconvening of Conference in 1992 or 1993 is one possibility of ensuring adequate follow-up. An intersessional working group would have to be established and report to the reconvened Conference.

3. Draft language for resolution, agreed by non-aligned caucus, Jan. 11, 1991:

Recalling resolution 45/50 of the United Nations General Assembly, decides that the Conference be recessed and that a second session be convened no later than June 1992. . . .

[D]ecides that a Working Group be established to study and make recommendations on the organization of control, institutional mechanisms, legal and all other aspects of a comprehensive nuclear test ban treaty, including the establishment of a sanctions regime for violations of the Treaty

Decides that the Working Group shall meet in New York and shall consist of the following [15] states.

Decides that the Working Group should adopt its own procedures and program of work, and that it should report on the progress of its work to the next session of the Conference . . . .

4. Pertinent Excerpt from President Alatas' "Non-paper," Jan. 16, 1991:

Acknowledging the complex and complicated nature of certain aspects of a CTB, especially those with regard to verification of compliance and possible sanctions against non-compliance, the States Parties were of the view that further work needed to be undertaken. Accordingly, they agreed to mandate the President of the Conference to conduct consultations with a view to achieving progress on those issues and resuming the work of the Conference at an appropriate time.

5. Draft Statement by the Conference President, prepared by some Western and some non-aligned delegates on Jan. 17, 1991 and circulated by Australia on Jan. 18, 1991, but never accepted by any countries or group of countries:

[F]urther work needs to be undertaken. Accordingly, it is understood that I will undertake consultations with States Parties with an objective of reviewing the progress in the overall CTB process, including that in the field of verification, and of seeking the views of the States Parties, concerning further actions to be undertaken by them.

6. Draft decision of the Conference, proposed by Indonesia, Mexico, Peru, Philippines, Sri Lanka, Venezuela and Yugoslavia, PTBT/CONF/L.1, Jan. 17, 1991:

Acknowledging the complex nature of certain aspects of a comprehensive test ban, especially those with regard to verification of compliance and possible sanctions against non-compliance, the State Parties were of the view that further work needed to be undertaken. Accordingly, they agreed to reconvene the Conference no later than September 1993 and to establish an intersessional working group, composed of 15 to 20 countries, in order to continue the consideration of verification of compliance of a comprehensive test-ban treaty. The working group will submit a report to the Conference at its reconvened session.

7. Decision of the Conference, Jan. 18, 1991: (See Appendix E for roll call vote):

[Same language as pertinent excerpt from President Alatas' "Non-Paper," above]

Appendix E:
Roll Call Vote on the Decision of the Conference, January 18, 1991

Countries Voting Yes (74)

Afghanistan
Antigua-Barbuda
Argentina
Australia
Bahamas
Bangladesh
Benin
Bhutan
Bolivia
Botswana
Brazil
Byelorussian SSR
Chile
Colombia
Costa Rica
Cote D'Ivoire
Cyprus
Denmark
Dominican Republic
Ecuador
Egypt
El Salvador
Fiji
Gabon
Gambia
Guatemala
Honduras
Iceland
India
Indonesia

Iran
Ireland
Jordan
Kenya
Laos
Lebanon
Libya
Malawi
Malaysia
Malta
Mauritius
Mexico
Mongolia
Morocco
Myanmar
Nepal
New Zealand
Nicaragua
Nigeria
Norway
Pakistan
Papua New Guinea
Peru
Philippines
Samoa
Senegal
Seychelles
Sri Lanka
Sudan
Sweden

Syrian Arab Republic
Thailand
Togo
Trinidad-Tobago
Tunisia
Uganda
Ukrainian SSR

United Republic of Tanzania
Uruguay
USSR
Venezuela
Yemen
Yugoslavia
Zambia

Countries Abstaining (19)

Austria
Belgium
Bulgaria
Canada
Czechoslovakia
Finland
Germany
Greece
Hungary

Israel
Italy
Japan
Luxembourg
Netherlands
Poland
Romania
Spain
Switzerland
Turkey

Countries Voting No (2)

United Kingdom
United States

PTBT Parties Not Voting (22)

Cape Verde (announced it would have
   voted yes)
Central African Republic
Chad
Equatorial Guinea
Ghana
Guinea-Bissau
Iraq
Kuwait
Liberia
Madagascar
Mauritania

Niger
Panama
Republic of Korea
Rwanda
San Marino
Sierra Leone
Singapore
South Africa
Swaziland
Tonga
Zaire

Index

Advanced Research Project Agency.
(Department of Defense), 22
AEC. *See* Atomic Energy Commission (United
States)
Afghanistan, 27, 30–31, 47
AFSC. *See* American Friends Service
Committee
Akashi, Yasushi, 4(n6), 82, 101–102
Alatas, Ali, 134(photo), 144(photo), 158,
177(n109)
and amendment conference continuation,
139–140, 152–153, 154–155, 157, 159,
160, 161–163, 164, 168, 171–172(n2)
and amendment conference continuation
compromise, 165, 166, 181
and amendment conference voting, 169, 170,
171
Conference Chair election, 112–113, 139
General Committee, 151, 173(n49)
speech, 148–149
Albania, 19
Alfonsin, Raul, 46, 67(n35)
Algeria, 186
Amendment conference, 139–171
background documents, 102–103, 109,
124(n53)
Clerici proposals, 88–89
Committee of the Whole, 156–157
and Conference on Disarmament, 107, 150,
151, 166, 205(n53)
decision-making, 108–109, 110–114,
125(n73)
depositors' control of procedure, 78, 80–82,
105
formal requests, 2, 60–61, 64, 69(nn 96,
98), 71(n117), 213–214, 215
and Fourth NPT Review Conference, 63, 75,
76, 78, 79–80, 131
General Committee, 151, 153, 154, 155,
173(n49)
and global arms control agenda, 183–184
and Gulf Crisis, 134, 157–158, 162–163,
165, 166, 174(n66)

January meetings, 82–83
location, 75, 76, 79, 84, 87, 120, 125(n86),
179–180
Mexican UN resolution (1989), 79–80, 81,
86
non-aligned caucus, 149–151, 157, 159,
160–161
non-aligned voting participation, 146–148,
167, 180
non-governmental organizations
participation, 88, 109, 115–117, 151,
177(n109)
openness, 88, 116
PGA strategies, 73–77, 94(n7)
public statements, 148–149, 158–159
requesters' caucus, 75, 77, 156
Soviet policies, 74, 83, 88, 109, 197–
198(n5)
timing, 52, 55, 63, 75, 78, 79–80, 81, 86,
87
treaty provision for, 2, 48, 179
UN involvement, 76, 81, 82, 83, 110, 180
U.S. Congressional support, 74, 75, 77, 91,
94(n11)
verification protocol draft, 156, 174(n60),
180, 214
See also Amendment conference
continuation; Amendment conference
financing; Amendment conference media
coverage; Amendment conference
proposal; British amendment conference
policies; Mexican amendment conference
strategies; Organizational Meeting; U.S.
amendment conference policies
Amendment conference continuation, 75, 76,
139–140, 180
Alatas strategy, 140, 171–172(n2)
composite resolution, 165–166, 167, 181–
182, 197–198(n5)
compromise proposals, 152–153, 154–156
and Conference on Disarmament, 148, 163,
182
Danish commitment, 161

221